FOOLPROOF

FOOLPROOF

Why Safety Can Be Dangerous and How Danger Makes Us Safe

GREG IP

headline

First published in Great Britain in 2015
by HEADLINE PUBLISHING GROUP

1

Cataloguing in Publication Data is available from the British Library

Hardback ISBN 978 1 4722 1417 1
Trade Paperback ISBN 978 1 4722 1418 8

Offset in Goudy by Avon DataSet Ltd, Bidford-on-Avon, Warwickshire

Printed and bound in Great Britain by CPI Group (UK) Ltd, Croydon, CR0 4YY

HEADLINE PUBLISHING GROUP
An Hachette UK Company
Carmelite House
50 Victoria Embankment
London EC4Y 0DZ

www.headline.co.uk
www.hachette.co.uk

To Nancy, who keeps us safe

CONTENTS

Contents

Friday, the thirteenth of October, 1989, had been a quiet day in the stock market; so quiet that some traders went home early. Then around 3 p.m., news broke that a takeover of an airline company had fallen through. The news unleashed a cascade of selling, and by day's end the Dow Jones Industrial Average had plummeted 7 percent.

The "mini-crash," as it was soon dubbed, has since been largely forgotten. At the time, though, it was rather frightening. It came almost two years to the day after the worst crash in history, Black Monday, and nerves were still raw. That weekend, officials from the Federal Reserve conferred with their foreign counterparts, then put out word that they stood ready to pump money into the financial system. When markets reopened Monday, no such action proved necessary; the Dow quickly recouped half of Friday's drop.

The mini-crash was very much on the minds of the country's brightest economists when they met the next day at the Royal Sonesta Hotel in Cambridge, Massachusetts. The conference topic was financial crises. Attendees included Ben Bernanke and Mervyn King, future heads of the Fed and Bank of England, respectively, and Paul Krugman, future Nobel laureate. None needed convincing that finance had become more treacherous. The puzzle was why the economy kept humming.

Larry Summers, who would later serve as Treasury secretary to Bill Clinton and adviser to Barack Obama, had a theory. Technological and financial innovation, he told the group, had indeed made finance more bubble-prone. He sketched out a scenario of how a crisis and deep recession could recur. Still, he concluded, since the Great Depression, the federal government had erected firewalls between the financial system and the real economy where ordinary people worked and invested: the vast federal budget, deposit insurance, and, most important, an activist Federal Reserve: "It is now nearly inconceivable that there would be no active lender of last resort in time of crisis."

The next panelist, Hyman Minsky, a professor at Washington University in St. Louis, for decades had flogged an iconoclastic theory of business cycles that fellow scholars had largely ignored. Since the 1960s, he said, the authorities had staved off another depression by reacting to every crisis with some combination of government borrowing and Federal Reserve lending. But each success, he warned, simply compounded the behavior that made the system crisis-prone. "Success is a transitory phenomenon," he warned. He conceded, somewhat grudgingly, that "transitory" could last an awfully long time. It had been some fifty years since the last depression.

The last speaker on the panel was Paul Volcker, who had stepped down two years earlier as Fed chairman. He agreed with Summers that the world had more tools for dealing with crises. But his own take was closer to Minsky's. He drew attention to a cartoon in that morning's *Boston Globe* pegged to the Fed's promise to pump money into the economy. It portrayed a dollar bill marked "United States of Amnesia." "We seem to be on something of a hair trigger in using these tools," he observed. "This leaves me with the disturbing question of whether by using these tools repeatedly and aggressively we end up reinforcing the behavior patterns that aggravate the risk in the first place."

Twenty years later, we have the answer to Volcker's question. The federal government was indeed effective at ironing out the ups and downs of the economy and dealing with periodic financial mayhem; the years from 1982 to 2007 were uncommonly tranquil. But the skill with which the economy's overseers had preserved that tranquillity had, as Volcker feared, nurtured risk taking until the stage was set for a devastating crisis.

This has been quite the decade for catastrophe. The world has witnessed not one but two financial meltdowns, one centered in America, the other in Europe. There has been a parade of ever more costly and destructive natural disasters. Much of our hand-wringing has been about all the things we did wrong to bring this on: lax regulation and recklessness in American finance, the political fissures that undermined Europe's single currency, mistakes by the designers of the Fukushima power plant or the levees in New Orleans, the role of climate change in the storms, floods, and forest fires whose tolls mount each year.

My story, however, is not about human failure; it is about human success—and how that success led to many of those same disasters, and the lessons we should learn.

America's crisis was the result of the twenty-five years of economic stability that came before. The crisis that threatens to break up the euro was possible because of how convinced people were that the euro was permanent. The enormous toll taken by Hurricane Katrina, Superstorm Sandy, and the tsunami that knocked out Fukushima can be attributed to the determination and ingenuity with which engineers and settlers have built cities and livelihoods on the coasts, in the path of water. Levees and other works had been built along the Mississippi as far back as the early 1700s so that its banks and floodplains could be used for settlement, farming, and industry. As a result, when levees fail, more people are flooded. Japan has built seawalls along its coast to protect its cities and industry from tsunamis. This encouraged the growth of population and the siting of nuclear power plants along the coasts. The massive forest fires that now regularly rage across the western United States are due not just to climate change but to how thoroughly forest rangers in prior decades suppressed fire.

What all these things had in common was that they made people feel safe, and the feeling of safety allowed danger to reemerge, often hidden from view.

The notion that a sense of safety can lead to disaster is quite intuitive. After all, that's the essence of complacency: let your guard down, take too much for granted, and nasty surprises await. Teenagers famously have too much faith in their own immortality and ability. That's why they hurt themselves so often, in cars, sports, and romance. "Best safety lies in fear," Laertes tells his sister, Ophelia, by way of protecting her from Hamlet's sinister overtures. "Only the paranoid survive" is legendary Intel chief executive Andy Grove's advice to business leaders.

Ample research demonstrates this point. Fender benders and minor injuries are more common when roads are covered in snow or ice than when they are dry, but serious injuries and fatalities are actually less common because drivers are traveling more slowly and carefully. Conversely, antilock brakes and studded snow tires embolden drivers to brave more treacherous conditions at higher speed. They may reduce injuries, but not as much as their designers had expected, because they didn't count on the possibility that making people safer could cause them to drive differently. In professional sports, hard helmets have reduced some injuries such as skull fractures, but increased others such as concussions. Why? Because players hit one another with their heads more often, and harder.

I once took a curve on a snowy road too quickly because I

thought my rental car's front-wheel drive (at the time a relatively novel feature) would provide better traction than the rear-wheel drive I was used to. I ended up in a snowbank, luckily with just my pride damaged. Conversely, if I notice that one of my children hasn't done up his or her seat belt, I slow down. In the first instance, I cursed myself for letting the sense of safety cause me to take more chances. In the second, I am proud of my added caution. Yet these two instincts are mirror images of each other.

This isn't to say we have a false sense of security, because it isn't false: these things really do make us safer—all else being equal. However, all else is often not equal. As our environment becomes more complex, so do our interactions and the potential for unintended consequences and catastrophe.

The history of technology is replete with cautionary tales of excessive confidence in safety. The *Titanic*'s crew sailed at top speed through ice-infested waters believing their ship to be unsinkable. The crew didn't acquire such hubris solely because of their ship's special safeguards against sinking; it was a product of their times. The ship's captain had, some years earlier, said he could not imagine what conditions would sink a modern ship. This wasn't based solely on his imagination. There had previously been no obvious instance of a similar ship sinking because of such a collision.

The *Titanic* has its modern analogs. The Deepwater Horizon had one of the best safety records in BP's fleet of drilling rigs; indeed, some of the company's executives were on it one night in April 2010 to learn more about that record. The rig's safety record turned out to owe more to luck than to BP's culture; that night, its luck ran out. It was destroyed by an explosion, killing eleven and triggering one of the worst oil spills in history.

In 2009, Air France flight 447, with 228 passengers and crew aboard en route from Rio de Janeiro to Paris, passed through a region of intense thunderstorms, then abruptly disappeared. When investigators finally recovered the black boxes two years later, they learned that the copilot had tried to climb too sharply, causing the Airbus A330 to stall and rapidly lose altitude. Exactly why remains a mystery, but one theory of investigators fingers the safeguards built into jetliners that have helped make aviation so safe. A "fly-by-wire" aircraft like the Airbus is equipped with computers that override pilots' commands if they are putting the aircraft in danger, for example by stalling. On Flight 447, though, ice on the aircraft had shut down the autopilot and lifted the restrictions on pilots' actions. And when the aircraft sounded a stall warning, the pilot ignored it, perhaps believing such a situation impossible.

Even when we reduce risks to ourselves, that behavior may put others at risk. One study of cars equipped with antilock brakes found they were involved in fewer front-end collisions but more rear-end collisions, apparently because drivers were braking harder. It is difficult for anyone to model in their mind how their actions affect anyone else's. Nor is it necessarily their responsibility. When fire threatens suburban homes in Texas or California, the forest managers' immediate duty is to protect the lives at stake. Yet in suppressing such fires, they encourage people to live near the brushland and allow forests to grow denser, which provides the fuel for even bigger fires.

Memory and experience shape our behavior. The more vivid our sense of danger, the greater care we take. On Wall Street, those who take risks can reap spectacular rewards. Those with longer memories hang back; their performance and profits suffer, and customers go elsewhere. Thus, trading is a young person's profession.

This explains why rogue traders, blowups, and Ponzi schemes appear with distressing frequency on Wall Street. It's also why, within years of a flood or a hurricane, people drop their flood insurance and again start building expensive homes next to the water. If you go down to Pass Christian, a resort town in Mississippi on the Gulf of Mexico, you'll see condominium complexes built within blocks of where a shopping center was destroyed by Hurricane Katrina in 2005. That shopping center itself was built on the site of an apartment complex flattened by Hurricane Camille in 1969.

That the gravity of danger fades with time is simply human nature. To combat that tendency, risk managers, engineers, and regulators build the lessons of history into their designs and rules so that, for example, hotheaded cowboys won't bring down an entire bank or, for that matter, the whole economy.

The history of civilization is the history of us trying to foolproof existence, to create safety and stability out of a dangerous and unstable world. Since ancient times governments have justified their existence, and often their repression, on delivering economic and political stability, from the Roman Empire to modern China. In the economic realm, stability has been the goal since there has been any concept of macroeconomic policy. Nowadays, central banks consider stability of the financial system as important as stability of the economy; they regularly issue "financial stability reports" and confer with one another at the Financial Stability Board.

But societies and economies, like bacterial colonies, are not inherently stable. They are constantly changing, evolving, and usually getting better in the process. Stability is blissful, but it may also be illusory, hiding the buildup of hidden risks or nurturing behavior that will bring the stability to an end.

Our efforts to make life safer come into conflict with an equally irrepressible desire to make things bigger and more complicated. As our cities, transport systems, and financial markets become more interconnected and complex, so have the opportunities for disaster. This is as true of technology and nature as it is of economies. "An incident-free system becomes mute" is how

René Amalberti, a French doctor, risk expert, and former air force general, puts it. In aviation, crashes have become so rare that it is increasingly difficult to anticipate the sorts of events that can now bring down an airliner—which explains why crashes these days, such as the disappearance of Malaysia Airlines flight 370 over the Indian Ocean in 2014, are often so strange. This is how the mundane, everyday mistakes of humans can coalesce into a systemic crisis that can capsize an entire economy. Our environment evolves, and successfully preventing one type of risk may simply funnel it elsewhere, to reemerge, like a mutated bacteria, in more virulent fashion. In fact, bacteria illustrate this. Millions of people become sick or die each year because excessive use of antibiotics causes bacteria to mutate into resistant strains.

The systems we've developed to learn from history can unintentionally magnify this tendency. Financial institutions, for example, monitor their risk with a formula called "value at risk," or VaR. Vastly simplified, VaR asks how much money would be lost if securities or interest rates fluctuate as much as they did at their most volatile moment in the recent past. A long period of calm will thus naturally lead a bank to raise its exposure. As that exposure grows, so does the potential loss if volatility exceeds expectations. Those losses will in turn trigger a rush to sell those securities, making the volatility even worse.

This misplaced faith in historic stability helps explain the financial crisis. Banks and their regulators assumed mortgages were generally safe based on models that went back a few decades, and contained no episodes of falling home prices. This of course increased their appetite for mortgage lending, which fueled the home price bubble. Given enough time, the assumption that prices would never go down made it all but inevitable that prices would in fact fall.

I did not anticipate the financial crisis, yet feel I should have.

I began my career as a financial journalist in 1989, and have been covering chaos and crises ever since. The mini-crash happened just a few months after I graduated from college, and I still remember wondering what would happen when markets reopened on Monday. I was also skeptical about the wisdom of protecting investors from such turmoil. I asked a Fed governor that fall: should the Fed repeatedly intervene when the market was in trouble? Well, I remember her answering, it's a central bank's duty to act when the financial system is threatened.

In the following decades, I saw a fiscal crisis convulse interest rates and the dollar in my native Canada, an exchange rate crisis erupt in Europe in 1992, the Asian financial crisis, the near failure of Long-Term Capital Management in 1998, and then the rise and fall of the technology bubble. By 2007, I was looking for the next crisis everywhere: in home prices, leveraged buyouts, the trade deficit. I was not, however, looking for catastrophe. I had by now developed a deep respect for the authorities' ability to counteract mayhem; I assumed that the economy, though it might get bumped around a bit, would come out okay.

A similar thought process was going on in the world's central banks. Even before he took office as Fed chairman in 2006, Bernanke was meeting with the Fed's staff to grill them on what preparations they had made for the next episode of financial instability. His colleague Frederic Mishkin, an expert on banking who had studied the Great Depression, examined what would happen if housing prices fell 20 percent. The Fed, he argued in a lengthy presentation to other central bankers, would lower interest rates quite quickly, the economy would shrink only 0.5 percent, and unemployment would barely rise.

A similar dynamic unfolded in Europe. Its pursuit of integration was in great part a response to periodic political and economic crises, starting with the Second World War. "Europe will be forged in crises, and will be the sum of the solutions adopted for those crises," said Jean Monnet, a French public servant who was one of the fathers of the European Union. European countries had often tried to peg their exchange rates, but the pegs would periodically break apart in a hailstorm of speculative attacks, most spectacularly in 1992. A single currency, the leaders concluded, would make such speculative attacks a thing of the past.

The euro succeeded beyond its architects' wildest imaginations. Within a few years of its launch in 1999, northern money began pouring into southern economies as lenders lost their fear of devaluation. Interest rates in Italy, Spain, and Greece plunged to German levels. Yet this very success planted the seeds of the later crisis by allowing those countries to accumulate staggering amounts of debt. This was not supposed to be a problem. As late as 2010, Jean-Claude Trichet, president of the European Central Bank, declared that when one country in the euro zone needed to borrow from another, it was "kind of automatic.... You are helped by the very fact of belonging to the euro area." In fact, the financing was anything but automatic, and when northern lenders began to worry that southern borrowers might not repay, they pulled their money from southern banks, sold their southern bonds, or stopped lending to southern companies.

There is no shortage of blame to go around in the postmortems of these events. The *Titanic*'s captain should have responded to warnings of ice in the North Atlantic, the big banks and credit rating agencies were appallingly shortsighted about the risks involved in mortgage-backed securities, and the NFL downplayed the threat to its players' health from repeated concussions for far too long.

If it were only bad behavior at work, the answer would be straightforward: pass more rules, and enforce them vigorously. But by seeing these events solely as a morality play, we're going to miss something very important and make it harder to solve them.

Oftentimes, it's not the nefarious stuff that does us in; it's the well intentioned.

Those well-intentioned efforts to safeguard humanity from economic, environmental, and technological harm pay substantial dividends. The fact that there is a tradeoff between these benefits and their unintended consequences doesn't tell us whether the tradeoff is positive or negative. Determining where the border lies, and whether we can ever get the balance between safety and risk right, requires examining history and evidence with an open mind. That's what this book sets out to do.

CHAPTER 1

Progressives, Engineers, and Ecologists

In the early years of the twentieth century, two disasters struck the United States, one man-made, one natural. In 1907 a terrifying panic swept New York's financial markets and tipped the country into a short, sharp recession. Three years later and thousands of miles to the west, massive forest fires broke out that burned across Montana, Idaho, and Washington, eventually consuming nearly five thousand square miles of forest, destroying several towns, and killing at least eighty-five people.

Until then, western settlers accepted fire and businesses accepted bank panics as the unavoidable by-products of a civilization pressing against its physical and industrial frontiers. Fires resulted when settlements, railroads, and farms pushed deeper into forested lands, just as panics arose when industry and agriculture expanded too rapidly. The two disasters marked a turning point in how Americans coped with chaos.

The United States had endured more than a dozen distinct financial panics between its founding and 1907. This didn't have to be. There was available a solution: a central bank that could lend to banks besieged by depositors demanding cash. Americans experimented twice with central banks in the eighteenth and nineteenth centuries. But suspicions of centralized power ran deep, and in both cases Americans chose to let those banks die. They preferred freedom (even if it meant disorder and uncertainty) to control (even if it brought order and security).

The Panic of 1907 shifted opinion decisively the other way. "It is the duty of the United States to provide a means by which the periodic panics which shake the American Republic and do it enormous injury shall be stopped," Robert Owen, a senator, argued the following year.

Owen had experienced such injuries firsthand. He grew up in Virginia, the privileged son of a prominent railroad executive, then saw his family's fortune wiped out in the Panic of 1873 and its aftermath. After his father died, his mother, who was half Cherokee, moved the family back to Indian territory, where she had been born. Owen worked as a teacher and an Indian agent before founding a bank in Oklahoma in 1890. The failure of several large companies triggered a panic in 1893 that cost Owen's bank half its deposits and, he later recalled, inflicted "injuries which required years to repair in the industrial and commercial life of the nation."

The experience transformed Owen into a fervent advocate of a central bank. In 1898 he visited Germany, France, England, and Canada and came back convinced that their central banks could do what the United States could not: quickly respond when "financial fear threatens the country." He entered the Senate in 1907 and went on to cosponsor the legislation that would create the Federal Reserve in 1913. The next year the nation's top bank regulator declared, "Financial and commercial crises or 'panics' ... with their attendant misfortunes and prostrations, seem to be mathematically impossible."

The fires of 1910 similarly altered the country's attitude toward natural disaster. Up until then settlers had emulated the Indians who had occupied the land before them and used fire to clear land for grazing. But the early twentieth century saw a shift in attitudes toward natural resources. The logging industry wanted the trees for lumber; Theodore Roosevelt wanted them for national parks. The fires of 1910, deadlier and bigger than any the country had known, brought the two, who were at odds on everything else, together in their view that fire was an appalling waste of precious resources.

Gifford Pinchot, a confidant of Roosevelt and the first chief of the U.S. Forest Service, wrote a few months after the fires: "Today we understand that forest fires are wholly within the control of men.... The first duty of the human race is to control the earth it lives upon." Fighting fire, he argued, was essential to economic progress: "Conservation stands for the prevention of waste. There has come gradually in this country an understanding that waste is not a good thing and that the attack on waste is an industrial necessity." He and his successors transformed the infant fire service into an organization devoted to preserving the woods for the use of industry and ordinary people; fighting fire became its principal mission.

A century later, panics and forest fires are still with us. In 2008 a devastating global financial crisis erupted and tipped the entire world into its worst recession since the 1930s. Meanwhile, massive forest fires have once again become routine: in 2002 the Rodeo-Chediski fire destroyed nearly half a million acres of forest in Arizona, a toll that would be exceeded five more times in the following decade.

Does this mean central bankers and forest managers were failures? From the point of view of their mandates, they've been hugely successful at putting out fires, both in the forest and in the economy. Yet it was that very success that planted the seeds for future disaster and that illustrates the fundamental contradiction in humanity's quest for safety and stability: oftentimes our efforts to make our surroundings safer trigger offsetting behavior that frustrates those efforts.

The economy, the environment, even the human body all adapt to their surroundings. If the surroundings seem safer, the systems tolerate more risk. For a century humans have bent these systems to our will and enjoyed long stretches of stability. But those long stretches invariably end at some point, usually in ways that can't be anticipated.

In the case of forests, putting out small fires makes large fires more devastating, since fire suppression allows more leaves, brush, and other dead tree matter to accumulate on the forest floor, leading to denser forests. The result is that when a fire becomes established, the copious fuel allows it to burn much more intensely.

Scientists who study the rings of ancient trees and the charcoal found in the sediment in lake bottoms know that throughout most of the past two thousand years, more forests burned when the climate was hot and dry and fewer burned when it was cool and wet. That pattern abruptly changed in the twentieth century: the climate grew hotter and drier, but the incidence of fire declined as forest managers countered the natural tendency of the landscape to immolate. The ferocity of fires in recent decades is the consequence of a warming climate combined with the fuel provided by forest density that has been allowed to develop over decades of fire suppression.

As for the economy, there is no shortage of theories about what produced the crisis of 2008. One popular culprit is private greed—financiers foisted mortgages they knew would fail on foolish home buyers and left the taxpayer to pick up the tab. Another is government: pursuing a vision of home ownership for all, politicians and activists prodded poor families to buy homes they couldn't afford. Or maybe the crisis was the result of one of the mass obsessions that periodically sweeps the population, from tulip bulbs in seventeenth-century Holland to Internet stocks in twentieth-century America.

All these forces played a part, but they present an incomplete picture. As the coming chapters will show, the most important factor was the sense of safety that resulted from years of successfully fighting crisis and recession.

The twenty-five years before the global financial crisis were unusually peaceful for the economy; recessions were rare and mild, inflation was low and stable, and periodic financial crises, whether the stock market crash of 1987 or the Asian financial crisis of 1997, were contained by the global fire brigades—the Fed, the Treasury, and the International Monetary Fund. Economists called this era the "Great Moderation," and credited it to changes in how businesses operated—using fewer inventories, for example—and a more disciplined, more nimble Federal Reserve, able to snuff out both inflation and recession. The global economy in 2008 was like a forest that hadn't burned in decades; it was choking with the fuel of leverage, risk, and complacency.

Making everyday life safer and more secure is one of the purposes of government, and for the past century it's been quite successful: our roads and our skies have gotten steadily safer, death rates from infectious disease have plummeted, absolute poverty has shrunk, and, at least until 2008, savage recessions had become a thing of the past.

Fear serves a purpose: it keeps us out of trouble. On the other hand, it's not much fun: a life lived in fear is also a life deprived of adventure, exploration, and growth. This tension suffuses modern life. Parents vacillate between walking their children to school every day to protect them from predators, and worrying they'll grow up sheltered and unable to cope with life.

This tension also bedevils the people whose job it is to steer our economy and manage our surroundings. Philosophically, they fall into two schools of thought. One, which I call the engineers, seeks to use the maximum of our knowledge and ability to solve problems and make the world safer and more stable; the other, which I call the ecologists, regards such efforts with suspicion, because given the complexity and adaptability of people and the environment, they will always have unintended consequences that may be worse than the problem we are trying to solve.

Engineering itself is an ancient profession. Engineers had a hand in the early economic progress of the United States when the Army Corps of Engineers helped develop inland waterways. As a philosophical approach to government, though, engineering's rise began with the Progressive Era in the late nineteenth and early twentieth century. At this time, two important social forces together worked to elevate the belief that enlightened managers could foolproof society against the capriciousness of the market and the environment.

The first force was astonishing advances in the social and natural sciences. Spurred by the spread of industrialization and mechanization, both business and economics became more scientific. The discipline of economics was more than a century old when the British economist Alfred Marshall published his path-breaking *Principles of Economics* in 1890, but as Marshall noted, as a science it was "in its infancy." The complexity and specialization of modern industry, he wrote, gave a "new precision and a new prominence to the causes that govern the relative values of different things. . . ."

Marshall made famous the supply and demand curves that every economics undergraduate today knows on sight. Those elegant curves impose visual order on the seemingly random behavior of consumers and producers. Meanwhile, medicine was achieving similar breakthroughs in understanding the human body. Paul Ehrlich, a German chemist, devised the first compounds aimed at a single pathogen and in 1906 predicted that mankind would eventually be able to develop a "magic bullet" (*magische Kugel*) for every pathogen, a prediction that in coming decades seemed fulfilled by breakthroughs in antibiotics and vaccines.

These tools persuaded experts that with enough study and

will, the complexities of nature and the economy could be both understood and managed. Expertise became institutionalized: the American Economic Association was founded in 1885, the Society of American Foresters in 1900, the American Sociological Association in 1905, and the American Planning Association in 1909.

This coincided with a second, political force. As America's economy industrialized, more wealth and power accumulated in the hands of millionaire capitalists and gigantic corporations, which by the late nineteenth century had produced a backlash. The product of this revolt against Gilded Age capitalist excess and the institutionalization of knowledge was Progressivism, the philosophy that government could be a force for both equity and efficiency.

Two presidents—Theodore Roosevelt and Woodrow Wilson— dominated the Progressive Era. Under Roosevelt, laissez-faire retreated as the guiding principle of economic management, replaced by a more activist, muscular state. Roosevelt turned the Sherman Antitrust Act, largely toothless since its passage in 1890, loose on anticompetitive monopolies, passed legislation to regulate food and drugs and interstate commerce, and expanded the system of national parks. Often his actions were informed by progressive ideas of scientific management. At the Forest Service, Roosevelt's friend Pinchot was steeped in principles of forest management he had learned in Europe, where forests were treated as farms—resources to be cultivated and harvested, not left to burn.

On the big economic question of the day, monetary reform, Roosevelt was inconsequential. He was largely a bystander during the Panic of 1907, and in fact welcomed the fear it struck in bankers' hearts, a sentiment that convinced contemporaries that he was financially illiterate. The panic, however, did energize central bank proponents such as Owen and led to the creation of a national commission on monetary reform. Like Owen a decade earlier, the commission traveled to Europe and came back recommending the creation of a central bank modeled on those in England, France, and Germany.

Woodrow Wilson shared Roosevelt's suspicion of big business, but as the former president of Princeton and the only PhD to occupy the White House, his views of the role of government sprung from social science. He wanted to apply the best ideas he had heard, often from foreigners, to the modern management of America's economy.

One of his influences was Walter Bagehot, a British essayist and editor of *The Economist* who had extolled the role of professional administrators in government. His 1873 book *Lombard Street* is a manifesto for how a central bank must act as "lender of last resort." When there is a general panic, Bagehot counseled, the central bank should lend freely against collateral at a penalty rate. Wilson was quite taken with *Lombard Street*; it abounds, he said, with "flashes of insight and discovery."

So when Wilson became president in 1913, he was already convinced of the need for a central bank; the only question was who would run it. Owen, now chairman of the Senate Banking Committee, wanted government appointees in charge; Carter Glass of Virginia, his counterpart in the House of Representatives, preferred that banks hold sway. Wilson and Congress eventually settled on a hybrid. Wilson signed the Federal Reserve Act into law just before Christmas 1913, calling it a "constitution of peace": "What we are proceeding to do now is to organize our peace, is to make our prosperity not only stable but free to have an unimpeded momentum." Before dashing off to a long-planned holiday on the Gulf of Mexico, he penned a quick note of thanks to Owen, for shepherding "a very difficult and trying piece of business" through a deeply divided Congress: "The whole country owes you a debt of gratitude and admiration."

The basic tools now existed for engineers to manage the

economy: new regulatory powers, a central bank, even an income tax. What they lacked was a consensus on how vigorously to use these tools, or what they ultimately hoped to accomplish. The Fed's first leaders argued over how expansive its remit should be. Many preferred that it limit itself to tiding banks over during periods of tight liquidity. But Benjamin Strong, head of the Federal Reserve Bank of New York and the system's de facto leader, envisioned a wider writ: the Fed eagerly stepped forward to finance the federal government's First World War effort. When the war was over, he used high interest rates to squeeze inflation out of the economy, triggering a short, savage depression; but

In the 1920s, the newly created Federal Reserve portrayed itself as a bulwark against economic disaster. (Image courtesy of the Federal Reserve Bank of San Francisco Archives)

after that, he was much more eager to prevent such downturns. He initiated the use of open market operations—the purchase and sale of government bonds—to temper the swings in credit and thus in the economy.

This worked well throughout the 1920s, and leading economists concluded that the problem of depression had been abolished. Banks reassured customers with posters comparing the Federal Reserve to a mighty dam. In the fall of 1929 Irving Fisher, the country's most respected economist, declared that stocks had reached a "permanently high plateau."

Those may be the most infamous words spoken in the history of economics. In 1929 the economy fell into the longest, deepest depression on record. Exactly what caused the Great Depression is fiercely debated even to this day. One theory that emerged in the early 1930s was that the engineers had overreached. Several Austrian-born economists led by Friedrich Hayek argued that economic booms bred overinvestment in dubious or unprofitable projects, and reasoned that the economy *required* a slump to clear away this overhang of unneeded assets. "Depressions are not simply evils, which we might attempt to suppress," wrote another of the Austrians, Joseph Schumpeter, "but forms of something which has to be done, namely, adjustment to change." Anything that remedied the Depression would interfere with this necessary adjustment.

This ecological view was shared by Andrew Mellon, Herbert Hoover's Treasury secretary. He welcomed the cleansing effect of the Great Depression. Hoover recalls being told by Mellon to "liquidate labor, liquidate stocks, liquidate the farmers, liquidate real estate . . . it will purge the rottenness out of the system. High costs of living and high living will come down. People will work harder, live a more moral life. Values will be adjusted, and enterprising people will pick up the wrecks from less competent people."

If ecologists like Hayek and Mellon accused engineers of

doing too much, engineers believed they had done too little. Yes, the Fed had been quick to pump cash into the banks after the initial market crash, and then to lend to healthy banks facing runs brought on by the failure of less healthy banks. But this was not enough to overcome the contractionary forces, many emanating from overseas, causing thousands of banks to fail. Fisher, for instance, laid the blame for the Depression at the feet of the Fed, for allowing deflation to take hold. As prices and wages fell, debt, which was fixed in value, became unbearable. The Fed, he said, had to restore prices and end deflation through expansionary monetary policy. Not many listened: the Depression had robbed Fisher of his fortune and his audience.

Herbert Hoover, elected president in 1928, was torn between these two schools. He was a Republican who believed in letting market forces play out, but he was also, by profession and temperament, an engineer. It was the engineer's duty, he later wrote, to clothe "the bare bones of science with life, comfort and hope." As Warren Harding's commerce secretary in 1921 he had arranged for the regular compilation and publication of economic statistics that would make economic engineering feasible. As president, Hoover thought Mellon meant well, but he dismissed his prescriptions and fought the Depression as best he could, for example setting up the Reconstruction Finance Corporation to lend to banks struggling with outflows of deposits.

This was not enough; the downward spiral of prices and output continued until Franklin Roosevelt took office in 1933 and implemented a banking holiday, devalued the dollar against gold, and proceeded to overhaul the Fed and vastly expand the role of government.

The notion that the economy could be managed was still relatively new, and controversial. Economists had no overarching theory of how the broad economy worked—what we now call macroeconomics. Alfred Marshall had showed how individual markets worked, what we now call microeconomics. If demand for some commodity was perturbed, its price would fall until demand was restored, a condition called "equilibrium." The overall economy was presumed to behave the same way: if the demand for labor suddenly shrank, wages would decline until full employment was restored. Prolonged periods of involuntary unemployment weren't possible. Since the economy was largely self-regulating, there wasn't much need for the federal government to intervene to right the ship, which is just as well since the government was tiny.

In the 1930s, though, the Great Depression demonstrated that economies did not self-equilibrate. Government could make things much better, or much worse. This was the revolutionary insight of the British economist John Maynard Keynes. In *The General Theory of Employment, Interest and Money*, published in 1936, Keynes described business investment as driven by "waves of optimistic and pessimistic sentiment." If businesses were pessimistic enough, even interest rates of zero could not coax them to invest. Individuals might rationally save more to protect their own financial security, but if everyone saved more and spent less, everyone's income would go down, no one would be better off, and the economy would stay depressed. Keynes called this the "paradox of thrift." It meant the economy could end up in a bad equilibrium rather than a good one.

Thus was born a role for the government: if private individuals and businesses would not borrow and spend, the government would have to, and thereby push the economy back to "full employment," which meant that everyone who wanted a job could find one.

Between them, Fisher and Keynes provided an intellectual framework through which government could steer an economy away from both booms and depressions. Politically, the time was ripe;

the economic devastation of the Great Depression made the public more amenable to activist government. Franklin Roosevelt didn't just expand the government's responsibility for the economy: he also extended its oversight of nature. Since 1910, the Forest Service's leaders were convinced that the only thing that kept them from controlling fires was lack of men and material. Gus Silcox, who had personally fought the fires of 1910, became the agency's chief in 1933 and a few years later promulgated what became known as the "10 a.m. policy": once a fire had been detected, it should be brought under control by 10 a.m. the next day.

It was pure hubris, but its spirit fit the temper of the times — and Roosevelt's own inclinations. As Stephen Pyne, a historian of fire, has written, Roosevelt considered himself a gentleman forester; one of his last physical acts before losing the use of his legs was to put out a fire on the Maine shore that he had spotted from his boat on the Bay of Fundy. Silcox proclaimed the Forest Service a tool of economic development that would alleviate rural poverty and unemployment, and Roosevelt was happy to oblige. The Civilian Conservation Corps, one of the New Deal's largest job creation programs, put thousands of unemployed, unmarried men to work planting trees and fighting forest fires. In the 1940s, the prevention of forest fires had been elevated to a civic duty, hammered home with the help of Smokey Bear. In one 1946 poster, Smokey wears a tool apron, one paw holding a carpenter's square, the other on a toolbox, and declares, "Burned timber builds no homes — prevent forest fires." In another, from 1953, Smokey holds a shovel, points to a burning wasteland, and proclaims, "This shameful waste WEAKENS AMERICA!"

Engineers' quest to foolproof the environment extended from the forests to the water. From the late 1800s onward the federal government and the Army Corps of Engineers had taken on ever more responsibility for controlling the lower Mississippi. Devastating floods in 1912 and 1913 led to the first federal flood

In this 1953 poster, Smokey Bear warns of the economic harm that results when carelessness leads to wildfires. (The name and character of Smokey Bear are the property of the United States, as provided by 16 U.S.C. § 580p-1 and 18 U.S.C. § 711, and are used with the permission of the Forest Service, U.S. Department of Agriculture.)

control act, in 1917. The Depression only strengthened the conviction that the rivers should be harnessed for economic benefit. In 1934 the National Resources Board declared, "In the interest of national welfare there must be national control of all running water from the desert trickle that may make an acre or two productive to the rushing flood waters of the Mississippi."

Thus, at the end of the Second World War, the engineers had assumed responsibility for much of the environment and the economy. In 1946 the Employment Act was passed, giving the federal government responsibility to create "conditions under which there will be afforded useful employment opportunities for those able, willing, and seeking work, and to promote maximum employment, production, and purchasing power."

Within twenty years, though, fissures appeared in this new consensus. Neither the economy nor the natural world turned out to be as amenable to human management as the engineers had imagined. Gilbert White, an obscure government geographer who had been pursuing graduate studies part-time at the University of Chicago, noticed that the frenzy of levee and dam building in the 1930s had not solved flooding; instead it had created a new problem: more homes, factories, and farms had sprung up on the floodplain, so more destruction ensued when floods overtopped the levees. In his dissertation, completed in 1942 but not widely circulated until years later, he wrote, "Floods are 'acts of God,' but flood losses are largely acts of man."

In forestry, ecologists began to chip away at the Forest Service's militarized culture of fire suppression at all costs. In 1962 the Kennedy administration appointed Starker Leopold, a zoologist and the son of one of the founders of the conservation movement, to head up an advisory committee on how best to manage the ecosystem inside the national parks. Leopold's report, released the next year, called for the reintroduction of fire as a device for habitat management, much as it was used on the grasslands of East Africa. Controlled fire was "the most 'natural' and much the cheapest and easiest to apply," his report said.

In economics, a similar shift was under way. Scholars, many working out of the University of Chicago, argued that government management of the economy was backfiring by failing to consider how people would adapt. Though federal regulation had continued to expand, George Stigler argued that regulators often ended up serving the regulated, not consumers. Stigler's student Sam Peltzman made an even more audacious claim: regulations aimed at making consumers safer might be doing the opposite. In 1975 he published a provocative study that claimed that seat belts were causing drivers to drive more recklessly, resulting in more pedestrian deaths.

Scholars were soon finding similar behavior in fields as diverse as shipping and football, and labeling the phenomena "risk compensation," "risk homeostasis," and "human factors." The economist's term was "moral hazard": the notion that when you protected people from the consequences of risky behavior, they take more risks. The upshot was that every well-intended effort to make us safer had unintended consequences that did the opposite.

Macroeconomic engineering faced a similar critique. Keynes's disciples figured they could use the levers of monetary policy (i.e., interest rates) and fiscal policy (i.e., the budget) to stimulate demand and hiring, and keep the economy at full employment. And for a while, it worked. But eventually, this strategy began to drive up inflation. In 1967 Milton Friedman predicted that as workers got used to higher inflation, they would demand higher wages—negating any additional demand for labor. By the 1970s, he was proved right as both unemployment and inflation rose, and recessions worsened. Friedrich Hayek's star rose as Margaret Thatcher, Ronald Reagan, and other conservatives embraced his deep suspicion of government meddling. He shared the Nobel Prize in 1974 and used his acceptance speech to attack his colleagues' fondness for economic engineering: "To act on the belief that we possess the knowledge and the power which enable us to shape the processes of society entirely to our liking, knowledge which in fact we do *not* possess, is likely to make us do much harm."

By the early 1980s, fiscal engineering—attempting to fine-tune the economy with a burst of spending here, a tax cut there—was dead; academic economists had disavowed it, political leaders shunned it, and with budget deficits ballooning, the public couldn't afford it.

But monetary engineering—tweaking interest rates just enough to keep both inflation and recession at bay—not only survived; it was more popular than ever. Paul Volcker, Alan Greenspan, and other central bankers gained folk-hero status. For twenty-five years, unemployment and inflation steadily fell, and recessions became less frequent.

This was no small thing. Every year not spent in recession, every percentage point less of unemployment, represented hundreds of billions of dollars of added income and wealth. Was there a downside? Most economists couldn't see one. One did, though, and he was not a disciple of Hayek but of Keynes. Hyman Minsky was born in Chicago in 1919 to two devout socialists who had met at a party celebrating the hundredth birthday of Karl Marx. Minsky, too, started out as a socialist. He was involved with the youth wing of the American Socialist Party, and during his army service in the 1940s, he helped occupied West Germany's Social Democrats keep their independence from the Communist Party. As a graduate student at Harvard he worked closely with both Schumpeter, a leading scholar of the Austrian school, and Alvin Hansen, Keynes's most influential disciple.

Minsky agreed with Keynes that the economy needed a big, active government to avoid depressions. But he also thought Keynesian models gave short shrift to the financial system. They assumed that the central bank had full control of the money supply, credit, and interest rates. Minsky argued that the volume of money and credit didn't depend just on the central bank but on financial innovation. If, to control inflation, the Fed restricted the growth of lending by banks, then Wall Street's innovators would come up with mechanisms to go around banks and get credit to those who wanted to borrow. Innovation, he predicted, proceeded through three stages: the first, "hedge" stage, when it served business's legitimate need to manage risk; the second, "speculative" phase, when it served mostly to finance rising asset prices; and a final, "Ponzi" stage, when investors had to borrow more simply to pay the interest on past borrowings. The longer the Fed prolongs prosperity, the further finance progresses through these stages, and the more unstable the financial system becomes. "Stability is destabilizing" sums up Minsky's thesis.

Minsky thought engineers' efforts to control the economy would ultimately be self-defeating because they assumed that the next threat to the economy would look like the last one. Because of innovation, this would never be the case. By enacting policies aimed at restricting the growth of credit by banks, they would fail to see how it was migrating outside of banks. He compared central bankers to the French generals waiting for the Nazis behind the Maginot Line in 1940: prepared to fight the last war. Because the financial system is always evolving, "the next financial crisis will never be just like the last one."

That was in 1957; Minsky would spend the next forty years, until his death, expanding on the theory and repeating it to whomever would listen. A handful of devoted followers did listen, mostly on Wall Street; most economists did not. Academic economists earn recognition with meticulous, statistical analysis of data or a tidy theory built on elegant models; Minsky gave both short shrift. His papers were more like essays, somewhat repetitive and often turgid. Though Minsky was on the faculty at Washington University in St. Louis, he showed scant interest in teaching or research. Eric Falkenstein, one of his teaching assistants and later a fund manager, recalls that his advanced classes were all classes in "Minskyism." Rather than teach the models of macroeconomics, he preferred to tell stories of the great economists he had known or pluck stories from the newspaper to illustrate his thesis.

Laurence Meyer, then department chairman, denied him a

raise one year for poor performance; a furious Minsky refused to speak to him for years afterward. "We used to say, 'Hy's written one paper over and over again,'" Meyer later told me. "But I would have loved to have written that paper."

Apart from being a difficult person, Minsky had another problem: his theory wasn't very useful. Economists had done their best to mimic the natural sciences by building models that yielded predictable results. If the price of widgets went up this much, their sales would fall that much. If interest rates rose by x, employment would fall by y. Minskyism was antithetical to such elegant model building. Extrapolating established trends was, he believed, precisely what caused them to collapse. Confidence and credit would grow hand in hand, until some event caused them to break, and the fragility that had grown quietly alongside them over the years would be exposed. When? Minsky didn't know any better than anyone else. Crises by their nature were unpredictable. "He always thought a market collapse was just around the corner," Falkenstein recalled.

At least once, he was right. On Friday, October 16, 1987, Falkenstein made a big bet against the stock market using options. The market crashed the following Monday. Falkenstein sent his old mentor a letter, telling him, "I'm going to get rich off your theory!" Minsky was tickled. He predicted the crash would lead to a recession, though not a depression.

In this he and many economists were mistaken. The economy did just fine. That puzzle is what inspired the National Bureau of Economic Research, the U.S.'s premier economic research organization, to gather forty scholars together in Cambridge that day in October 1989, on the second anniversary of the crash. Nobody dismissed the potential for further crises. The fact was, however, that crises had come and gone while leaving surprisingly little mark on the economy. Markets had not been so turbulent since the 1930s, noted Paul Krugman, yet the economy had chugged along for seven years "without either turning into a runaway boom or stalling into a recession."

Minsky's message was that the good times would not last. "The financial instability hypothesis is pessimistic," he warned. "Capitalism is flawed in that thrusts to financial and economic crises are endogenous phenomena."

Despite his inclusion in the program, Minsky was still a relative outsider among these academic celebrities, and he drew little attention. Volcker was a different matter. Though out of office he still commanded huge respect. He was an inveterate worrier, with reason: he had already dealt with more crises than anyone else in the room. "I indeed think that the economy is becoming more crisis-prone, more overextended," he said, but then, there were far more tools to deal with it. The problem was that people were getting used to being bailed out by those tools. He remembers thinking, as president of the Fed bank overseeing the New York district in the 1970s, "What this country needs to shake us up and give us a little discipline is a good bank failure. But please, God, not in my district." Volcker thought it would be healthier if people were a bit more scared: "We need that greater sense of risk within a structure of stability and resiliency—and it is awfully easy to say that and awfully hard to do."

Volcker's worries were both prescient and richly ironic, for no one had used the tools of economic and crisis management so intensively and successfully as he during the 1980s. The result was a generation of low inflation and stable growth, and in time diminished fear. This was the combination that would eventually make possible the global financial crisis. It just wasn't apparent at the time.

"Please, God, not in my district": Before the Economy Could Destroy Itself, First Paul Volcker Had to Save It

Paul Volcker never had a grand plan to make the world a safer place; things just turned out that way. Starting in the early 1970s, when he first rose to prominence as a Treasury official, the world kept throwing problems at him. In 1971, it was collapsing confidence in the dollar's link to gold. He helped scrap that link. In 1975, it was the imminent bankruptcy of New York City. Volcker had just become president of the Federal Reserve Bank of New York, the most important of the Fed's twelve banks. Richard Ravitch, who headed the state's urban development arm, asked Volcker over dinner how to approach the Fed for a bailout. Volcker said to Ravitch, "If we do it for New York, we'd have to do it for everyone else." The city went elsewhere.

But these paled next to three interlocking problems that awaited Volcker shortly after he became Fed chairman in 1979. The first was inflation. It had been rising since the 1960s, and that year, revolution in Iran sent oil prices through the roof and inflation into double digits. Volcker set out to crush it by pushing interest rates to an all-time high of 20 percent. The second problem was that many Latin American countries had borrowed heavily in dollars, and high interest rates threatened their ability to pay the money back. The third problem was that if those countries defaulted, the big American banks that had lent them the money could collapse. Solving those three problems would consume most of Volcker's time in office and set the stage for the prosperity to follow.

During the 1970s, American banks were anxious to expand abroad. They took dollars earned by Arab oil exporters and lent them to Latin American governments to finance their trade deficits. By 1982, with the interest rates soaring, it was only a matter of time before something gave. Mexico was running out of foreign currency to service its bank loans. Volcker knew that if it defaulted, a big chunk of the American banking system would be instantly insolvent. So he bought time by having the Fed lend to Mexico to disguise its loss of foreign currency reserves. He hoped a new Mexican president could take office that fall and put in place the economic reforms necessary to restore confidence. But by August it was clear that this plan would not work: Mexico was going to run out of money long before a new president was in place. On Friday, August 13, Volcker began calling top officials in other countries to arrange bridge loans to tide Mexico over.

The next step was to persuade the banks to refinance Mexico's maturing loans for a few more months. For some months, Volcker had been meeting with Mexico's finance minister, Jesús Silva Herzog. Volcker arranged for Herzog and his debt expert, Ángel Gurría, to meet with their bankers in New York to try to work out a solution. The stakes were unbelievably high: if Mexico defaulted, some of those banks could be wiped out. Volcker did not think it appropriate to attend a meeting between Mexico and its creditors, and so it was up to Herzog to make the case. The first meeting, with a handful of banks and officials from the Fed and Treasury at the New York Fed, was tense. It led to a second, bigger meeting the next day with a much larger group of bankers.

Herzog was a charismatic and urbane man with a flair for drama. Arriving in lower Manhattan, Herzog looked up at the headquarters of big American banks and confided to Gurría, "I get the impression that every time we take a step on the sidewalk here in New York, these big buildings shake." He could be grave one moment and hysterically funny the next, which would be a crucial asset in what would prove a tense series of negotiations. At that second, larger meeting, he began by urging the bankers to act in their own interest by giving Mexico more flexibility to pay. "We're out of money, and we think it's in your interest not to force payment," he told them. "In fact, we think it's necessary for you to lend us some more money." As Gurría later recalled, all the bankers understood that if Mexico defaulted, they would have to write down their banks' loans. That would render many of those banks insolvent. They also knew that Brazil and Argentina weren't far behind. But if a single banker balked and called its loan, all the others would do the same, since the last to collect would likely get nothing. But then, nobody would get paid in full.

The bankers were angry, confused, and, mostly, hungry for information. Mexico's debts came in a bewildering array of types and sizes, from short-term loans to leases on oil rigs. Herzog did his best to answer questions, tossing the more technical ones to Gurría. But the truth was, they didn't have a lot of answers. As the meeting dragged on and the questions became ever harder to answer, Herzog decided to inject some humor into the meeting to ease his creditors' minds. "Listen here," he said, "my name is Jesus, and his is Angel. You're in good hands."

Volcker did not have a road map for resolving the crisis; his priority was that the banks not force Mexico into default, an event that could trigger a global banking panic in the midst of a deep recession. Thus, those initial meetings led to countless other meetings and negotiations, and eventually the banks agreed to roll over Mexico's debts and lend them enough money to pay the interest, thereby preserving the fiction that Mexico was solvent. The Fed and other regulators, in turn, decided not to force the banks to face reality and write down their loans to Mexico and other strapped countries to true value. If they had, Manufacturers Hanover, Bank of America, and perhaps Citicorp (the predecessor of Citigroup) would have been insolvent. The regulators' forbearance gave the banks the rest of the decade to earn enough profits to absorb the losses.

Volcker had staved off one banking panic, but another soon loomed. Continental Illinois, then America's seventh-largest bank, had grown rapidly, and by early 1984 it was in big trouble. So Volcker swung into action again. As deposits fled Continental, the Fed replaced them with loans of its own.

In theory, this was the Fed's job: if a healthy bank was in danger of collapse because panicked depositors were pulling their money and funds were rushing out, the Fed could print money out of thin air and lend it to the bank to stave off collapse. But Continental, by that point, wasn't healthy. It had grown too fast and had too little capital. Most banks funded themselves primarily with deposits from ordinary individuals that tended to stay put because, up to $100,000, they were federally insured. But Continental relied mostly on large, uninsured deposits from institutions, companies, and wealthy individuals, which were quick to flee at the smell of trouble.

The Fed wasn't supposed to lend to unhealthy banks. Ordinarily, Continental's shareholders and uninsured depositors should have accepted the consequences of the risks they took. The problem was that Continental wasn't alone; banks across the country had been battered not just by the Latin American debt crisis but also by collapsing oil and farmland values. Nine of Texas's biggest banks failed in the 1980s. As Volcker saw it, if Continental went down, several even bigger banks would be next. So Volcker did more than just lend to Continental; he urged the Federal Deposit Insurance Corporation to protect deposits beyond the $100,000 cap. When other banks could not be persuaded to take over the slowly capsizing bank, the FDIC did, becoming its largest shareholder—an unfamiliar role for an agency whose main job was to regulate and when necessary close banks, not run them. The rescue of Continental prompted a congressman to observe that a new class of banks now existed: "too big to fail."

The crises didn't end with Volcker. In 1987, a few months after his successor, Alan Greenspan, took office, the stock market crashed. Greenspan slashed interest rates while his colleagues persuaded banks to keep lending to crippled Wall Street dealers. A total meltdown in the markets was narrowly averted; the economy never skipped a beat. The mini-crash of 1989 was also a nonevent, perhaps thanks to the Fed's assurance of assistance.

Volcker's actions in 1982 and again in 1984, and Greenspan's in 1987 and 1989, set the template for how policy makers would react to crisis for twenty-five years. Inflation would be kept low and stable. With that proviso, the Fed would do what it could to prevent both recessions and financial collapse. But what were the unintended consequences of this pattern? That's what vexed Volcker when he spoke at that conference in Cambridge back in 1989.

I met Volcker one afternoon in late 2013 at his office in New York's Rockefeller Center. Outside, the lights on the center's Christmas tree had begun to twinkle. Behind him stood stacks of books about the financial crisis; scattered around were mementoes of his long career in public service, which had continued even after he had left the Fed some twenty-six years earlier. At the time of our visit he was preoccupied with his own prescriptions to fix the financial system, such as banning banks from trading with their own money and slimming down the bloated ranks of American regulatory agencies. At age eighty-six, his memory of key events in the 1970s and '80s remained crystal clear; names and events came back to him as we talked.

I noted that he sternly disapproved of moral hazard and had frowned on the Fed's bailout of so many companies during the recent crisis. So I asked why it was okay then to bail out Continental Illinois in 1984. He said, "You're always worried about the effects elsewhere. Continental Illinois was not the only bank in trouble at the time." Others, he said, included Chase Manhattan and Bank of America.

Then I brought up his remark from Cambridge in 1989: "As president of the Federal Reserve Bank of New York, I often said to myself, 'What this country needs to shake us up and give us a little discipline is a good bank failure. But please, God, not in my district.'" He smiled. That, he said, was "just a confession of my personal weakness."

I asked him whether he thought constantly intervening in the financial system, as he and his successors had, to protect the economy could have given people an increased appetite for risk because they were more confident that the economy would be rescued. He tilted his head, narrowed his eyes, and glared at me. "I'm not going to accept full responsibility," he said. Well, I asked, how about partial responsibility? He laughed. "No."

Indeed, it is easy to misinterpret the link between Volcker's and Greenspan's interventions and the eventual crisis. Critics, for example, often say that by saving financiers and investors from their own idiocy, they guaranteed that those individuals and institutions would repeat the behavior until they paid a price. But that's not correct. The truth is far more subtle. As we shall see, Volcker and his successors did not sit on their laurels each time they saved the economy from disaster. When they were finished bailing out a struggling bank or rescuing the financial system from collapse, they set themselves to rooting out the causes of the crisis to avoid a repeat. But while individuals, companies, and even entire countries such as Mexico usually paid a price for taking too many risks, the system as a whole learned the opposite lesson: the economy was largely insulated from its most destabilizing elements, and that stability lulled everyone into thinking it was okay to take on more risk. In 1979, when Volcker took office, business and household debt stood at 95 percent of gross domestic product (GDP), or annual economic output. By the start of 2008, it stood at 171 percent.

It's often said that the financial crisis was brought on by deregulation, such as the repeal of Glass-Steagall, the Depression-era law that split commercial banks from securities dealers. But this is an oversimplification. In the decades before the financial crisis, there was plenty of both regulation, such as increased capital requirements, and deregulation, such as the repeal of Glass-Steagall. Some deregulation, to be sure, was meant to better enable banks to compete. But regulators, in the process, thought they were correcting the flaws in earlier rules that made banks more fragile. Glass-Steagall, they thought, had caused the best-quality borrowers to issue bonds instead of takeout bank loans, leaving banks with the riskiest borrowers. Allowing banks to underwrite bonds and other securities would correct that flaw.

More important than outright deregulation was benign neglect — the decision not to regulate — of the alternative forms of lending that were taking banks' place. Their efforts did make banks safer; but for the economy as a whole, safety was illusory because much of the risk had been pushed outside the banks, such as to mortgage companies like Countrywide Financial and off-balance-sheet investment funds. This wouldn't have mattered if those so-called shadow banks had remained small; but they didn't. By the time of the 2008 crisis, many were bigger than banks.

Volcker was prepared to prop up banks because they had always been at the core of the financial system, were closely regulated, and enjoyed explicit government support via deposit insurance and loans from the Fed. He did not think shadow banks should get the same treatment.

Yet the migration of risk to shadow banks began as a consequence of Volcker's efforts to fix banks. From his earliest years in office, he was worried that banks were taking too many risks and weren't adequately regulated. Early in his tenure at the New York Fed, he was paid a visit by Walter Wriston, the legendary chairman of Citicorp (now Citigroup), the largest and most innovative bank at the time. Wriston had come, with his chief financial officer in tow, "to explain to me why Citibank didn't need any capital at all," recalls Volcker. Wriston argued, "If we run into some problems, we'll take it out of the profits for that year. There's not a chance that we'll have the losses that exceed our profits in a year, so we don't really need any capital. And the only reason we keep any capital is some of the old fogies on my board insist that we do." Volcker recalls being "appalled how little capital they had. Not just Citibank but the banks in general had let their capital erode during that period. When I became chairman of the [Fed], I went on kind of a campaign to get banks to increase capital."

Capital serves as a shock absorber: it absorbs losses from bad loans, thereby protecting depositors' money (and the deposit insurance fund). Capital comes in many forms, usually common equity but also preferred equity and certain types of debt. Imagine a bank has $100 of loans and decides to fund them with $95 of deposits and $5 of capital. If just 6 percent of the loans go bad, the value of the bank's loans drops to $94, less than it owes depositors; its equity will be wiped out and it will be insolvent. The solution for banks' excessive risk taking, as Volcker saw it, was to force them to hold more capital, so that bad lending decisions would not sink them.

To the Walter Wristons of the world, this seemed like a terrible idea. Bankers hate capital standards (requirements on how much capital they must hold, expressed as a ratio of capital to assets), and with good reason: they make banking less profitable. With a 5 percent capital standard, if a bank sells $1 of new stock, that dollar can support $20 of new loans, as opposed to just $10 of loans if the standard is 10 percent.

By the early 1980s, with so many banks saved from insolvency only by regulators' forbearance, it was clear that Wriston had been wrong, and Volcker was determined not to let weak capital bring down the banks again. He began the process of raising capital standards in 1985. Naturally, the banks protested that this put them at a competitive disadvantage to foreign banks with laxer requirements. To level the playing field, in 1986 Volcker teamed up with his counterparts in Britain to make the changes in concert. By 1988, under Greenspan, the effort had gone global; the United States joined most other major countries in passing the first of the Basel Capital Accords (named for the Swiss city where bank regulators met). Henceforth, banks would have to have $8 of capital for every $100 of assets, up from between $4 and $6. There were exceptions: government bonds, considered riskless, would require no capital; mortgages, considered safer than business and consumer loans, would require only $4.

The increased capital standards survived a hail of opposition by banks and their allies in Congress and were phased in from 1988 to 1992. They were widely blamed for aggravating the recession

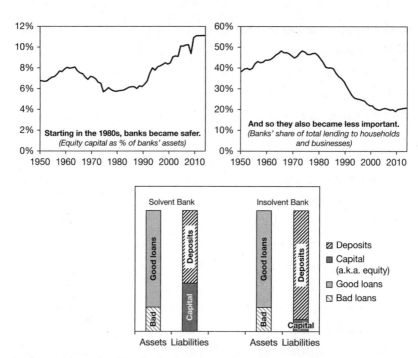

In the 1980s and 1990s, banks became safer as their equity capital rose, but their importance as a source of credit shrank as other types of lenders took their place. The lower diagram illustrates how less capital makes a bank more vulnerable if loans go bad. (Sources: Federal Deposit Insurance Corporation and author's calculations based on data from the Federal Reserve)

of 1990–91 and holding back the recovery. "Thank Basel for Credit Crunch" read an op-ed by Richard Breeden and William Isaac, former heads of the SEC and FDIC, in 1992.

Despite its unpopularity in some circles, this strategy did seem to shore up the banks, but with an unintended consequence. Higher capital requirements and tougher regulation meant that traditional deposit gathering and loans were becoming more expensive. The financial system became adept at coming up with alternative ways to gather up savings and lend them, the practice later dubbed "shadow banking." The most important was the capital markets. Big companies had long been able to bypass banks by issuing bonds and commercial paper to big investors such as pension funds and mutual funds.

In the 1990s, innovations made it possible for developing nations and households to bypass banks as well. For countries, the best bypass route was Brady bonds, named for Treasury secretary Nicholas Brady. Banks, groaning under billions of dollars of impaired loans to emerging economies, needed a way to get them off their balance sheets. Brady hatched a plan that would let them convert their loans to bonds, and then sell them to investors. The Brady bond program was a crucial step back toward health for America's big banks. It also gave birth to the emerging market bond industry. As a result, emerging economies would henceforth borrow not from banks, with the attendant risks to banks' solvency, but from the capital markets. This didn't eliminate sovereign debt crises such as the Asian financial crisis, but it made them less likely to be a threat to America's financial system; American banks' exposure to Mexico in 1994, and East Asia in 1997, was far smaller than in 1982.

A similar feat was accomplished with securitization. Banks had always been able to sell individual loans, usually to other banks. But starting in the 1970s Lewis Ranieri of Salomon Brothers hit upon the idea of packaging many mortgages, and later credit card receivables or auto loans, together into a single "mortgage-backed security" (MBS) or "asset-backed security" (ABS) and selling it to investors just like a corporate bond. The original purpose was to increase the supply of mortgages by enabling banks and thrifts—a sort of bank with more restrictions on its lending—to make loans, sell them, and use the proceeds to make new ones. Regulators found that securitization served another purpose: it removed potentially risky loans from the hands of both damaged and healthy banks. The Resolution Trust Corporation, set up in 1989 to dispose of loans inherited from failed thrifts, securitized them, giving a powerful kick start to the sector. So did Fannie Mae and Freddie Mac. Once they determined that a loan met specific underwriting standards, they guaranteed the MBS against default.

By the 2000s, banks were transforming regular loans into securities that could similarly be sold off to investors or held on their own balance sheets. For example, a syndicate of banks might make a loan to a business, then sell that loan to mutual funds.

The growth of capital markets and securitization meant that the U.S. economy became steadily less dependent on banks. In 1979, banks supplied 46 percent of the American households' and businesses' credit. By 2007, that share had fallen to 20 percent. Shadow banks such as finance companies and investment banks had stepped into the gap, making lots of new loans that were then securitized, or underwriting corporate bonds. Regulators considered this a good thing. Since prior crises had always involved banks, a bank sector that was better regulated and that had farmed out much of its riskier activity to the capital markets ought to be safer. Events of the early 2000s seemed to confirm this. In 2003, Greenspan noted, with satisfaction: "Even the largest corporate defaults in history (WorldCom and Enron) and the largest sovereign default in history (Argentina) have not significantly impaired the capital of any major financial intermediary."

Greenspan would later blame Fannie and Freddie and their implied government backing for the crisis. But at the time, he thought they helped make the banking system safer. By promoting securitization, as Greenspan saw it, they had "contributed to the transfer of credit risk from highly leveraged originators of credit—especially banks and thrifts—to less-leveraged insurance companies and pension and mutual funds, among other investors."

Given the traditional focus on banks, it is perhaps not surprising that up until 2007, regulators were sanguine. Bank capital was robust. The riskiest mortgages were being originated not by banks but by finance companies such as New Century Financial and Ameriquest, then securitized by investment banks and sold to investors all over the world. Other than Fannie and Freddie, there wasn't much reason to worry that a mortgage crisis would bring down the financial system. It seemed that the response to the various crises of the 1980s had made the financial system genuinely safer.

It wasn't just the banking crisis of the 1980s that taught economic leaders lessons. Each of the subsequent crises left them determined to avoid a repeat. Consider, for example, the stock market crash of 1987. Stock trading was facilitated by specialists and market makers—dealers who would buy and sell for their own accounts. At the market's nadir many suffered crippling losses on the stocks they had bought that then went down in value. Subsequent reforms created circuit breakers to halt sudden drops in the markets, while the dealers who handled stock trading were required to bulk up their capital. Stock markets faced numerous bear markets over the subsequent decades, but not since 1987 have they again come close to total meltdown.

In 1998, when Russia defaulted and Long-Term Capital Management, a giant hedge fund, threatened to fail and inflict chaos on the markets, the Fed cut interest rates three times and brokered a bailout of LTCM by the banks that were its principal creditors. The Fed was alarmed at how little it, and the banks it oversaw, knew about LTCM, and so it began instructing banks to keep much closer tabs on the leverage its hedge fund customers were allowed to accumulate. Although the failure of two in-house hedge funds helped bring down Bear Stearns & Company, hedge funds were not much of a contributor to the later crisis.

Foreign crises also triggered changes aimed at making the global economy more stable. In the early 1990s Mexico, as it had in the 1970s and 1980s, borrowed heavily from foreigners, this time in the form of short-term Treasury bills whose value was linked to the dollar rather than via bank loans. When the peso collapsed in 1994, the cost of servicing that debt soared, and the United States and International Monetary Fund bailed Mexico out. Mexico learned its lesson, and thereafter kept a floating exchange rate and stuck to borrowing in its own currency. When the rich world sank into crisis in 2008, Mexico's central banker observed, with relief, "This time it wasn't us."

Individual firms learned lessons, as well. While almost forgotten now, the collapse in 1990 of Drexel Burnham Lambert, home of the junk bond king Michael Milken, was the largest closure of an investment bank in the United States. Drexel had borrowed by issuing commercial paper, essentially a short-term loan from an investor rather than a bank, secured not by collateral, like a house or a Treasury bond, but merely by its promise to repay. Secured financing is supposed to be safer because if the borrower goes bankrupt, the lender can seize the collateral. That's why you pay a lower interest rate on your mortgage, which is secured by your house, than on your credit card, which isn't secured by anything. A study by several Fed economists in 2010 noted that securities firms, analysts, and supervisors took those lessons from Drexel's failure on board. Firms began to limit their use of unsecured commercial paper and instead touted their use of secured loans backed with collateral such as Treasury bonds. Bear Stearns, for example, boasted in its 2006 annual financial report that it made "extensive use of secured funding."

Bear Stearns's secured financing consisted of so-called repo loans. "Repo" probably makes you think of a man in a bad suit repossessing your car, and a repo loan isn't that different. An investment bank like Bear Stearns would borrow for a few days or a week from a money market mutual fund and secure the loan with securities such as Treasury bonds.

Secured funding was supposed to be a foolproof way to support more lending without making the financial system more dangerous. But there weren't enough Treasury bonds to serve as collateral for the growing mountain of repo loans. So securities firms began using mortgage-backed securities that were designed to be as safe as Treasurys, and had the same top AAA rating. In 2008 lenders were nervous enough about AAA-rated MBSs to refuse to refinance repo loans that used them. Bear Stearns collapsed in 2008 largely because it couldn't refinance its maturing repo loans, which, given the lessons learned from Drexel, simply wasn't supposed to happen.

Drexel's experience amply illustrated how a financial innovation that seemed at the time to reduce risk once it became widespread enough, did the opposite, and raised risk throughout the system. Another example was the use of mortgage-backed securities. Because American banks tended to be regional, they were acutely vulnerable to localized housing busts. Deep downturns in Massachusetts and Texas had sent many local banks over the edge. MBSs made it possible to pool loans from around the country, diluting the effect of a housing bust in any region on the overall portfolio. Because historically prices never fell on a nationwide basis, investors were much more comfortable holding a diversified portfolio of mortgages. The diversification benefits of MBSs both reduced the cost of borrowing for everybody and expanded the influx of credit into the mortgage market. Investors, believing that nationwide home prices could never go down, acted in a way that guaranteed they would.

Certainly, some bankers and investors suspected that home prices were poised to fall and that MBSs sold as safe would turn out not to be. But they were in the minority, and were either ignored or chose to stay quiet. The majority persisted in believing that the mortgage market would remain largely trouble-free, as it historically had—as evidenced by how many of the people closest to the business, from frontline bankers to chief executives, had their personal wealth and their companies tied up in it.

By foolproofing the banks, policy makers figured they'd vanquished one of the two great threats to economic stability. The other was inflation, which did damage in a number of ways. First, pushing it down usually required a recession and higher unemployment. Second, keeping up with the rising cost of living was deeply dispiriting; by the late 1970s, the public consistently named inflation a bigger problem than unemployment, and that discontent practically drove Jimmy Carter from office. Third, inflation was one reason the banks by the early 1980s were in such bad shape. As inflation rose in the 1960s and '70s, so did interest rates. Banks and thrifts were stuck with loans made when interest rates were low, but now had to pay much higher interest rates to attract and keep deposits, saddling them with huge losses.

Not surprisingly, policy makers concluded that the best way they could restore prosperity and stability was to defeat inflation. First, Volcker knocked down inflation from 13 percent to 4 percent, at the price of a deep recession from 1980 to 1982. It was up to Alan Greenspan to finish the job.

Greenspan took office in 1987 and, as he told me many years later, had one preoccupation above all, to prevent any backsliding on Volcker's progress on inflation: "That would have been a disgrace." True to his intent, just weeks after taking office, Greenspan persuaded his colleagues to vote for a half percentage point increase in the Fed's discount rate, a largely symbolic but highly visible preemptive strike against inflation. Shortly afterward, Greenspan received a personal note from Volcker: "You have now become a central banker." Greenspan's determination to finish the job Volcker had begun resulted in another recession, from 1990 to 1991, after which inflation slid further, to below 3 percent, where it stayed.

Low inflation produced a virtuous circle. The longer it stayed low, the more businesses and households set wages and prices on the assumption that this would persist. Low inflation thus became self-perpetuating. This had many small, microeconomic benefits: fewer distortions (e.g., in the tax code), and less time and effort spent by businesses deciding how much to change their prices. But the macroeconomic benefits were even greater. When inflation was high and volatile, the Fed would drag its feet about cutting interest rates even if unemployment was high, fearing a rapid reacceleration in price pressure. But once inflation became anchored at such a low level, the Fed felt far more comfortable cutting interest rates when threats to growth materialized. This became apparent when the Fed briefly slashed interest rates in the fall of 1998 to deal with the turmoil of Long-Term Capital Management. Inflation barely budged. It cut them even further and faster in 2001 and 2002, after the collapsing dot-com bubble and then the 9/11 terrorist attacks. The 2001 recession was the mildest since the Second World War.

With steady growth and stable inflation, the 1990s became known as the "Goldilocks" economy: not too hot, not too cold. In 2002 economists Mark Watson and James Stock came up with a grander label. They fed a wealth of data into their computer models and identified a remarkable decline in the volatility of growth, inflation, and interest rates since 1984, dubbing this period "the Great Moderation." Theories abounded as to why the business cycle had been tamed: some said it was good luck, including fewer oil price shocks. Some credited better business practice, including tighter control of inventories. Ben Bernanke, an economist steeped in the theory and history of monetary policy who joined the Fed in 2002, credited one factor above all: the Fed had become far more adept at nipping inflation in the bud. The more inflation remained under control, the more the Fed could devote its attention to unemployment. Businesses were keeping better control of inventories precisely because inflation was lower. Oil price spikes still occurred, but they were less likely to trigger a wage-price spiral when people had faith the Fed wouldn't let that happen.

But low inflation also had a dark side. The same stability it brought to the overall economy also fed the imbalances from which crises would come. Some of this was simply a matter of arithmetic. Textbook models of stock and bond valuation show that the more predictable the outlook for profits, the more investors will pay for a future dollar of those profits. (The same math applies to bonds and houses.) For example, shares of Coca-Cola traditionally trade at a higher price-to-earnings ratio (P/E) than other companies because its profits are so stable. That logic, applied to the economy as a whole, could justify a much loftier stock market as well.

In the late 1990s Abby Joseph Cohen of Goldman Sachs became the most famous and widely followed strategist on Wall Street for her persistently bullish, and correct, calls on the stock market. Cohen was by training an economist, and inflation was at the core of her bullishness. According to her theory, when inflation is low and stable, booms and busts are less pronounced and investors have more confidence that expected profits will in fact materialize. They will thus pay more for those profits. The historical average ratio of stock prices to company earnings (the P/E ratio) was 14, but Cohen would note that in the 1960s, when inflation was low, the ratio was 22.

In practice, though, high valuations can be fickle: they last only so long as stability does. Once the outlook becomes more uncertain, perceived risk rises, causing valuations to collapse. This became clear when Cohen's forecasts took a beating in the subsequent bear market.

Low inflation was also a propellant for higher home prices. When inflation is high, so are interest rates. This has the effect of pushing up the payment the borrower must make, which reduces the size of the mortgage he can take on. That burden steadily declines as the borrower's income climbs along with inflation. Low inflation reduces the payment and enables the buyer to afford a much larger mortgage and thus a pricier house.

While it was true that high inflation was corrosive to financial stability, so, perversely, was low inflation: inflation was low and economic growth stable in the 1920s in America, and in 1980s-era Japan. In both cases, the result was a stock market bubble. Greenspan himself pointed this out in the aftermath of the dot-com bubble in 2002. As inflation had become tame, recessions had become less frequent, so investors and home buyers were willing to pay higher prices for assets, which exposed them to big losses if anything went wrong. "It seems ironic," he said, "that a monetary policy that is successful in inducing stability may inadvertently be sowing the seeds of instability associated with asset bubbles." The Fed, of course, could cure this problem by letting inflation rip, then clamping down, triggering more recessions—and keeping a lid on the prices of homes and stocks. This was more or less what happened in the 1970s and early 1980s. That course of action, Greenspan wryly observed, "can be readily dismissed."

The successful containment of both inflation and banking instability was not enough to bring on a crisis; attitudes about risk had to change. And that they did. By making the economy seem safer, the Great Moderation also changed attitudes about debt.

The Great Depression had left a lasting wariness of debt. When, in the postwar period, the newly prosperous middle class bought homes, cars, and appliances and rediscovered installment credit, the rapid growth in consumer debt brought no end of angst. "The bald, unadorned figures of consumer-credit expansion smell of a credit binge," *Fortune* magazine warned in 1956, in an article for which Alan Greenspan, then a young consultant, provided the data. "The turn in consumer credit would powerfully accelerate a general recession."

By the time of the Great Moderation, however, views had begun to shift. Debt was, after all, only one side of the balance sheet—the liability side. On the other side were valuable assets: homes, cars, and college degrees. By the 1980s and '90s, regulators began to suspect they had made it too hard for many Americans to borrow. Many states, for example, had usury laws limiting how much interest banks could charge. Since banks could not charge risky customers enough to compensate for the possibility of default, they simply didn't lend to them. Starting in the early 1980s, state antiusury laws were repealed and lenders began extending credit to groups that had long been denied, in particular minority and lower-income families. Loan denial rates dropped sharply, marking the birth of the subprime loan market. In the mid-1990s, Bill Clinton pushed hard to ease financial barriers to home ownership; his National Home Ownership Strategy pressed lenders and regulators to lower down payment requirements and reduce transaction costs in an effort to boost home ownership, "fueled by the creativity and resources of the private and public sectors."

That making home ownership easier would be politically popular was neither surprising nor new. What is striking when we look back at the 1990s and 2000s is that economists, who knew very well the risks of excessive debt, were so sanguine. How could this be? It turns out that there were two key reasons for their embrace of debt.

One was described in a 2005 study by several Fed economists that documented a striking phenomenon. Even as the overall economy became less volatile, individual households were experiencing more volatility. Layoffs, life changes, and abrupt reductions in hours meant they were more likely to suffer sudden declines or loss of income. But, these economists noted, something had reduced the impact of these events on the overall economy. Financial innovation had enabled consumers to keep spending even when their income plunged. The deregulation of interest rates meant credit was no longer turned off like a tap when the Federal Reserve tightened, while developments in asset-based lending, automated underwriting, and novel loan products enabled households to make big purchases when in previous eras they would have had to tighten their belts. Whereas consumer spending was highly correlated to incomes in the 1960s, there was little to no correlation between the two in the early 2000s. The conclusion: giving consumers more tools to borrow with made the overall economy less volatile and kept the Great Moderation going.

Nobody thought for a minute that financial distress for lower-income households had disappeared—far from it. In a separate paper those same three economists documented that between the 1970s and 2000s, the typical household was much more likely to see its income cut in half. But the evidence seemed to be that financial innovation, especially in the mortgage market, was helping defray the ill effects of that volatility.

A second reason economists were sanguine about debt was the Fed's ability to respond to financial panics. Economists knew that if people borrowed more, bankruptcy became more likely. As long as the lenders were paid for that risk, that was okay. The question was, could borrowing—even if it ended in bankruptcy for the borrower—ever bring the entire economy down? Economists were confident that it would not. As Frederic Mishkin, a Fed governor, argued on the eve of the financial crisis, a quick-acting Fed could prevent even a 20 percent drop in housing prices from doing any serious economic damage.

Brad DeLong, an economist at the University of California at Berkeley who had served in Clinton's Treasury from 1993 to 1995, described many years later why he and his fellow Democrats pushed deregulation: "It had then been more than sixty years since financial disruption had had more than a minor impact on overall levels of production and employment.... The poorer two-thirds of America's population appeared to be shut out of the opportunities to borrow at reasonable interest rates.... Depression-era restrictions on risk seemed less urgent, given the U.S. Federal Reserve's proven ability to build firewalls between financial distress and aggregate demand. New ways to borrow and to spread risk seemed to have little downside.... It seemed worth trying. It wasn't."

The rise in household debt over the course of the Great Moderation was no coincidence: a more stable economy meant that taking on more debt was much less dangerous than before. True, you could still lose your job and default on your loan because of some personal misfortune, but it wasn't likely to happen because of a wrenching recession.

It was a persuasive story. Yet Paul Volcker, the inveterate worrier, couldn't quite buy it. One evening in February 2005 he took the podium after a dinner at Stanford University. It had been eighteen years since he'd left the Fed, but he had never really left public service. Having been busy investigating accusations of corruption in the United Nations' oil-for-food program, he opened with some stern advice for the politicians, CEOs, and academics in the audience: "If you have any doubts about some aspects of your own background...do not use e-mail. You can't erase that stuff."

After the laughter died down, Volcker turned to another of his perpetual preoccupations: the threat of a crisis. There was a lot of optimism around, he acknowledged. He did not share it. "Underneath that favorable and placid surface," he said, "there are some really disturbing trends. Some huge imbalances, disequilibria, risks. Call it what you will. And altogether the circumstances seem to me as dangerous and intractable as I can remember, and I can remember quite a lot." He went down his list of worries: America's gaping trade deficit financed principally by foreign central banks, the fiscal threat of retiring baby boomers, soaring home prices that had relieved those boomers of any compulsion to save, and, most of all, a troubling complacency about it all. He concluded: "Big adjustments will inevitably become necessary....And as things stand, the danger is that it will be a financial crisis eventually rather than policy foresight that will force the changes."

Volcker was better at foretelling crises than describing what they would look like. The budget, the trade deficit, and inflation were topmost in his mind that evening; none mattered when the crisis arrived. Volcker put the odds of a serious drop in the dollar at 75 percent; in fact, the dollar went up during the crisis, not down.

Volcker had the details wrong, but in his gut he was right about the big picture. And he wasn't the only one. So were his successors. Every summer the Federal Reserve's Kansas City district hosts a conference in the wilderness resort of Jackson Hole, Wyoming. A hundred or so of the world's economic elite—central bankers, Treasury officials, bankers, and academics—get together to sip wine in the shadows of the Teton Range, hike trails, and ponder some of the world's weightiest issues. In the summer of 2005, the conference was devoted to the legacy of Alan Greenspan, approaching the end of his eighteen years as the Fed's chairman.

Greenspan had spent several weeks preparing his speech, a retrospective on what he had learned about central banking. He also wanted to point out something that was bothering him: investors seemed willing to lend money to pretty risky borrowers and get very little in return. But how loudly should he sound the alarm? "I wanted to flag it but not get on a hilltop and scream 'stop.' It seemed unseemly for an outgoing, lame duck chairman to start throwing bombs," he recalled years later. "I just wasn't going to do it."

And so the warning took the form of a few lines tucked into the speech, draped in the oblique jargon for which Greenspan was famous: "History has not dealt kindly with the aftermath of protracted periods of low risk premiums." Translation: when lenders accept so little return in exchange for risk, bad things usually follow.

A few months later, Ben Bernanke was nominated to succeed Greenspan. Bernanke had spent most of his life in academia, followed by three years as a Fed governor and a few months as George W. Bush's chief economist. Many outsiders fretted that he lacked the financial markets experience necessary for dealing with a crisis. This was a somewhat blinkered view. As a leading scholar of the Great Depression, Bernanke knew more than virtually anyone about how a broken financial system could damage an economy. Nonetheless, even he recognized that the nuts and bolts of the financial system were not his strong suit, and he immediately set out to correct that.

"Even before the crisis, I was worried about financial crises," he later recalled. He had studied the many smaller crises of the preceding decades. He had heard executives on Wall Street fretting over the frenzy for ever-riskier deal making. He suspected that this might lead to a chaotic event in the markets. "We envisioned a serious market break that would not necessarily destroy the economy but might create a recession."

Shortly before formally taking over as Fed chairman, Bernanke asked the Fed staff what they had on crisis management. They had compiled a manual, which mostly consisted of memos on what the Fed had done in previous crises, such as the 1987 stock market crash, and phone numbers of key regulators. Bernanke quickly concluded that the file was of little use, stuck it in a pile, and never looked at it again. Instead, he convened a meeting of the Fed's top staff to explore how to prepare, and out of that emerged an ad hoc committee of staffers who would, each quarter, brief the board on threats to the financial system.

The Fed was hardly alone in taking these preparatory measures. Numerous other central banks, and the International Monetary Fund, had been regularly publishing "financial stability reports" to highlight potential crisis threats. All suffered from the same problem: ignorance of the risks then propagating in the shadows of the financial system. The Fed knew that subprime mortgages and more exotic instruments such as collateralized debt obligations and credit default swaps existed, but as one study later found, rarely did any of these seem important enough to be mentioned in monetary policy makers' regular meetings.

So, by 2007, there was widespread awareness that homes were probably overvalued but little concern that this would produce a systemic crisis. Twenty-five years of experience and reform had moved most of the risks out of the banking system, provided new tools such as secured repo loans to contain risks, and slain inflation, the single biggest threat to financial stability anyone alive had ever known. People felt safe, safer than they had in years.

That was what worried Greenspan that day in 2005. But even he felt himself succumbing to the feeling, against his better judgment. When he returned to his seat amid a standing ovation that morning in Jackson Hole, he noted the contrast between his stated worries and the complete absence of fear in his own gut. He remembers thinking: "How many times have I seen this before?" Then why, he wondered, did he feel the same complacency that everyone else in the room felt?

CHAPTER 3

Now Is the Time to Panic: What to Do When Safety Fails

In the summer of 2006, two years before a panic swept the financial markets, a similar sort of panic swept the supermarkets. That August, an elderly woman in Nebraska was hospitalized with food poisoning and died shortly afterward. Within a few weeks another death and dozens of cases of sickness were confirmed. Federal investigators soon concluded that the victims had been infected by E. *coli* from eating fresh spinach. On September 14, the Food and Drug Administration issued a general warning to the public not to eat bagged spinach and eventually expanded the warning to all fresh spinach and products containing it, by far the most far-reaching advisory it had ever issued. "If you don't know if it's pre-packaged or not, avoid it," the agency's top food safety officer warned.

The response was dramatic. Supermarkets cleared spinach from their shelves; restaurants and delis stopped serving it. Consumers switched to lettuce. When one woman served her children creamed spinach, they accused her of "premeditated murder." The panic struck just as thousands of acres were ready for picking in California. Farmers plowed their crops under, while retailers tossed bags of spinach into dumpsters. Sales of bagged spinach plunged 74 percent. They didn't fully recover until 2008.

It took six months for the FDA and state authorities to track down the source of the outbreak: a shipment of 1,002 pounds of spinach harvested in California's Central Coast region, then processed the next day by an organic food processor. Investigators were never able to pinpoint the original source of the E. coli although they found identical samples in wild pig and cattle feces in a pasture near where the spinach had been harvested. But while the outbreak was under way, the FDA, not knowing its origin, cast a wide net.

The spinach recall was to food what the subprime mortgage crisis was to finance: a watershed event that prompted wholesale regulatory changes. There had been proposals stalled in Congress for years to require growers and processors throughout the food supply chain to take preventive steps against contamination and audit their suppliers to aid in tracing sources of contamination. Together with several other foodborne illness outbreaks, the spinach incident melted industry opposition, and in 2011 the Food Safety Modernization Act passed.

The food chain and the financial system have a lot in common. Each is a complex, omnipresent part of the economy. Both are also, most of the time, incident free and thus assumed to be safe. Learning that some food is tainted with a deadly bacteria is like hearing that your bank or money market mutual fund owns toxic mortgage assets: it undermines the premise that the system is safe, and the response is often panic.

The premise of safety is, most of the time, true. Even during outbreaks of foodborne illness, the vast majority of food is fine. But the slight possibility that a portion may be tainted is unacceptable when the public is accustomed to taking its safety for granted, and the response is to discard everything: a small amount that's bad and a vast swath that's good. That is what makes it so damaging: not just the fact, but even more the perception, that what should be safe, isn't.

Starting in 1986 the Natural Resources Defense Council, an environmental group, began studying the potentially carcinogenic properties of Alar, a pesticide sprayed on apples to improve their appearance and the length of time they stayed on the tree. In January 1989, the EPA declared Alar a health risk though not an imminent one, and would not seek to phase out its use for eighteen months. In February, it became the subject of a sensational *60 Minutes* installment, in which host Ed Bradley solemnly called it "the most potent cancer-causing agent in our food supply." The reaction to the broadcast was swift. Schools yanked apples and apple juice off their menus. Parents threw out applesauce. South Koreans boycotted Florida grapefruits, believing, wrongly, they had been sprayed with Alar. An American supermarket chain yanked all the apples off its shelves after trace amounts, none exceeding government standards, were found in its apple juice. "We're dealing with perceptions here," said a spokesman. "We're not dealing with reality." Some 5 million to 7 million boxes of apples—worth around $50 million—went unsold, and that fall the federal government offered to buy up $15 million worth to cushion the hit to growers.

At first blush, the reaction seems irrational. At the time, Alar was legal; the manufacturer withdrew it from the market after the *60 Minutes* broadcast, and the EPA, at the manufacturer's request, banned its use on crops. The EPA continues to permit it to be sprayed on plants that aren't eaten. Although scientific evidence did link it to cancer, the risk was cumulative. To match the doses received by laboratory rats that developed cancer, a child would have to consume 4,000 gallons of apple juice per day for life. So even if Alar posed a threat, it wasn't imminent, unlike, say, the threat from *E. coli*; eating a single Alar-sprayed apple would not make you sick. Indeed, federal agencies urged consumers not to reject apples, only a tiny portion of which had ever been treated with Alar.

But from a different point of view, the "panic" was rational. No one has to eat apples or drink apple juice; substitutes are readily available, as they were for spinach in 2006. Rejecting all apple products was, for an individual, a small inconvenience to avoid the risk that any might have Alar. Similarly, it was a small price for retailers to pay to avoid the potential reputational damage of serving something consumers don't consider safe. As we will see, a similar logic prevails during financial crises. Experts often intone, "This is no time to panic." But for an investor with no tolerance for loss and unsure which assets are tainted, panic has a certain logic.

The food system is certainly not prone to the sort of systemic event that nearly capsized the global economy in 2008; in that sense, the premise that the system is safe is more often true for food than for finance. Yet even for food, that sense of safety is partly illusory. Some pathogens are so ubiquitous and difficult to kill that the food supply will never be free of them. *E. coli*, listeria, salmonella, and other pathogens are in many things we eat— it's just that the vast majority of the time no one gets sick, because people consume too little, they're in robust health, or for reasons not fully understood. Nor is it understood why some foods, such as cantaloupes, are so often implicated in outbreaks, and others, such as pineapples and watermelons, are not. "What's the difference between cantaloupe and pineapple? Yet we've never had an outbreak with pineapple," says David Gombas, a scientist for United Fresh, a trade group of fruit and vegetable growers. "Watermelon sometimes comes from the same field as cantaloupe. Why doesn't anybody get sick from watermelons?"

The complexity of the food production chain also provides ample opportunity for contamination. Raw ingredients are produced at farms around the world and shipped thousands of miles to restaurants, stores, or food processors, who combine the ingredients and then ship them on again, to either the consumer or another food processor. Pathogens may be in the soil or water used at the farm, they may be on the hands of the workers picking or packaging the food, they may be on the equipment or in the facility used to wash, package, or transport the food, or in the store or restaurant where it is prepared and sold to the final consumer.

This complexity means that even experts struggle to determine where the threat has originated. In April 2008, consumers began to fall sick with salmonella, which the Centers for Disease Control said was probably from eating tomatoes. Over the next few months, reported cases soared to more than 1,400, with more than 200 hospitalized. As investigators from the FDA fanned out, the warning about tomatoes was expanded to more than forty states. Shipments from Mexico were stopped at the border. Burger King stopped serving tomatoes on its hamburgers, and tomato salsa disappeared from Chipotle's menu. Walmart, Kroger, and Whole Foods Market yanked tomatoes from their shelves and canceled orders. Prices for a box of tomatoes slid from $18 or $19 before the announcement to $4 afterward, and as little as $1 in some states. "We're abandoning production in the field, and the marketplace is in absolute collapse," an official for a tomato growers' association complained.

But tomatoes, it turns out, weren't the culprit. A month after its original warnings, the FDA figured out that raw jalapeño and serrano peppers were to blame, and it lifted its advisory against eating tomatoes. By then, the damage had been done: a third of Georgia's spring crop was left to rot in the fields. Growers in Florida lost $600 million and in Georgia, $100 million, according to a lawsuit that growers brought against the FDA.

Industry and regulators have worked hard to foster belief in the complete safety of the industry. In the process, ironically, they may raise expectations in perverse ways. Consumers are advised not to eat frozen cookie dough raw. But people have been infected by *E. coli* from eating the raw dough, and so it is now pretreated with a "kill step" before being packaged and shipped. These examples show how the industry copes not just with the danger posed by its own practices, but with the danger customers pose to themselves.

Why do we go to such lengths to create this sense of certainty? The answer can be found in behavioral economics, an amalgam of traditional economics and psychology that in recent decades has yielded valuable insights into bubbles and panics. The main finding of this research is that people evaluate risks quite differently than the idealized "economic man" would.

Consider, for example, the following test. (Don't worry, it's more like an inkblot test than a math test; there's no right answer.)

Option one: I give you an envelope containing $500, no strings attached.

Option two: I flip a coin. Heads, I give you $1,000. Tails, nothing. Which option do you prefer?

In economic terms, the bets are worth the same amount. If you flipped a coin hundreds of times and won $1,000 each time it came up heads, on average each coin flip would be worth $500. This is called its expected value. Since, in this example, the two bets have the same expected value (what we call a fair bet), someone indifferent to risk would be equally happy with either option. But if you're like most people, you choose option one. In fact, even if I raise the value of the prize for flipping heads to $1,200, you will still probably pick the first option.

That simply demonstrates that real people are not "risk neutral": they value certainty so much that they will give up economic value to achieve it. This observation was first made by the Swiss mathematician Daniel Bernoulli in 1738 and has been confirmed repeatedly in real life and experimental settings. Amos

Tversky and Daniel Kahneman, two Israeli psychologists, concluded after a series of experiments that the expected value of a gamble would have to be worth twice as much as the sure thing before people found it equally appealing. In other words, the typical person wouldn't pick the coin flip over $500 in an envelope until he was promised $2,000 for winning the coin flip.

So people put enormous value on probabilities of 100 percent. As probabilities move away from 100 percent, that changes. Tversky and Kahneman demonstrated this by altering the game described above. In their study, subjects were offered two options. The first was a gamble with an 80 percent chance of $4,000 (expected payoff $3,200); the other was to walk away with a sure $3,000. Eighty percent of subjects chose the sure thing, even though its expected payoff was lower.

Then, subjects were offered a different pair of options. The first was a gamble with a 20 percent chance at $4,000 (expected payoff $800); the second had a 25 percent chance of $3,000 (expected payoff $750). This time, 65 percent of subjects took the first option.

The findings seemed contradictory. In the first version people were risk averse: they chose the bet with the higher probability of winning, even though it was worth less. In the second, they chose the gamble that was worth more, even though it had a lower probability of winning. But in fact there was no contradiction; the experiment simply showed that the probability of 100 percent has a special appeal. Choosing between a sure thing and an almost sure thing is not the same as choosing between an improbable thing and a slightly more improbable thing. This explains, for example, why companies or individuals will often settle out of court for enormous sums even if they expect to win at trial: they are paying to eliminate the small risk of a devastating financial penalty or a criminal conviction.

Why do we hate uncertainty? The economist's answer is the

theory of diminishing utility, a fancy way of saying that each dollar of income provides less pleasure than the last. Going from middle class to rich is nice but going from middle class to destitute is horrible, and most of us would give up the first rather than risk the second. But even when our family's welfare isn't at stake, there's an emotional cost associated with the unknown that affects our behavior.

The economist Richard Thaler ran a series of experiments like the following. Coffee mugs were randomly distributed to half the students in a class, then all students were invited to trade so that those who value the mugs the most could buy them from those who valued them the least. On average, students demanded twice as much to sell what they already had as they would pay for something they did not yet have. Thaler dubbed this "the endowment effect": people put greater value on something when they own it than when they don't. They also feel worse about losing something they already own than failing to get it in the first place. The reasons why vary: you may have mental associations with something that you don't want to give up; you may worry about regret, or retribution, for giving up something you once had. Uncertainty—not knowing whether you will have more money, or less—taxes the psyche.

Moreover, our tolerance for loss changes. The more imminent and tangible the possibility, the more painful it becomes—and the greater the value we place on certainty. George Loewenstein, an economist at Carnegie Mellon University, notes that we are generally terrible at predicting how we will react to a stressful event before the event actually occurs. He and several colleagues offered a class of college students two dollars each to tell a funny story in front of the rest of the class the following week; they were all free to change their minds. Two-thirds of those who agreed to tell a funny story chickened out when the date arrived. None of those who initially declined to tell the story changed their minds. Among a different group of students who were shown the terrifying elevator scene from the horror movie *The Shining,* far fewer agreed to tell the story in the first place. Fear, they concluded, significantly elevates risk aversion. Countless other experiments confirm the same finding.

These findings help explain the enormous value we place on safety, and why panics happen when that sense of safety is threatened. Throwing out perfectly good spinach or apples entails a small, known loss in return for the certainty that you will not get sick in the unlikely event that they are contaminated.

The findings also explain several features of the financial landscape — for example, why stocks over time return more than bonds. If their returns were the same, the vast majority of people would stick with bonds because their returns are more certain. In effect, bonds have to become a really unfair bet before people switch to stocks. The findings explain why we buy insurance, too. By definition, insurance companies must expect to collect more in premiums than they pay out in losses to make money, which means that the customer buying a policy is taking an unfair bet. He's willing to do so because he values the certainty that comes with eliminating the possibility of loss. And they explain why the financial system is periodically seized by panic, and why that panic is so destructive, as it was in 2008.

Nobody knows this better than Gary Gorton, an economist at Yale University. He may be the country's leading authority on bank panics, and he has advanced probably the single best explanation for what caused the financial crisis and why it was so destructive. If anyone should have seen it coming, it was Gorton. The great irony is that he didn't. Not until his life was being torn apart by the crisis did he realize he was in the middle of what he had spent his career studying.

Gorton took a circuitous route to economics. He went to the University of Michigan intending to pursue a PhD in Chinese literature, then dropped out, unable to see the purpose in such a degree. He worked as a union organizer, started law school then dropped out, worked as a machinist's apprentice at an auto assembly plant for a few months, and drove a taxi at night. Then one day in a bookstore he picked up a microeconomics textbook, became engrossed in the mathematics, and decided to apply to graduate school for economics.

Gorton chose bank panics as his dissertation topic. At the time, economists understood that bank panics could lead to a contraction in the money supply and a depression, but there hadn't been much empirical research on exactly how panics occurred. His thesis adviser tried to discourage him—"He said, 'That's too hard, you'll never finish.'" And indeed, he continued to work on it even after he left graduate school and landed a job at the Federal Reserve Bank of Philadelphia as an economist.

Gorton gleaned several important insights from his research. First, a central purpose of the financial system is to supply people with a safe asset. The value of an ordinary asset, such as a stock or bond, fluctuates with new information, such as about profits or interest rates. A safe asset is so safe that its holder doesn't need to know anything about it; it is, in Gorton's words, "information insensitive." A typical example is money, or a bank deposit. You don't have to know anything about the person paying you with a twenty-dollar bill to trust it. Second, financial innovation leads to the creation of new sorts of safe assets. Third, panics occur when people believe that safe assets are no longer safe. It happened repeatedly with bank panics in the nineteenth and early twentieth centuries, and it happened in 2008—with the help of safe assets that Gorton himself helped to create.

Gorton's early research focused on banks in the early 1800s. A bank, like any other company, has a balance sheet: on one side are assets and on the other are liabilities: money it owes, such as loans. Most companies think of their assets as central to what they do and their liabilities as a mere annoyance. Ford, Johnson & Johnson, and Walmart all issue bonds, for example. But what makes those companies valuable is not their liabilities but their assets: factories, intellectual property, and stores.

Banks are different. Their assets are loans they have made, which are obviously useful; however, so are their liabilities, because they consist of deposits, which are an extremely convenient way for ordinary people to pay for things and store their savings. A bank that never made a single loan would still be providing a valuable service because its deposits would be safe assets for its customers: readily accessible and requiring no due diligence.

In the early 1800s, banks' principal liability was bank notes; indeed, most currency was issued by private banks. Not until the creation of the Federal Reserve did the issuance of currency become a federal monopoly. Typically, a depositor would deposit gold or some other asset with a bank and receive bank notes in return as proof of his claim on the bank. The depositor could then use those notes to buy goods from someone else. Eventually, someone who had received the note many steps removed from the original depositor could bring it back to the issuing bank and receive its face value in gold.

Gorton was particularly interested in how different banks' notes were valued, and what happened if they couldn't convert them back to gold. A dollar issued by one bank was supposed to be worth the same as a dollar issued by another. In practice, if the bank was in a different state, its dollars would be worth less, reflecting the hassle of returning to the bank to convert the note to gold or silver. More important, if depositors doubted whether the bank could redeem its bank notes, their value would decline. Indeed, if note holders worried about the bank's solvency, they rushed en masse to redeem their notes. Few banks kept enough gold and silver on hand to redeem all their notes. Faced with mass redemption requests, a bank would "suspend" convertibility— simply stop redeeming its notes. In extreme cases, it would fail, i.e., close its doors. If depositors thought other banks were in the same straits, a generalized run would develop, becoming a full-blown panic.

Gorton tracked down a trove of nineteenth-century newsletters that listed the discounts at which bank notes were trading, relative to face value. He learned that contrary to popular belief, only a small number of banks that suspended convertibility actually failed. Those that reopened were usually able to repay all their depositors. The greatest loss to a depositor was during the panics of 1873, at a mere two cents on the dollar. From this, Gorton concluded that panics were about lack of information: people weren't sure which safe assets were now unsafe, and thus redeemed them en masse. In time, though, many safe assets were proven to be safe.

Gorton also learned that safe assets morphed over time. If the public's demand for safe assets outstripped the supply, clever financial innovators would come up with ways to produce other safe assets. Indeed, the whole history of finance is about trying to find a way to make risky assets safe.

The first bank notes weren't truly safe because the bank that issued them might not be able to redeem them in gold. Thus, people had to think twice before they accepted a bank note, and bank notes' values fluctuated. That changed in 1863–64 with the National Bank Acts, which created new, nationally chartered (as opposed to state chartered) banks that could issue national bank notes only if they could back them with federal government bonds instead of silver or gold, or state bonds. Since the underlying collateral was the same, all national bank notes traded at par. They had become truly information insensitive.

Eventually, the public's demand for money outstripped banks' ability to supply bank notes backed by government bonds. This produced another innovation: the checking account. Instead of issuing customers notes, banks let savers hold their money as deposits and write checks on them. Deposits seemed pretty safe — until a bank either was, or gave the impression of being, at risk of failure. Then, instead of savers trying to convert their bank notes to gold, they tried to convert their checking deposits to bank notes. The creation of the Federal Reserve in 1913 and deposit insurance in 1933 solved the problem of runs on deposits by providing a common federal backstop for banks. Savers no longer had to distinguish between banks' deposits; they were all equally safe. The safe asset problem, it appeared, had been solved.

But toward the end of the last century, a shortage of truly safe assets once again emerged. The problem arose because of what superficially seemed like a good thing: everyone, in particular foreign investors such as central banks, wanted to lend to the American government.

Foreigners' ownership of American Treasury bonds and bills shot from 20 percent in 1994 to 50 percent in 2007. Their ownership of debt issued, or guaranteed, by Fannie and Freddie — technically private but treated as part of the government — rose from 6 percent to 21 percent in the same period. Just as in the 1800s, this insatiable demand for safe assets led clever people on Wall Street to come up with substitutes.

When Gorton and two coauthors tracked the history of safe assets, they learned that the assets remained remarkably constant from 1952 to 2010, at about 33 percent of total assets. Some of those safe assets were public, such as Treasury bonds, and some were private, such as bank deposits. What was really striking was the transformation within the private category. Bank deposits slid from about 80 percent in the 1950s and '60s to 27 percent on the eve of the crisis. What took their place? Money market mutual funds, asset-backed securities, and commercial paper. The difference was critical. Bank deposits, up to the federal deposit insurance limit, truly are safe. These new assets had been engineered to seem as safe as bank deposits, but they really weren't, and that distinction would prove critical during the crisis. But Gorton would not make the connection until the crisis had begun.

In 1984 Gorton began teaching at the Wharton School, where he began studying the practice of banks "securitizing" their loans. Securitization involves bundling a bunch of loans into a single security, which is then sold to investors, enabling the bank to make more loans. It was a way to transform risky assets into safe ones. Lewis Ranieri said the beauty of a mortgage-backed security was that the buyer "did not have to know much, if anything, about the underlying mortgages. You have just taken an ugly object, a home loan, and dressed it up."

In the 1990s, Gorton found a way to cash in on his expertise. American International Group, an insurance company that had gotten its start in Shanghai in 1919, had grown into one of the world's largest and most admired financial conglomerates. Perhaps its least known but most cutting-edge division was AIG Financial Products, based in Connecticut, which was getting into the growing business of financial derivatives. AIGFP had a custom of inviting academics to visit and do research at the firm, and through a fellow Wharton professor, they asked Gorton to do that. Instead, Gorton went to work for AIG itself on an exotic new financial innovation.

Shortly before he joined AIG, J.P. Morgan had written the first "credit default swaps," or CDSs. This was essentially an insurance contract that earned the bank a premium in return for promising to pay the lender in full if the issuer of a bond defaulted. It occurred to Gorton that this was a product he could help with. By developing models of how likely a loan or an MBS was to default, he could help AIG decide how much to charge for the insurance against that default.

The first big customers to benefit from Gorton's work were European banks. Like most banks, they had to hold capital to guard against losses on loans, but if they bought insurance against the borrower's default from a company like AIG, they could reduce their required capital. Later on, AIG began selling insurance on mortgage-backed securities. An MBS was often sliced into "tranches." As mortgages were repaid, money went first to the owner of the top tranche. If any mortgages defaulted, it was the lowest tranches that took the loss. This meant that it would take a cataclysmic level of defaults before the top tranches sustained any losses. Those tranches were deemed so safe they deserved the highest credit ratings available: AAA or AA. Tranches were often pooled into a new security called a collateralized debt obligation (CDO), which was, itself, then sliced into tranches. AIG made a point of selling protection only on the highest-rated tranches of MBSs and CDOs.

By 2006, AIGFP had begun to worry enough about the quality of underwriting that it stopped selling protection on subprime-backed MBSs and CDOs. Cracks appeared in the system as indexes tied to subprime mortgages began to fall. By 2007, those cracks spread and began to show in the market. Gorton realized that the financial system was undergoing a bank panic much like those he had studied, but with a difference. Instead of ordinary savers rushing to redeem their bank notes and bank deposits, institutional investors were rushing to redeem repo loans and commercial paper because they were backed by subprime mortgages. He put those thoughts down in a long paper that he presented in August 2008 at the Federal Reserve's annual Jackson Hole retreat. In it, he described the crisis as "essentially a banking panic. Like the classic panics of the 19th and early

20th centuries in the U.S.," this one was because of a "lack of information": lenders weren't sure which securities were suffering defaults or who held them, so they pulled back broadly from the banks and shadow banks that held them.

Gorton recalls looking out at the audience of central bankers and academics and thinking, "They've studied monetary policy for twenty years and they have no idea what I'm talking about."

I met Gorton one warm, sunny morning in October 2013 in his office, which at the time was on the main floor of a classically styled building that looks like a miniature Parthenon. The halls were lined with framed, defaulted bond certificates, including one issued to finance the Panama Canal. In his office he keeps a framed copy of the last pound notes to be issued by the Royal Bank of Scotland, in 1986, back when it could issue its own currency, much as American banks once did. Behind his desk was a white board covered with abstruse mathematical formulas, work product, he said, of a paper about securitization then in process. Dressed in an open-necked shirt, corduroys, and fashionable black-rimmed glasses, he seemed the quintessential Ivy League academic.

Over lunch, I suggested to Gorton that AIG, by selling credit default swaps on mortgage-backed securities, seemed to be doing what banks used to do: creating safe assets. The AIG swaps relieved investors of having to worry about the idiosyncrasies of each security; they were assured of getting all their money back thanks to insurance they bought from AIG, just as bank deposits were protected by federal deposit insurance.

Gorton at first disagreed, but then agreed this was true. By selling protection on a bank's portfolio, he said, "you are making it safe, in the eyes of regulators or investors, so you are contributing to this process of creating safe assets."

Perhaps if Gorton had made that connection at the time, he would also have realized how vulnerable AIG was to the sorts of runs he had studied for the past thirty years. Despite his calculations that the odds of default on the MBSs that AIG had insured were minuscule, their value was plummeting nonetheless.

What went wrong? In financial as in food panics, some things really are toxic, and many more things are just feared to be toxic; both get dumped. Both factors played a part in AIG's demise. Though Gorton still defends his models, the CDOs AIG insured turned out to be much less safe than those models anticipated because defaults on the underlying, lower-quality MBS tranches were highly correlated: when one went bad, others tended to as well. However, the AAA-rated MBSs AIG insured were, as Gorton predicted, quite safe; one of Gorton's PhD students, Sun Young Park, later combed through prospectuses and trustee reports of $1.9 trillion worth of subprime bonds issued between 2004 and 2007. As of late 2014, the realized principal loss on the AAA-rated tranches was just a fifth of a cent on the dollar. But during the panic, they were not perceived to be safe, and their prices (and the CDOs' prices) plunged.

Under the terms of its credit derivative contracts, AIG had to post collateral—that is, set aside scarce cash to prove it could pay what it owed—as the price of what it insured went down. AIG's own credit rating, AAA as recently as 2005, was repeatedly cut, triggering requirements to post even more collateral. Gorton's last visit to AIG came shortly after he spoke in Jackson Hole. He sat on the trading desk and listened to AIG's traders shrieking at their counterparts over the phone about how much the securities were really worth and therefore how much collateral AIG had to post: "No one wants to pay anything. Arguments over prices were legitimate. No one knew what the prices were."

As the MBS fire sale continued, AIG was hemorrhaging cash to meet collateral calls. It would have followed Lehman into bankruptcy, except that the next day the Fed and the Treasury took control of the company, eventually ponying up $182 billion to meet the company's obligations. The public's outrage boiled over in 2009 when it learned that AIG's customers—big banks such as Goldman Sachs—had been paid enough by the federal government, together with the collateral from AIG that they kept, to receive the full $62 billion face value for the subprime securities AIG had insured, at a time when their market value was only $29 billion. The atmosphere turned even more poisonous when word emerged that taxpayer money had been used to pay AIG's employee bonuses. A senator urged AIG's employees to commit suicide. Bernanke was furious over AIG, saying he "slammed the phone more than a few times" during its bailout.

For Gorton, that period was hell. After the *Wall Street Journal* reported on his role in designing AIG's models, he received death threats in the mail and considered moving his family out of New Haven. When he learned that a neighbor had asked his children during a regular car pool about AIG, he told the neighbor testily, "I'll tell you about AIG, just don't ask my kids about it."

He left AIG in 2008 and has since devoted himself to teaching, research, and studying the crisis.

While AIG clearly fell victim to a panic, that panic wasn't necessarily irrational. People are used to losses on risky assets such as stock mutual funds. But safe assets such as bank deposits, money market funds, and repo loans are different. They represent certainty. When that certainty is threatened the reaction is immediate, and powerful. One result is the phenomenon of "fire sales": investors' willingness to sell securities for far less than their intrinsic worth. Generally, if you hold a security that you think is worth 100 cents, it makes little sense to sell it for less. But what if the current market price is, say, 90 cents? Lenders may worry about your solvency and demand that you repay your loan. Your board of directors or your regulator may ask you if you own any of these notorious securities. To repay your lender or keep your job, you sell them. That drives the price down even further, putting other holders in a similar position.

In the years before the financial crisis, many investors had purchased mortgage-backed securities rated either AA or AAA, in other words, very safe. Until 2007, these securities generally traded at close to 100 cents on the dollar. But as subprime mortgage defaults mounted, prices began to drop. At the height of the panic, a popular index implied that the price of AAA-rated MBSs had fallen to between 20 and 60 cents on the dollar.

This had a lethal effect on the apparent health of banks. Over the course of 2008, the value of the securities on American banks' books sank by a staggering $70 billion. The fear that such losses might render some banks insolvent only worsened the panic.

Was any of this rational? By 2009, the price of AAA-rated mortgage-backed securities had recovered to about 80 cents, and as Sun Young Park's research found, eventually paid off at close to 100 cents. By early 2010 banks' security holdings had more than recovered all the losses reported in late 2008.

This might suggest that the pricing of securities in the depths of the crisis was irrational. Yet at the time, before the Treasury and Federal Reserve had pulled out the stops to save the financial system, it was easy to imagine them going to zero and countless banks failing. This perception was reinforced by a rule that took effect in 2007 that such assets be "marked to market," in other words that banks record them on their books at the value they could fetch that day in the market, not what they expected to eventually recoup. Mark to market accounting serves a sound regulatory purpose: it deters banks from trying to hide or postpone the truth about bad loans or investments. The downside is that it amplifies the impact of fire sales by forcing everyone to behave as if a price driven heavily by panic is in fact the true value. A bank quite certain that the fire sale price is wrong would still be rational to sell at that price rather than risk being regarded as insolvent.

There was no more poignant illustration of what happens when the feeling of safety is violated than the fate of the world's oldest money market mutual fund. You've probably never heard of Bruce Bent, but you have almost certainly used his invention. In the 1970s Bent was toiling away on Wall Street when he noticed that bank depositors consistently got lower rates of interest than big investors who lent big sums to companies and other borrowers in the money markets. Setting out to create a fund that would give all savers access to those same, superior rates, he and a partner launched what became known as Reserve Primary Fund, the world's first money market mutual fund. By 2008, 52 million Americans had some $3.8 trillion invested in such funds.

On the afternoon of Sunday, September 14, 2008, Bruce Bent and his wife boarded a plane in New York bound for Italy, a trip to celebrate the fiftieth anniversary of the day they'd met. When he arrived in Rome early the next morning, splashed across the newspaper headlines was the news that Lehman Brothers had gone bankrupt. That news set in motion a series of events that would cost Bent the company he'd spent his life building and land him and his son in court. That headline and its consequences reveal precisely what makes financial crises so destructive: the sudden discovery or perception that something thought to be safe—whether a bank deposit or shares in Bent's fund—in fact is not.

That morning, Reserve Primary Fund was holding $785 million of short-term debt issued by Lehman Brothers, making up 1.2 percent of the fund's $62.4 billion in assets. The calling card of the money fund was that, unlike other funds whose share price (or net asset value) fluctuated from day to day, the money fund's was supposed to be always one dollar, repayable on a day's notice.

The fund's ability to repay shares at a dollar each on a day's notice depended on two things: the fund not sustaining large losses on any securities, and those securities being liquid enough to be sold to meet even large redemption requests. With Lehman bankrupt, the value of that paper was now a huge question mark. That morning, unable to value its Lehman paper, Reserve also found itself deluged with redemption requests from customers clamoring to get their money back. Patrick Farrell, the fund's chief financial officer, was stuck at Chicago O'Hare airport that day, his flight to New York delayed. He called a colleague at Reserve who told him redemption requests had so far reached a staggering $18 billion, and that the fund had only $3.8 billion available to meet them.

"Holy crap," said Farrell. "You know, those customers are not going to get their money today."

His colleague responded: "Pat, that's going to be the kiss of death."

Bent called his son, Bruce II, from his hotel room in Italy to decide what to do next. Since the money fund had been invented, only once had a fund "broken the buck"—that is, failed to redeem shares for less than a dollar—and it was far smaller and less well known than Reserve. Many had come close, but in all instances the funds' sponsors had infused enough of their own money into the fund to cover the loss and maintain the dollar share value. Bent and his son explored whether they could do the same, and the company even prepared communications for announcing its intention to do so. But by the end of Tuesday, with Lehman debt now priced at zero cents on the dollar, they concluded they could not, and announced that Reserve's shares were now priced at 97 cents instead of one dollar.

Federal Reserve and Treasury officials had spent the weekend trying to imagine and prepare for every collateral effect of a Lehman bankruptcy. One thing they apparently did not consider was that a money market fund might break the buck. That announcement arguably sowed as much panic as Lehman's bankruptcy itself.

Within a week, investors yanked a total of $349 billion from almost every money market fund not invested solely in Treasury bills, regardless of whether it had exposure to Lehman. Some thirty-six of the one hundred largest U.S. prime money market funds were eventually supported. Meanwhile, the funds themselves stopped buying commercial paper, the short-term IOUs that everyone from General Electric to obscure investment funds had come to rely on to fund everything from equipment inventory to subprime mortgage-backed securities.

The panic came to a halt three days later when the Treasury Department created an insurance program to guarantee money funds for a fee and the Federal Reserve announced that it would buy the commercial paper the funds could no longer sell. That halted the panic, but the damage had been done: within a month, the total stock of commercial paper had shrunk by 15 percent, to $1.43 trillion. Imagine America's banks calling in one-sixth of the loans to their best customers; that is the equivalent of what investors did by redeeming their commercial paper.

What did Reserve Primary Fund do wrong? Bruce Bent had long considered commercial paper risky, and for most of its existence the fund had been conservatively run, investing primarily in bank certificates of deposit and government securities. But in 2006 Reserve began investing in commercial paper, which soon represented half the fund's assets, making possible higher yields that acted as a magnet to investors. By early 2008, Reserve had lent money not just to Lehman but to Bear Stearns and Merrill Lynch. Reserve had strayed from its original vision.

At his trial, Bent described Lehman's bankruptcy as "just beyond belief." Lehman's paper retained its top rating from Moody's and Standard & Poor's until the day of its bankruptcy;

the Securities and Exchange Commission had overseen Lehman through a special oversight program, with staffers on site; and the SEC's chairman had pronounced Lehman's capital sufficient. But many other investors had been skeptical of such assertions and avoided Lehman paper; arguably, Bent should have done the same.

Still, there were at least two other assumptions grounded in decades of experience that suggest why Lehman's failure and Reserve's breaking the buck came as such shocks. The first was that Lehman would not be allowed to fail. Indeed, in the prior four decades, no financial firm even close to Lehman's size or importance had been allowed to collapse. As we saw in Chapter 2, when the collapse of a big bank threatened the economy, Volcker worked hard to prevent it, lending to Mexico and leading the bailout of Continental Illinois. In the years thereafter, regulators had intervened to protect the uninsured depositors of the fourteenth, thirty-third, and thirty-sixth largest banks.

Because banks are at the core of the financial system, they were already backstopped by the government via deposit insurance and the Fed's lender-of-last-resort authority. Thus, Volcker felt they deserved different treatment than the rest of the financial system. But in March of 2008 regulators crossed that line as well. Bear Stearns, the fifth-largest of the stand-alone investment banks (Lehman was fourth), had been days away from collapse as lenders refused to roll over their short-term repo loans. One of them was Reserve. The fund had lent "repo" money to Bear Stearns, but after its managers saw the company's CEO unpersuasively seek to reassure investors on television on March 12, the company decided to pull out. Just a few days later, the Fed took the unprecedented step of lending Bear enough money to stay afloat until it could be sold intact to J.P. Morgan Chase & Co. Lenders to Bear didn't lose a penny.

The Fed then took another unprecedented step: it gave the

four remaining investment banks—Goldman Sachs, Morgan Stanley, Merrill Lynch, and Lehman—access to the discount window, a privilege previously accorded only to regular banks. Given this recent history, it was understandable that most people on Wall Street, including Lehman's own executives and the managers at Reserve, did not expect Lehman to be allowed to go bankrupt. Michael Luciano, a portfolio manager at Reserve, later told a congressional inquiry that he had assumed that if the government wouldn't let Bear fail, it wouldn't allow the others, which were larger and more important, to fail either.

For the Fed and the Treasury, the decision to let Lehman fail was the most tortured of the crisis. In its aftermath, officials have insisted they had no choice, that the Fed had no legal authority to lend to Lehman because it lacked sufficient collateral to secure such a loan. Evidence has since surfaced to suggest that at least some Fed staffers thought Lehman might in fact be solvent. Yet at the time, it is also clear that some officials thought letting it fail would serve a useful purpose: it would purge the financial system of the moral hazard that the rescue of Bear Stearns had created and that had drawn reproof from many quarters. Over the course of the summer, Treasury had tried to make it clear that no similar rescue would await Lehman. Inside the Fed, feelings were more conflicted; Tim Geithner, president of the New York Fed, was adamant that the Fed should keep the bailout option open, but some staffers agreed that bankruptcy was better than a bailout. One staffer said the Fed must not contribute its own money to assist a takeover of Lehman as it had with Bear Stearns because the "moral hazard and reputation cost is too high." Letting Lehman go bankrupt would be a "mess on every level, but fixes the moral hazard problem." Bernanke and Hank Paulson, the Treasury secretary who would have had to sign off on a bailout, felt similarly.

Certainly, the "too big to fail" label should never have been allowed to take root; it was an implicit taxpayer subsidy to big firms and their executives that put smaller firms at a disadvantage. But once the status had been accorded, its abrupt withdrawal triggered panic.

The failure of Lehman shattered assumptions about the safety of all the major financial institutions. If Lehman wasn't too big to fail, nobody was: not Goldman Sachs, Morgan Stanley, Citigroup, or any other institution.

The second assumption that had been allowed to take root was that money market funds were basically the same as bank deposits. That, more or less, was how their shareholders treated them. Rate of return was much less important than safety and immediate access to funds. "We could get our cash any day that we would need it," explained one investor in Reserve. "And it gave us safety because the money market fund was a dollar in, you get your dollar out."

Of course, these investments weren't bank deposits. Funds were not legally obligated to maintain the dollar per share value. But in practice, the reputational damage of breaking the buck was so great that sponsors—the management companies who ran the funds—almost always put their own capital in rather than allow it to happen. It later emerged that, between 1972 and the lead-up to the crisis, there had been 146 instances of a fund sponsor intervening to preserve the dollar per share value of a money market fund. As I mentioned earlier, only once had a fund actually broken the buck and been forced to liquidate. The sponsors in these cases were doing the right thing for themselves and their investors, but in the grand scheme of things, these backstage interventions worsened the eventual crisis, because they reinforced the illusion that investors would never lose money in money market funds.

Over the course of the next five years, other institutions would suffer the same fate as money market funds: the illusion of safety would be abruptly torn away from European government debt during the euro crisis, as we will see in Chapter 5, and the same thing very nearly happened to U.S. Treasury debt in 2011 when Congress temporarily refused to raise the statutory limit on how much the Treasury could borrow. The process of disenchantment illustrated something very important about the financial system and how it comes to crisis. A huge part of what the financial system does is try to create the fact — and at times the illusion — of safety. Usually, it succeeds; no one has lost money on an insured bank deposit. On those rare occasions when it fails, the result is panic.

Bruce Bent had devoted much of his life to promoting a product that would create both the fact and feeling of safety, for savers anywhere. September 14, 2008, marked the beginning of the end of a business he had spent much of his life building. Over the next few months, the funds were liquidated. Securities regulators charged him and his son with fraud for their actions that day: they had told investors they would maintain the fund's dollar per share value when in fact, regulators alleged, they never intended to, because they couldn't. The Bents' response was that after announcing their intention to support the fund's share price, the global economy fell off a cliff, making the intention impossible to carry out. In 2012, a jury acquitted Bent and his son of fraud charges. Bent's son was convicted of one count of negligence. And investors? When all the books were closed, Lehman remained Reserve's only losing position. Investors ultimately got back 99 cents, for a total loss of just under 1 cent per dollar.

More Risk, Please: The Unintended Consequences of Football Helmets and Antilock Brakes

Even by the standards of the National Football League, October 17, 2010, was a violent day. In three different games that Sunday, five players were taken off the field after violent helmet hits left them with concussions, or other injuries. As Cleveland Browns left wide receiver Josh Cribbs took the ball, curved right, and headed up the center of the field in the second quarter, he met several Pittsburgh defenders who began to pull him down. Coming from his left in a blur of speed, Steelers linebacker James Harrison closed in and drove his helmeted head into Cribbs's. Cribbs collapsed onto the field in a quivering heap as Harrison rose to his feet and pumped his fists in triumph. Just minutes later, Harrison did the same thing to the Browns' Mohamed Massaquoi; as Massaquoi caught the ball, Harrison drilled him from the side with such force that the sound of their helmets colliding could be heard over the roar of the crowd. Massaquoi sank to his knees, then toppled backward to the ground. Some three hundred miles away, in Philadelphia, the Eagles' star wide receiver DeSean Jackson was just catching a pass when the Atlanta Falcons' Dunta Robinson drove his head into him. Both men collapsed and had to be helped from the field; both suffered concussions that kept them from playing for the next few weeks. On the same day near Boston, Brandon Meriweather of the Patriots delivered a crunching helmet blow to the head of the Baltimore Ravens' Todd Heap just as Heap was catching a pass.

The spectacle of so many star players being sidelined ignited a simmering debate about whether such aggressive tackling had any place in the league. The NFL was at that time already battling controversy over concussions. More than 4,500 mostly retired players and their families sued it for ignoring evidence that repeated concussions could cause dementia, leading the league to settle for $765 million.

That week, the NFL decided to send a message. It fined all three offending players from $50,000 to $75,000 each (though the fines of all three were later reduced) for hitting with their helmets, and threatened thenceforth to suspend any player who committed a similar foul.

That move triggered an equally angry response, this time from the players. After all, the offenders had only been playing as they were all expected to play—hard. The league didn't just tacitly condone such violence; it reveled in it: for decades, *Monday Night Football* opened with the image of two helmets colliding and exploding.

"They give me a helmet, I'm going to use it," said Miami Dolphins linebacker Channing Crowder. Harrison told a local radio station, "I don't want to see anyone injured, but I'm not opposed to hurting anyone." In response to the fine, he threatened to quit the game. Cribbs was surprisingly conciliatory about the whole episode, as were many other regular targets of helmet-to-helmet hits.

A few days later, Mike Ditka, a former coach of the Chicago Bears, offered up his own remedy: lose the helmets. "I don't think people would strike with the head nearly as much if you didn't have a helmet on your head," he told ESPN Radio. "You would learn to strike with a thing called shoulder pads."

Was Ditka right? Have helmets, designed to save players from injury, done the opposite? It sounds heretical, but in fact the question has preoccupied safety experts for decades, not just in sports, but in automobiles and finance. Almost any activity we undertake—driving on a rainy road, skiing down an icy slope, investing in a new venture—involves some risk of physical, environmental, or financial harm. Reducing that risk increases our appetite for the activity, and in the process counters the benefit of that innovation.

This presents a fundamental challenge to would-be foolproofers. For helmets, antilock brakes, and derivatives to do their jobs, we must take into consideration how they change our behavior. If they don't alter our underlying appetite for risk, it can be hard to make us safer.

The inherent violence of football has always been both part of its appeal and a source of controversy. When football was first played, in 1869, players didn't wear uniforms, much less helmets. And it was violent. In 1905, after a season of severe injuries, President Theodore Roosevelt called on the heads of college programs to clean up the game. The first head protection consisted of a leather cap with earflaps and interior padding designed primarily to keep the hair or ears from being yanked. The caps were uncomfortable and tended to stink: the leather often absorbed moisture from damp weather and perspiration. In 1939, the John T. Riddell Company of Chicago introduced the first plastic-shell helmet, which was harder and longer-lasting than leather. The next year, it added the first face mask.

The helmets reduced injuries, from knocked-out teeth and

broken noses to jaw fractures. But coaches saw the helmet as more than just a form of protection; it could also serve as a weapon. They taught players to put their heads down and use it to "spear" the opposing player, a tactic made possible thanks to the protection provided by the helmet. "We teach our boys to spear and gore," Woody Hayes, the legendary coach for Ohio State, told a group of reporters in 1962, according to *Sports Illustrated*. "We want them to plant that helmet right under a guy's chin."

Helmets reduced some of the ugliest injuries, while leading to more injuries of a different sort. When a player is struck in the face, his neck flexes back, absorbing some of the force. But when he puts his head down to spear an opponent, the neck and spine form a single axis and the force of the blow is fully loaded onto the spinal column. A study comparing football injuries in the four years from 1959 to 1963 to the four years from 1971 to 1975 noted that the number of youths playing football had gone up roughly 60 percent, to 1.275 million. In the same period, the number of deaths declined 10 percent, to 77, but the number of permanent quadriplegias more than tripled, to 99, and the number of lesions causing cervical fracture-dislocations (i.e., broken necks) quadrupled, to 259. The authors blamed these developments on "the development of a protective helmet–face mask system that has effectively protected the head, and by doing so has allowed it to be used as a battering ram in tackling and blocking techniques, thus placing the cervical spine at risk of injury."

In February 1976, the National Collegiate Athletic Association banned spearing, defined as the "deliberate use of the helmet in an attempt to punish an opponent." Following the rule change, spinal injuries fell dramatically.

But as the NFL's ongoing concussion controversy shows, football continues to exact a high toll on the health of its players. Helmets do prevent skull fractures and subdural hematomas—

bleeding between the brain and the skull that often leads to death. Concussions are different. When a player's head is stopped because of a collision or fall, the skull comes to a halt but the brain, which is floating inside the skull, keeps moving, hitting the inside of the skull, causing the concussion. The padding inside a helmet is intended to compress when the head is struck, allowing the head to decelerate rather than come to a sudden stop. This should reduce the risk of concussion, unless the player, by wearing a helmet, hits his opponents harder or more often.

"Helmets attenuate forces much better than ever before," Robert Cantu, a neurosurgeon at Boston University and an expert in catastrophic brain injury, told me. "So players can use their heads in a way that doesn't cause them pain, the way it would have twenty years ago." This is particularly helpful for a small player, who is more likely to bring down a heavier player using his head than by wrapping his arms around him.

The NFL is aware of this, which is why it prohibits spearing. In reality, though, "the law's not being enforced by officials, and blocking and tackling with the head is still commonplace," Cantu added. "And it's in that action that the majority of these concussions are sustained. You will see thousands of offside penalties happen before you see a spearing call. The officials just haven't been doing it, and so far they are not being held accountable for not doing it."

Other sports followed a similar trajectory. Hockey players are regularly struck by other players, by the boards, the puck, and by sticks. Head injuries were common, and numerous careers were cut short when a stick, puck, or fist to the eye blinded a player. In the 1960s, Stan Mikita, a star center for the Chicago Blackhawks, began curving hockey stick blades by heating them in hot water. Pucks could now be fired at 100 miles per hour; goaltenders started wearing masks. In 1968 Bill Masterton, a center for the Minnesota North Stars, was knocked backward by two players for the Oakland Seals, fell back, and smashed his unprotected head on the ice. He lost consciousness, was treated on the ice, and rushed to the hospital, where he died thirty hours later.

Helmets became mandatory for new National Hockey League players in 1979. Thereafter the number of head fractures went down, while the number of spinal injuries went up. The conclusion of several specialists was that a more aggressive style of play, perhaps encouraged by the wearing of helmets and full face masks, was causing players to hit one another harder in ways that made spinal injuries more likely. There is a "serious concern that players have become invincible warriors, wearing a suit of armor, doing battle in the ice arena—that violence and aggression are part of the game," two authors wrote in 1993.

The complicated consequences of helmets that so vex professional sports is part of a much larger debate that has long preoccupied and divided engineers and ecologists. The federal government had begun to assert its oversight over the economy and the environment during the Progressive Era, and in the 1960s, that oversight expanded significantly, most noticeably onto the highways. The catalyst was the publication in 1965 of *Unsafe at Any Speed: The Designed-In Dangers of the American Automobile* by Ralph Nader. Nader had worked for Daniel Patrick Moynihan at the Department of Labor, and his book exposed how the auto manufacturing industry had knowingly built dangerous features into their cars, such as chrome on the dashboard that reflected sun into drivers' eyes and hood ornaments that were unnecessarily dangerous to pedestrians.

Nader's critique zeroed in on the Chevrolet Corvair, whose design, he said, was intrinsically unsafe and prone to oversteering. Nader might have remained an obscure activist and author of an unread book had General Motors not embarked on a campaign to challenge his credibility, hiring a private investigator to dig into his background. The result was a lot of publicity for Nader and his book. GM's president later apologized to Nader.

Unsafe at Any Speed triggered several congressional hearings and was instrumental in the passage of the National Traffic and Motor Vehicle Safety Act in 1966, which for the first time gave the federal government authority to set standards for automobile and highway safety. Among the first standards passed were rules requiring seat belts for all occupants, energy-absorbing steering columns, a padded instrument panel, and dual braking systems.

But just as government control of the economy and the environment had by this point come under fire, so did safety regulation. Leading the backlash was Sam Peltzman, the University of Chicago economist we met in Chapter 1.

I visited Peltzman one afternoon at his office at the university's business school on the city's South Side. Seventy-three years old, he had retired some time ago from active teaching but was still writing and speaking. Peltzman dresses like a hippie. He favors loud checked pants, Hawaiian shirts, and sports jackets in blinding fuchsia or lime green. His office is littered with coffee cups and packages of coffee, and mementoes from his Brooklyn upbringing; on one wall hangs the front page of the *New York Daily News* when the Mets won the World Series in 1969 and a sign salvaged from the old Dodgers' stadium pointing the way to the women's restroom.

Peltzman grew up in the Bensonhurst section of Brooklyn surrounded by union members who "venerated the New Deal and Roosevelt." In 1948, they backed either Harry Truman or the Soviet-sympathizing third-party candidate Henry Wallace. Peltzman, then eight, remembers being for Dewey. He went to City College of New York, then Chicago. "I was the first in my family to go to college," he told me. "I didn't know what the economy was until I took my first course. What I had going for me was contrary inclinations."

After graduate school, Peltzman took a teaching job at UCLA, and that was where he first scandalized the regulatory establishment. In 1962 the Food and Drug Administration began requiring much more testing before a new drug could be approved for sale in the United States, the aim being to keep drugs such as thalidomide, a morning sickness drug that turned out to cause birth defects, off the market. In a controversial 1973 paper, Peltzman reckoned that these rules were hurting consumers far more than they helped, because many people with preventable illnesses had to wait for new drugs. The paper caught the eye of Milton Friedman, who praised it in his *Newsweek* column. Peltzman told a BBC interviewer that there had not been enough "thalidomide tragedies." Called before Congress to explain what he meant, he said he merely meant that faster introduction of new drugs would alleviate a lot of misery, but it would have costs, such as the occasional thalidomide tragedy. Avoiding thalidomides meant that many people were quietly dying of treatable illnesses.

Peltzman's next big salvo at the regulatory establishment came in 1975 with the publication of his paper "The Effects of Automobile Safety Regulation." Peltzman wanted to know whether the many auto safety innovations passed since 1966 had had the intended effects. He analyzed the claimed reduction in fatalities made for various safety devices at the time of their introduction and compared them to what actually occurred. Those claims, he concluded, implied a 10 to 25 percent reduction in deaths of vehicle occupants per vehicle mile traveled. He then looked at the trend in automotive deaths and concluded that while driver deaths had indeed gone down, that reduction had been offset by a rise in pedestrian injuries and property damage.

Peltzman felt his results were a straightforward illustration of an elementary principle of economics. Risky driving has a price:

the possibility of getting hurt in an accident. Seat belts and other safety devices reduce that price; by making risky driving "cheaper," people will do more of it: "If sufficiently few accidents are prevented by these devices and they lower the probability of death and injury per accident, the induced increase in driving intensity will increase the total number of accidents."

Peltzman's study would eventually be cited hundreds of times. It earned him the nickname Seatbelt Sam, and the term "Peltzman effect" was coined to explain everything from accidents in NASCAR racing to penalty minutes in ice hockey. Peltzman didn't stop with autos. In 1986 he decided to investigate the effects of the 1938 law that led to the requirement that certain drugs deemed dangerous could be sold only by prescription. He noticed that the incidence of accidental poisoning by drugs went up (after adjusting for the availability of physicians) in subsequent decades. He didn't say that regulation was causing people to poison themselves more often, but it certainly wasn't reducing the incidence. He speculated that prescriptions encouraged people to take more potent drugs, which made accidental poisoning more likely.

Gerald Wilde, a psychologist at Queen's University in Kingston, Ontario, went even further than Peltzman and argued that each person had a personal "risk thermostat" that adjusted his behavior until his preferred level of risk was achieved. Make a car safer, and the thermostat would instruct the driver to go faster until his risk of death returned to where it had been in his old car. Wilde illustrated his point with the case of Sweden changing from driving on the left side of the road to the right side in 1967. The following year, death and injury rates plunged. Wilde's explanation was that drivers perceived the roads as much more dangerous and drove more cautiously, which produced the reduction in accidents. But in time they acclimated to the switch and their perception of danger fell away, with the result that driving habits and fatality rates returned to their prechangeover level within two years.

The scholarly backlash against automobile safety soon generated a backlash of its own. Leading the counterattack was Leon Robertson, an epidemiologist at the Insurance Institute for Highway Safety, an industry think tank devoted to reducing road deaths and injuries (and insurance claims). The institute had recruited Robertson from Harvard Medical School in 1970 to bring a more scientific approach to its safety research.

One of his early research projects found that drivers in Maryland were much less likely to be injured in cars produced after the 1968 model year, which met new state and federal automobile safety standards including seat belts, and those drivers were no more likely to hit pedestrians than were drivers of pre-1968-model-year cars. So he was deeply skeptical when he saw Peltzman's results. He claimed Peltzman's paper had multiple methodological flaws: failing to fully account for changes in alcohol consumption; treating motorcyclists as pedestrians; and failing to distinguish between cars, which were covered by the 1968 standards, and trucks, which were not. Once these adjustments were made, he said that fatalities were 15 to 20 percent lower as a result of the regulatory changes. He scolded Peltzman for ignoring the findings from Maryland and from the Australian state of Victoria, among the first jurisdictions with a mandatory seat-belt law, where occupant deaths declined and pedestrian deaths didn't change.

Robertson was even more withering in his criticism of Wilde, arguing that people didn't crash often enough, or know enough about the actual risks around them—e.g., how many drivers they passed that were drunk—to calibrate their behavior as finely as Wilde's thermostat implied.

Peltzman and Robertson never met; their fight transpired in

scholarly journals and articles. But it was nasty. Peltzman disputed Robertson's adjustments and his interpretation of the data from seat-belt laws in Australia. Yet what irked him most was that Robertson had no overarching theory of human behavior, only statistical relationships uninformed by any alternative theory for driver behavior like his own. He accused Robertson of seeking the result that suited his biases: "Selective editing of data motivated only by displeasure with a particular result can almost always be pursued to success."

To Robertson, the obsession with theory was precisely the problem. Of Peltzman, he said disdainfully: "The reification of a theory to the point of ignoring data that contradict its hypotheses is not uncommon among scientists. However, the scientist who does so often loses credibility along with his basic theory." In his critique of Wilde, he wrote that risk compensation "is almost invariably trotted out today to bolster the views of opponents of many safety measures, such as the compulsory wearing of bicycle helmets. Unfortunately, economic research is too often anti-regulation ideology cloaked in esoteric mathematical formulae to give it the appearance of genuine science."

Robertson was certainly onto something. The battle over safety regulation was about more than statistics; it was also a struggle between philosophies. Engineers, epidemiologists, and scientists had more faith that technology and enlightened policies could make life less dangerous, and their research tended to support the benefits of regulation and debunk that of Peltzman and his fellow travelers. Economists, psychologists, and ecologists more broadly believe that incentives matter a lot to human behavior and that regulation had unintended consequences, that risk appetites are inbred, and efforts to eliminate risk were likely to fail.

The safety critique also had libertarian undercurrents. Many opponents of seat-belt laws cared less about their efficacy than that they infringed on citizens' right to risk their own necks. (Not surprisingly, New Hampshire, whose motto is "Live Free or Die," is the only state that does not require drivers to wear a seat belt.)

Determining whether Peltzman was right was stymied by a methodological problem. To know whether the presence of a safety device altered someone's behavior would require observing two identical subjects in identical circumstances, except that one would have the device and the other wouldn't. In real life, too many variables intruded: economic conditions (since people had a greater economic incentive to drive fast when they had a well-paying job), law enforcement (seat belts that weren't worn didn't reduce deaths), distance traveled and types of roads (interstates were safer than two-lane highways), traffic density (people crash more often in denser traffic, but die less because the traffic moves more slowly), the demographics of the driving population (the very young and very old crashed more often), and underlying attitudes about risk having nothing to do with cars.

One complication was that certain types of people might be more likely to buy, and use, safety devices. Clifford Winston, an economist at the Brookings Institution, theorized that safety-conscious drivers were more likely to purchase cars with antilock brakes and air bags; the reduction in injuries would thus be attributable to the drivers' preexisting characteristics, not the technology. He and his coauthors undertook a study in Washington State that found that antilock brakes and air bags didn't reduce the number of crashes or crash severity, suggesting that those who relied on these measures were driving more dangerously, offsetting the safety benefits.

As more data and more refined methodology became possible, the pure Peltzman effect proved elusive. A study in 2001 by Liran Einav and Alma Cohen looked at the effect of forcing drivers to buckle up by examining traffic fatalities in states before and after they passed mandatory seat-belt laws. They concluded that enforcing seat-belt laws did increase their use and did reduce fatalities among occupants—with no increase in pedestrian deaths.

So did this mean the Peltzman effect didn't exist? Was it, as Robertson suggested, ideology masquerading as science? As it turns out, a Peltzman effect does exist, but not in the way Peltzman first theorized. And this became obvious with the advent of a product at first hailed as the greatest safety innovation since seat belts.

Originally devised for use on aircraft, antilock brakes promised a new level of automobile control in dangerous situations. Conventional brakes, when applied on a slippery surface or with too much force, always risked "locking" the wheels, so that rather than maintaining traction between the tires and the road surface, the tires skidded, thus reducing traction. Antilock brakes sense when the wheels are about to lock up and prevent the driver from continuing to apply pressure. Rather, the pressure is applied in rapid, intermittent bursts, as many as eighteen times per second, which slows the wheels down without allowing them to lock.

When in 1970 Ford rolled out the Lincoln Continental Mark III, one of the first production cars to include antilock brakes, the company promised a new standard not just in luxury but in safety: "the safer, straighter way to stop a car." By 1978, the German manufacturer Bosch had introduced electronic antilock brakes, and within seven years ABS was becoming standard on high-end vehicles. The systems have since become ever more popular, sophisticated, and expensive. Bosch's professional drivers test its systems in northern Sweden on a frozen lake with a surface like glass.

On test tracks, antilock braking systems dramatically reduced stopping distances and crashes. They also enabled the driver to steer around obstacles while braking. This generated enormous and widespread enthusiasm. In Germany, universal adoption of ABS was predicted to reduce the rate of severe crashes by 10 to 15 percent.

But initial studies of real-life experience were deflating: they found virtually no reduction in crashes. Why? In one, a taxi company in Munich equipped some of its fleet with ABS and compared the results with the rest of the fleet three years later. The startling outcome: ABS-equipped vehicles had just as many collisions as the others. It appeared that drivers who had ABS were driving faster and braking harder. A different study found that cars with ABS had fewer frontal but more rear-end collisions. By stopping faster, drivers with antilock brakes were making themselves safer but making others' behavior more dangerous.

Other researchers came up with different findings: no increase in rear-end collisions, but an increase in run-off-the-road incidents and rollovers. Perhaps, the explanation went, drivers were putting too much trust in their brakes and taking curves too aggressively. Or maybe not: perhaps when cars without ABS went off the road they were more likely to be stopped by a tree; drivers with ABS could steer around the tree but then they would roll over.

Maybe the problem was that drivers didn't understand how to use ABS: they thought it reduced stopping distances on all surfaces, when in fact it lengthens distances on some. In the early 1990s the Baltimore police department purchased Ford Tauruses with antilock brakes, but found officers crashed them just as often as the old cars. "We hear it all the time," one officer told the *Baltimore Sun*. "They tell us, 'I hit the brakes and the pedal started wobbling under my foot, so I tried them again. And again and again. Then I hit that tree.'" A Ford spokeswoman told the newspaper that the pedals are supposed to wobble. "When you start pumping them with your foot, well, it takes longer to stop. Somebody needs to tell the officers that."

In 1998 Leonard Evans, a research scientist at General

Motors, published an exhaustive review of GM's experience with cars that were equipped with ABS in 1992 and several other studies, three of which he wrote or cowrote, covering wet and dry, fatal and nonfatal, single- and multivehicle crashes, rollovers, hitting pedestrians, and other incidents. The result was more than a hundred specific observations. On wet roads, risks went down roughly twice as often as they went up; on dry roads, risks went up three times as often as they went down.

Evans went beyond the data. A regular lecturer, he would quiz audiences on how they thought ABS affected their behavior. Based on several hundred responses, he concluded that no one drove slower because of ABS and many drove faster, himself included: "I have driven faster on many occasions because my vehicle was ABS-equipped. For example, when driving on slush on a narrow two-lane road, with oncoming traffic a few feet to my left and a deep drainage ditch a few feet to my right." To check his suspicions, he obtained police records from Oregon and found that drivers of the new-model GM cars with ABS had 60 percent more speed-related offenses than non-speed-related offenses; for drivers of earlier-model-year versions of the same cars the difference was only 36 percent.

Why, then, was the Peltzman effect so apparent with antilock brakes but not seat belts? Adrian Lund, who succeeded Leon Robertson at the Insurance Institute for Highway Safety, says it's because of how the technology affects the task of driving. People often forget they are wearing seat belts. "When I finally got my mother-in-law to wear a seat belt she went to get out of her car and the belt stopped her. That's what happens with the belt. It doesn't affect the driving task," Lund told me. "But if you give people studded snow tires, we know from empirical evidence they will drive faster on snow. They don't drive faster enough to lose all the benefit, but they do drive faster. Because it's feeding back into the driving task."

This seems to explain the antilock brake experience. A driver who knows his car is equipped with antilock brakes feels he has more control over the car in dangerous situations and can thus drive faster. Most of the time he's right, and the brakes do keep him out of trouble on a wet road. But occasionally he's wrong, and the false confidence the brakes give him result in an accident he could have avoided if he had driven differently, or not driven at all. Lund recalls driving a car equipped with ABS for the first time, on a visit to Saab in Sweden. He was on snow, and couldn't get the car to stop. "I didn't hit anything, I just kind of drifted into the curb, which brought my speed down. I said [to Saab], this is very disconcerting. They said, 'You have to get used to it.' I said, 'That's not what you're telling people, you're saying they're miracle brakes.'"

This is a crucial insight. Whether a safety enhancement generates offsetting behavior depends a lot on what the enhancement enables us to do. Even when we're belted in, a car crash is an awfully unpleasant experience; few drivers would knowingly run a greater risk of one just because they thought they were more likely to survive it. But we might drive faster if we thought our cars had technology that made an accident less likely in the first place.

The same dynamic can explain the behavior of financial traders. Remember those credit default swaps that Gary Gorton helped AIG sell to European banks? Banks bought them with the explicit aim of having a riskier balance sheet than they otherwise could.

More than thirty years later, Peltzman now acknowledges that a key conclusion of his original study was wrong: drivers do not change their behavior enough to offset the entire benefit of new safety technology. But he maintains that they do offset some of it. The National Highway Traffic Safety Administration figured that raising seat-belt usage to 90 percent of the population from 68 percent (where it stood in 1996) would save 5,536 fatalities per year. Yet Einav and Cohen concluded that seat belts would save only a third as many lives. Indeed, real-life experience rarely finds that new safety devices produce benefits on the promised scale.

Nonetheless, fatalities on the roads have steadily declined, a fact that Peltzman readily acknowledges. The question is, why? Even if mandated regulations explain some of the decline, they can't explain all or even most of it. Peltzman notes that fatalities fell at about 3.5 percent per year in the decades before Nader's book was published in 1965, and continued falling at roughly the same rate thereafter.

The explanation lies in the original concept behind the tradeoff between safety and risk. When a risky activity becomes

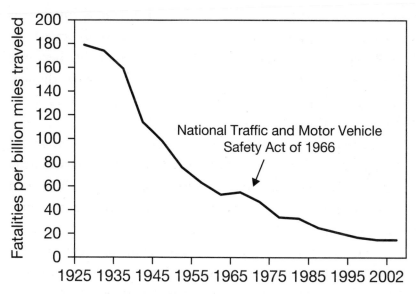

Automobile fatalities have declined steadily since 1925, with the introduction of federal safety regulation showing only a minor effect. (Source: data courtesy of Sam Peltzman, University of Chicago)

safer, people do more of it—assuming that their underlying appetite for risk stays the same. But risk appetites can change. Over time, people may insist that a particular activity be safer before they will take part in it.

That's what John Adams, a retired geography professor at University College London, believes is going on with traffic. Adams started his professional career as an environmental activist protesting the construction of new freeways around London and ended it as a vocal opponent of mandatory seat-belt laws and an expert in human behavior and risk.

Adams notes that in Britain, as in America, deaths per kilometer driven have fallen fairly steadily since 1950, with no apparent difference as Britain introduced lower speed limits, tougher laws against drunk driving, and mandatory seat-belt laws.

The bigger reason traffic deaths have declined, says Adams, is not mandated safety but society's changing tolerance for risk. In 1971, a survey of five schools at different locations in Britain found that 80 percent of seven- to eleven-year-olds walked to school without an adult. When Adams repeated the survey in 1990, the proportion had dropped to 9 percent for children ages seven and eight. This was due primarily not to fear of child abduction but fear of traffic.

As society becomes more affluent, one of the things it spends its additional income on is more safety. This is one reason highway traffic death rates are far higher in poor countries than in rich ones. Adams likes to show photographs of the Lagos–Ibadan Expressway in Nigeria. Though it looks like any freeway in Britain, if more dilapidated, it is frequently brought to a standstill by horrific accidents; one in August 2010 burned fifteen people to death. As Adams points out, "They are achieving their higher death rates with modern imported technology, with one hundred years of safety technology built into them. Nigeria has a seat-belt law, speed limits, drunk driving laws, prohibitions on mobile phones." What Nigeria doesn't have is Britain's lower appetite for taking risk on the roads; that may take time.

Risk appetite is also a function of age. History has yet to record a surefire method of persuading young people that they are not immortal. In the 1930s, there was an almost universal belief that since automobile accidents were overwhelmingly the fault of the "nut behind the wheel," the best form of accident prevention was driver education. Driver's ed courses became prevalent and by 1960 were often required in high school. Insurance companies offered premium discounts for drivers who had taken the courses. These presumptions seemed to be vindicated by early studies that found graduates of such programs had fewer accidents.

But more careful research debunked those findings. Students who are predisposed to drive more safely are also more likely to take driver's ed courses. Once that is controlled for, the better driving record disappears. In fact, some scholars concluded that driver's ed was leading to more accidents because it enabled young drivers to get their licenses sooner. Whatever increased ability young drivers derived from driver's ed was offset by overconfidence in that ability. One Norwegian study, for example, found that those who learned car handling on a slippery course had more skid-related accidents.

Similarly, financial literacy programs have sometimes succeeded in influencing people to make wiser choices and avoid rip-offs. But they do not necessarily keep them safe. This was poignantly illustrated by a pilot project on the South Side of Chicago that took place at the height of the subprime mortgage bubble, in 2006. The program targeted anyone with a low credit score or who applied for a mortgage with one of several risk factors: an interest rate that adjusted within three years, negative amortization (meaning the principal went up instead of down over time), prepayment penalties or closing costs in excess of 5 percent, and loans underwritten on the basis of stated (as opposed to documented) income.

Applicants who filled the bill had to attend a one- to two-hour session with a counselor who verified the borrower's information on the application and explained the terms and consequences of the loan as well as potential pitfalls. In all, 1,200 borrowers underwent counseling during the pilot program's brief existence. But as a study by Itzhak Ben-David of Ohio State University and four coauthors found, counseling seemed to have no impact on borrowers' willingness to take on a risky mortgage. For example, fixed-rate mortgages are safer than adjustable-rate mortgages because their rates can't go up; but just as many borrowers switched from fixed to adjustable as the other way around. The program did have some clear impacts: it found evidence of fraud in 9 percent of loan offers, and the possibility of being exposed drove many predatory lenders to stop doing business in the area. But it also drove out borrowers, who disliked the time and effort involved in counseling. In fact, the impact on both the demand and supply of loans was so great that, under pressure from community groups and mortgage brokers, the program was discontinued three years early, after less than a year. The lesson is that when people really want to borrow, it can be very hard to persuade them not to, even when they're told it's a menace to their financial health.

Risk appetite also helps explain why eliminating concussions in football has proved so difficult. While direct comparisons are tricky, concussions appear to be less common in rugby.

Andrew McIntosh, a sports injury expert in Australia, has compared the force that occurs in head-on collisions in American football with those in rugby and Australian rules football (a sort of hybrid of soccer, rugby, and American football), both of

which are played without hard helmets. He concluded that players were hitting one another with twice the energy in American
football than in the Australian version or rugby. There appear to
be two reasons. One is that because American footballers wear
helmets, they hit one another harder. The other is different risk
appetites. Fans of American football expect a more violent spectacle than fans of rugby or Australian football, and the games are
played accordingly. In rugby, the defenders use their arms to try
to drag the ball carrier to the ground, at which point a battle for
control of the ball ensues. They do not try to knock the player
down, and direct hits to the head are illegal. Rugby's international governing rules strictly limit the amount and type of protective gear players may wear; soft, thin headgear to protect the
ears is allowed but hard helmets are not.

Even in rugby, though, concussions are growing, a reflection
of the fact that as the sport has become professional, the players
have gotten bigger and faster (as they have in American football), which produces more forceful impacts and injuries when
players collide. It's a reminder that what people want from sports
is, first of all, excitement and thrills, just as what they want from
their cars is to reach their destination quickly. Anything that
makes the game or the drive safer inevitably becomes a means to
achieve that primary goal—and some safety will be sacrificed in
the process.

CHAPTER 5

The Trouble with Saving: From Gold Standard to Euro

You can learn a lot about a country from its language. In Germany, the word for debt, *schuld*, is the same as the word for guilt. That pretty much sums up German attitudes about saving (good) and borrowing (bad). The same ambivalence about spending explains why most German stores don't open on Sunday. Aldi, one of the country's best-known retailers, is a monument to frugality that once sold no-name bags of potato chips out of plain cardboard boxes. German tax collectors leave interest on savings accounts alone. One economist even speculates that the weakness of the future tense in German makes the future seem closer to its speakers, and thus more important to save for.

Germany's attitudes were on display over the course of the European debt crisis. While Greece, Portugal, and Ireland teetered on complete collapse, Germany was always the country most resistant to bailing them out. "Sell your islands, you bankrupt Greeks, and the Acropolis, too!" the German tabloid *Bild* scolded in 2010.

Germans, like many outsiders, blamed the European crisis on the habits of the crisis countries: Italians, Spaniards, Greeks, Portuguese, and Irish, who borrowed with abandon and then dragged the continent to the edge of an abyss when they balked at paying.

A high regard for saving is not restricted to Germany: it is a universal cultural constant—Aesop's fable of the grasshopper and the ant, Joseph's biblical instructions to Pharaoh to save during the seven fat years to prepare for seven lean years, the aphorism that a penny saved is a penny earned (which predates Ben Franklin). Saving embodies so many of the values we worship: thrift, self-restraint, foresight. It also represents prudence and safety. The householder who sets aside money now protects herself and her family against the vicissitudes of the future.

Trust the economists to demolish this tidy moral tale. An elementary though often forgotten law of economics states that for someone to borrow, someone else must save. One country's debt is another's asset. And Europe's crisis was as much the consequence of German saving as of Greek, Italian, and Spanish borrowing. Indeed, throughout history it has been savers' desire for safety that so often precipitates international crises.

Savers, of course, seldom see their culpability, because their link to the ultimate user of their money is often opaque. People with a bank deposit or a mutual fund may have only the vaguest sense of the loans the bank makes or the securities the mutual fund buys. This is by design. Savers and borrowers seldom match perfectly. Savers want the comfort of knowing they can get all their money back immediately. Borrowers would rather not give it back until they're ready, with as few strings attached as possible. It's the job of banks and other financiers to reconcile these divergent needs. When savers and borrowers live in different countries, the task gets even more complicated. One of the biggest challenges is this: in what currency will you be repaid? If a British lender lends an American 100 dollars, will the 100 dollars be worth as much when he gets them back in pounds? What if he lends in pesos? Or drachmas?

A banker must consider all these factors before making a loan in a different currency. If he suspects the currency will be devalued by inflation and government deficits, he will demand a higher interest rate, or he will look for some sort of commitment to ensure that the currency's value won't change. "Who would be prepared to lend with the fear of being paid in depreciated currencies always before his eyes?" asked Georges Bonnet, a French finance minister of the 1930s. In the early 1800s, Britain became the linchpin of a monetary system that made it vastly easier for savers to do business with borrowers around the world. In 1821, after the Napoleonic Wars, Britain made the pound sterling convertible on demand to gold. Throughout the 1800s, the willingness of Britons and their bankers to lend to another country closely corresponded to that country's adherence to gold. If the dollar, or peso, was redeemable for a fixed quantity of gold, then its value was effectively fixed against the pound sterling. British investors assumed that when a country issued paper money (i.e., not redeemable in gold), hyperinflation would ensue and credit would collapse.

At the time, Britain and America were perfect economic complements: Britain was a wealthy, industrializing country with plenty of spare savings that needed a place to be invested. The United States was a young country with vast economic potential and too little savings to invest in development. But British savers and their bankers, typically landlords, clergymen, professionals, and retired military officers, were a conservative bunch. They weren't after double-digit gains; they were happy with a 5 percent return and assurance that a 100 pounds sterling loan would be repaid with 100 pounds sterling, not some worthless paper foreign currency. By promising to repay in either sterling or dollars backed by gold, American borrowers attracted a torrent of British capital to finance canals, railroads, and other economic projects in the early 1800s.

During the Civil War, the United States was desperate for funds to finance its efforts and decided to issue greenbacks—paper money not redeemable in gold. That made it almost impossible for Barings, one of Britain's oldest and most prestigious merchant banks, to sell American bonds to British investors. When the state of Pennsylvania began paying off bonds in greenbacks instead of gold, a representative of the Rothschilds accused the state of pauperizing widows and orphans in England and Europe.

British savers returned in 1869 when Ulysses S. Grant took office and promised to return to the gold standard. They fled once again in 1877 upon introduction in Congress of a bill that would have allowed debts to be repaid in silver. British investors dumped their American bonds in favor of colonial bonds with interest and principal guaranteed in sterling. The bill that eventually passed allowed only limited silver coinage, and the United States returned to gold in 1879.

The late 1800s were, literally, the golden age of globalization as more countries joined the gold standard. By making a country safe for savers, the gold standard made it easier for it to borrow. It was a "good housekeeping seal of approval," as monetary historian Michael Bordo and his coauthor Hugh Rockoff put it. The gold standard also carried moral overtones: its proponents considered it morally superior to paper money, and saw an inability to stay on gold as a sign of foolish profligacy, a sentiment that lives on among gold's followers today. Countries that promised repayment in gold paid significantly lower interest rates. Chile, for example, paid under 5 percent on gold bonds but 7 percent on paper bonds.

However, by making it easier to borrow, the gold standard also made it easier to run up crippling debts. By insisting on repayment in gold, savers avoided one risk (depreciation) but took on another: default. The most spectacular example was

Argentina. It joined the gold standard in 1867, and between 1870 and 1889 capital equivalent to 19 percent of its GDP flowed in to develop its vast, fertile plains. But the debts Argentina accumulated proved difficult to repay. In 1890 Barings, unable to sell the bonds of the Buenos Aires Water Supply and Drainage Corporation, took a massive loss that nearly bankrupted it. Argentina suspended its commitment to gold, foreign savings up and left, and the economy collapsed. In the ensuing political unrest, the president was forced to resign. But Argentina restructured its debts, the British government bailed out Barings, and flows soon resumed.

The trust that British savers placed in this system was astonishing. By the eve of the First World War, British investment abroad each year approached 10 percent of GDP, and the income Britain earned on those overseas holdings was equal to nearly 10 percent of GDP. British investors felt more comfortable lending to foreigners than buying shares in British manufacturing.

But the stability the gold standard imparted to the world financial system was fragile, because it could require painful economic adjustments that some countries found intolerable. The value of a currency depends heavily on how its purchasing power is sustained at home, which in turn has to do with productivity (the more efficient business is, the less costs rise), inflation (faster-rising prices eat away at a currency's purchasing power), government deficits (a government may be tempted to finance them by printing money), and private saving (the less a country saves, the more it imports). Exchange rates work the way other prices do: they move up or down to restore balance. If one country's inflation is too high or it consumes too much and produces too little, its currency will decline to bring its costs back in line or force it to import less and save more. As chaotic as floating exchange rates (currencies that fluctuate against one another) are, they thus serve a vital economic purpose: they allow separate economic cultures to coexist.

Milton Friedman compared floating exchange rates to daylight saving time:

> Isn't it absurd to change the clock in summer when exactly the same result could be achieved by having each individual change his habits? All that is required is that everyone decide to come to his office an hour earlier, have lunch an hour earlier, etc. But obviously it is much simpler to change the clock that guides all than to have each individual separately change his pattern of reaction to the clock, even though all want to do so. The situation is exactly the same in the exchange market. It is far simpler to allow one price to change, namely, the price of foreign exchange, than to rely upon changes in the multitude of prices that together constitute the internal price structure.

The gold standard didn't permit such adjustments. A country that experienced inflation, for example, would see its costs rise. This would lead to falling exports and higher imports. If it did not sell enough exports to pay for its imports—that is, if it had a trade deficit—it would borrow the difference. If it could not borrow, it would pay for the difference by handing gold over to foreigners. As gold supplies dwindled, the country would have to raise interest rates to attract lenders and their gold, and cut government spending to reduce borrowing. That would drive down prices and wages—a process called deflation—reduce imports, and reinvigorate exports.

Deflation is an extremely painful process that frequently requires a recession, but it can also be the price of entry to a prestigious club. When Russia was preparing to join the gold standard in the late nineteenth century, its finance minister lamented, "We must export though we die."

Some countries simply could not endure the necessary sacrifice. Joining the gold standard caused so much hardship that it contributed to the Russian Revolution, Bordo and Harold James, another historian, reckon. Many Russians thought the tsars had sold out their interests to foreigners; Lenin claimed that foreign creditors controlled Russia's foreign policy.

During the First World War, Britain suspended the gold standard to allow massive government borrowing to finance the conflict, which led to a rapid rise in prices. When Britain returned to the gold standard after the war, wartime inflation had made the country deeply uncompetitive, necessitating a decade of painfully high interest rates and deflation in an attempt to return to the old gold standard level, a solution that more or less kept the economy in depression.

Gold had another insidious effect. A country reluctant to lose gold would seek to maintain a trade surplus, for example through high import tariffs. But this tactic would penalize other countries' exports and in effect force them to run deficits. If all countries sought surpluses, no one would import from anyone else and the global trading system would implode.

This is a problem common to all monetary systems, as can be illustrated with a real-world example from, of all things, a babysitting co-operative. In the 1970s, families on Capitol Hill in Washington agreed to babysit one another's children. Each family that babysat for another would be paid with scrip (an unofficial currency); it could then spend that scrip by asking another family to babysit for them. But as Richard James Sweeney, a government economist, and his wife, Joan Sweeney, described it, a problem arose: there was so little scrip to go around that members were reluctant to spend what they had by going out; instead, they all wanted to babysit: "Those who wanted to go out but didn't have scrip were desperate to get sitting jobs," the Sweeneys later wrote in an academic journal. "The scrip-price of babysitting couldn't adjust, and the shortage worsened. The co-op even passed a rule that everyone must go out at least once every six months. The thinking was that some members were shirking, not going out enough, displaying the antisocial ways and bad morals that were destroying the co-op."

It is telling that it took an economist to label savers, not borrowers, as immoral. To an economist, the babysitting co-op became just like an economy in which everyone wants to save and no one wants to borrow — in fact, this happens to fit the circumstances of the gold standard very neatly. During the 1920s, the United States and France accumulated gold by running trade surpluses while Britain and Germany lost gold, which tightened credit and depressed their growth. As the economic historian Barry Eichengreen has observed, France's attitude at the time was similar to Germany's today: the French attributed their trade surplus to having a stronger work ethic and more thriftiness than the British.

The babysitting co-op solved its problem by issuing everyone more scrip, which relieved the pressure members felt to stay home and hoard what they had. For the international financial system, the equivalent — issuing more gold to everyone — was obviously not possible; the supply of gold depends on how much miners can pull out of the ground each year. The alternative was to drop the promise of pegging currencies' value to gold so that currencies could move up and down, to better reflect countries' underlying competitive positions. That's what Britain eventually did. In 1931 it left gold, and the pound immediately fell about 25 percent against the dollar. The decline in the British exchange rate allowed it to restore competitiveness and to lower interest rates, which boosted demand. It also forced many of its trading partners to devalue; those that didn't devalue imposed foreign exchange controls or raised tariffs.

Economists now know that adherence to gold was a major contributor to the Great Depression. To maintain their parities, adherents were forced to keep interest rates higher and budgets balanced, which only tightened the vise on their domestic economies. Countries that abandoned gold escaped that vise and recovered much more quickly.

But at the time the world drew a different lesson: it associated the Depression with "beggar thy neighbor" devaluations, and the gold standard with stability, order, and prosperity. That's why the world's nations agreed to return to fixed exchange rates at the Bretton Woods Conference in 1944. The United States would fix the dollar in gold; every other country would fix its currency in dollars. The new model wasn't quite as rigid as the gold standard— countries could devalue against the dollar if necessary, usually with the permission of the International Monetary Fund—but it came close.

The new system started to break down when some countries began to accumulate large stocks of dollars and rising inflation in the United States undermined the dollar's value relative to gold. Foreigners rightly questioned whether the United States had enough gold to redeem their dollars, and began to exchange their dollars for gold. In 1971 the United States, running low on gold, "shut" the gold window—it would no longer freely exchange gold for dollars at its fixed price. Exchange rate chaos soon followed, with dollars, yen, francs, pounds, and deutsche marks all fluctuating wildly against one another.

No sooner had fixed exchange rates evaporated than Europe set out to restore them. France harbored particularly unpleasant memories of the franc's bouts of weakness in the 1920s. Valéry Giscard d'Estaing, France's president in the late 1970s, associated the currency stability of the gold standard a century earlier with steady growth and industrialization: "With their roots in a rural economy and their cultural leaning towards the fundamental values of savings and thrift, the French...thrive on stable money." Europe had already plunged down the road toward economic integration with the European Economic Community, an attempt to bury forever the conflicts of the past century by binding their economies ever more tightly together. Monetary integration, naturally, followed. Starting in the 1970s, the main countries in the EEC sought to peg their currencies to one another.

But speculators would regularly test a government's commitment to maintaining the low inflation, competitive policies, and balanced budgets necessary to keep its currency stable. And because so many countries couldn't keep inflation as low or saving as high as Germany, their currencies were regularly forced to devalue against the deutsche mark. What was the solution? As one study by the European Commission concluded in 1990: "Adoption of a single currency is the only sure way to overcome this credibility issue." And so in February 1992, in Maastricht, the Netherlands, Europe's countries signed a pact committing them to move to a single currency by 1999.

The euro's architects were aware that economic fundamentals had to be aligned, and so they set down tough criteria on inflation and budget deficits as conditions for joining.

As if to illustrate their point, the most devastating speculative attack in the region's history began in the fall of 1992. Convinced that Britain, Spain, France, and Italy had kept their exchange rates at artificially high values, speculators such as George Soros sold billions and billions of their currencies, and those countries fought back—first by spending some of their own precious deutsche marks to buy up their tainted currencies, and then by hiking interest rates to try to draw investor interest back. One by one, the weakest surrendered. On "Black Wednesday," the Bank of England stopped defending the pound, and it immediately plunged 7 percent. Within a day, both the Italian and Spanish currencies had also been devalued.

Predictions of disaster proved unfounded: spurred by the cheaper pound and lower interest rates, Britain's economy bounded ahead the next year. France, which had successfully defended the franc with sharply higher interest rates, slipped into recession.

By then Britain had had it with fixed exchange rates. But the rest of Europe took a very different lesson: only a single currency could put an end to such crises once and for all. Soros agreed. In a magazine article, he warned that Europe would come apart without a single currency: "A common market cannot survive in the long run without one because currency markets are notoriously unstable and currency speculation . . . can have a destabilizing effect on the economies involved."

French bankers feared that repeated crises like the one in 1992 would keep interest rates permanently higher and longed to get the single currency in place. Spain, Italy, and other traditional economic laggards, terrified of consignment to the economic backwaters, redoubled their efforts to qualify for the euro. Romano Prodi was elected prime minister of Italy in 1996 on a campaign of promising to do what it took to join the euro, and Italian voters backed him even though they expected the price to be years of austerity to shrink budget deficits and high interest rates to reduce inflation.

The most important change of heart was Germany's. It had always been ambivalent about the euro. Germany endured chronic monetary and economic instability between the world wars, lurching from hyperinflation to deflation and depression, which in turn set the stage for Hitler's rise. When the Allies rebuilt

Germany, they bestowed upon it a fiercely independent central bank to ensure that it could never again become a mechanism for political subjugation or militarization. The Bundesbank's insistence on raising interest rates to stamp down inflation repeatedly destabilized exchange rates within Europe. Even German leaders realized this was not an arrangement built to last, a point underlined after Black Wednesday, when British newspapers darkly linked the Bundesbank to the Nazis.

Otmar Issing personified German monetary orthodoxy. A prominent economist and member of the Bundesbank board, he had long opposed monetary union on the grounds that weaker countries would never meet the necessary conditions. But events following Black Wednesday changed his mind. Every time Germany's trading partners devalued, their products automatically got cheaper relative to Germany's. In the wake of the 1992 crisis, Issing fretted, companies in southern Germany, unable to compete with Italy, went bankrupt. "It created calls for tariffs, quantitative constraints, et cetera," Issing told me. He loudly warned that if the disaster were repeated, which he considered virtually certain, "the single market would have been destroyed."

Issing went from skeptic of monetary union to advocate, and in 1998 he was named to the board of the European Central Bank, which would become the new currency's guardian in 1999. Issing equated monetary stability with political stability. When Roman legions conquered western Europe, they took both their language, Latin, and their coin, the denarius, with them. When the European Parliament held a hearing to consider his appointment, Issing related how as an adolescent he imagined a merchant traveling from Rome to what is now Cologne, and even to London, able to use the same money. "The Pax Romana ensured political cohesion, the scarcity of gold ensured the stability of the currency," he lectured European parliamentarians. Then, evoking the collapse of the Roman empire, its money, and the Dark Ages, he added rhetorically, "And what did the centuries that followed hold in store for Europe?"

Many were skeptical of the euro. They felt Europe's economies were still too different to prosper in a monetary union. The bloated government budgets and rigid labor markets of the peripheral economies simply couldn't survive competition with their northern neighbors without the salve of periodic devaluations. Investors, they predicted, would force peripheral governments to pay painfully high interest rates and suffer permanently higher unemployment, which would eventually provoke rebellion from their voters. Soros worried that without more help for the unemployed, popular discontent would sweep away the euro.

And yet, the adoption of the euro did just the opposite. Interest rates in Europe's peripheral economies plummeted and growth boomed. In the 1990s, governments in the GIIPS (Greece, Ireland, Italy, Portugal, and Spain) paid as much as 5 percentage points more than Germany to borrow; by the early 2000s, that differential had completely disappeared. The confidence the euro had inspired in savers exceeded even what the gold standard had achieved in the late 1800s. Banks in northern Europe became enthusiastic lenders to customers in southern Europe, with Deutsche Bank and ING, Germany's and the Netherlands' largest banks, respectively, vastly increasing their lending to the GIIPS countries. In 1997, just 12 percent of German banks' loans were to borrowers in the GIIPS; by 2008, that had topped 25 percent. For Dutch banks, the proportion rose from 10 to 18 percent. Cross-border mergers soared. A merger or an acquisition "within the euro area is no longer an issue of correctly assessing long-term exchange-rate developments," Ernst Welteke, president of the Bundesbank, told a British audience in 2001.

Behind this surge in lending was a conviction that the traditional risks of lending to such countries had diminished. Locked into a single currency, lenders no longer had to worry that they'd

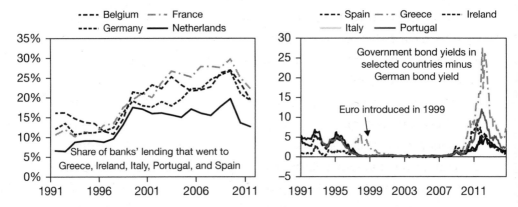

The euro led to a surge of lending by northern banks to southern countries and a plunge in the interest rates southern countries paid relative to what Germany paid. (Sources: bank lending chart data courtesy of the Federal Reserve Bank of San Francisco; interest rate data from OECD Main Economic Indicators)

be repaid with devalued currencies. And members of the euro zone, if not possessing the same Teutonic dedication to balanced budgets and hard work as Germany, were assumed to at least be getting close; default by a sovereign borrower was unthinkable. For countries on the outside, joining the euro became as much a seal of approval as joining the gold standard had been more than a century earlier. Cyprus, for example, a tiny island country that had long marketed itself as an offshore finance center, in particular to Russians and other eastern Europeans, needed entry to the euro so that the lenders who financed its banks' sprawling operations around the eastern Mediterranean need not worry about devaluation.

But confidence that the euro had made crises a thing of the past proved to be its undoing. The architects of the euro assumed that as countries joined, they would have to accelerate their fiscal and economic reforms to meet the standards of Germany. And they did—in order to join. But perversely, once they joined the euro, the opposite happened. Previously, savers' fear of devaluation meant they charged higher interest rates to weaker countries, which provided a spur to domestic reform. With the euro, as one study documented, that fear, and that spur, were gone. Spain abandoned efforts to make its labor market less rigid in 2002; the school dropout rate rose, corruption worsened. The inflow of money made it easy for the Cajas, Spain's politically connected, local government-owned banks, to vastly boost their lending to local developers, often for projects of dubious merit. Greece's excessively generous pension system was a major drag on its finances, and governments had sought to reform it starting in 1990 under pressure from the European Union as a condition of joining the euro. But once Greece joined, the political and economic pressure to act disappeared; the country's bonds yielded 22 percent in 1994, but by 2003, they were yielding 3.6 percent, the same as Germany's. In 2001, the government proposed raising retirement ages, reducing the pension benefit, and requiring longer work tenure to qualify for a pension, but it backed down in the face of massive protests.

Successive Greek governments chose to postpone action on its dire state finances, or simply sweep them under the rug. In Spain and Ireland, the influx of money found its way into local banks that then lent it out to homeowners and property developers. The result was a surge in housing construction and prices that far outstripped America's. Amid those booms, there was no pressure on southern economies to become more competitive; indeed, prices and wages continued to rise faster than in Germany, and the result was steadily eroding competitiveness and widening trade deficits.

This was all made possible by the inflow of savings from Germany. As I noted earlier, German savers may not have made the connection, because they put their money in banks, and the banks lent to the south. The euro gave German banks the confidence to do so at rates they never would have offered before, and allowed far bigger debts to build than would have been possible before the euro. These risks were largely invisible to both investors and Europe's leaders. Obsessed as they were with fiscal probity, they took comfort that budgets in Ireland and Spain were balanced and debts declining relative to GDP.

As late as 2010, Europe's leaders insisted that the euro meant that it no longer mattered whether one country borrowed from another, any more than it mattered how much Florida borrowed from New York. *But it did matter.* In the fall of 2009, a new Greek government revealed that the previous government had lied about its budget deficits. Overnight, Greece's debts went from manageable to unsustainable. In 2010 the rest of the euro zone and the IMF put together a massive bailout to keep Greece afloat and began working on a broader solution should other countries get into trouble.

This came at a price, though. Angela Merkel, the German chancellor, fretted that bailing out profligate countries would breed moral hazard: savers would continue to lend to such countries without checking on whether they could pay the money back. That October in Deauville, France, Merkel went for a walk on the beach with Nicolas Sarkozy, the French president, and persuaded him that as a condition of rescues, private investors in government bonds would have to take "haircuts," that is, get back less than 100 cents on the euro. In effect, sovereign debt would be no more sacrosanct than that of a railroad or a supermarket.

The Deauville Declaration became Europe's "Lehman moment," the point at which deeply ingrained assumptions about the safety of the financial system are shattered and unease turns into panic. The implications went well beyond Greek debt. Any northern investor holding a Spanish, Italian, Portuguese, or Irish bond realized that instead of depreciation, his principal worry in pre-euro days, he now had to worry about something far worse: default, which hadn't happened in Europe since the aftermath of the Second World War. The significance went even further: in Europe, big banks were all assumed to be too big to fail, since their governments invariably bailed them out. But if governments could fail, so could their banks. Anyone with money in a southern bank now risked losing it (as many discovered when Cyprus was bailed out in 2013 and depositors sustained losses).

Northern banks and other investors began to dump southern governments' bonds, causing their yields to skyrocket and undoing all the convergence the euro had made possible and more. Northern savers also began to yank their savings out of southern banks. The financial integration that had proceeded so rapidly from the introduction of the euro went into reverse.

The fixed exchange rates that preceded the euro had a bad habit of periodically disintegrating in the face of speculative attack, but their saving grace was that the resulting devaluation would correct the imbalance that had led to the crisis, much like devaluing against gold under the gold standard. Inside the euro, no such safety valve exists. As northern savings pulled out, southern countries had to slash government spending to shrink their deficits, and workers endured layoffs, wage freezes, and pay cuts as domestic sales dried up and employers struggled to regain their competitive position against Germany.

Two years after the Deauville Declaration, the European Central Bank sought to undo its damage when its president, Mario Draghi, promised to do "whatever it takes" to save the euro. This meant that if a private saver wouldn't buy Italy's or Spain's bonds, the ECB would. Much as the Federal Reserve responded to its Lehman moment by treating the big banks as too big to fail, the ECB responded to its own by declaring sovereign governments too big to fail. This proved remarkably successful: at the time of this writing, in early 2015, the ECB has yet to invoke this emergency authority to buy a single bond, and interest rates on southern governments' bonds have fallen substantially, although not to northern levels. Savers' precious sense of safety has—for now, at least—been restored.

But the damage has been done. To shrink their budget and trade deficits, southern economies have endured painfully high unemployment, sinking public support for European economic integration, and the rise of extremist, populist parties on the left and right that inveigh against immigrants, banks, and foreigners. These political tensions may set in motion forces that push some countries out of the euro.

It is possible to create an economic zone free of both exchange rate crises and debt crises; the United States is such a zone, where fifty states share a single currency and none has defaulted since the 1930s. But this stability comes at a price. American states have surrendered most of their control over the economy to the federal government. Whether California runs a budget deficit and Utah runs a surplus means little for the local economy because the federal government does most of the taxing and spending. No one cares if Illinois is too broke to bail out its banks, because the banks are backed by federal deposit insurance.

Europe is still far from this point. There is little prospect of national budgets being surrendered to a federal European government or bank deposits to a common deposit fund. And while the euro has survived, the tensions that produced its crisis persist: its northern and southern members remain very different economies. Restoring equilibrium would ideally not just involve southern countries cutting wages and government spending, but Germany increasing its own. But it has no interest in that, and still sees the region's crisis as the product of too much borrowing, not too much saving. Germany emerged from the euro crisis with the world's largest trade surplus, which makes it harder for other countries to correct their deficits. When the United States pointed this out, Germans responded with puzzlement and annoyance. "The German economy is competitive, with record-high employment—so it's really not understandable why we're being blamed for this success," said Michael Meister, a top legislator and ally of Merkel. The puzzlement is understandable; Germans have long thought of saving, restraint, and discipline as qualities to be admired, not vilified. They can no more imagine themselves responsible for the harm this inflicts on others than a driver who hits his brakes too hard takes responsibility for the driver who follows too close behind.

A similar problem afflicts the entire global economy. The crisis that befell America was in its own way the product of too much saving in other parts of the world. Indeed, this could be traced to the roots of a previous crisis, in East Asia, which was itself the result of a failed effort to eliminate the uncertainty of floating exchange rates.

Thailand entered the 1980s suffering from double-digit inflation, excessive private borrowing, and a gaping budget deficit. It put in place several strict policies to restore health, among them fixing the exchange rate of its currency, the baht. That stable exchange rate made foreign investors less worried about lending to Thai companies in local currency, believing that when the Thai borrower repaid the money, it would not have lost value because of a devaluation. It also encouraged Thai companies to borrow in dollars. Ordinarily, that's a risky proposition; if the baht went down, dollar-denominated loans would become far more expensive to repay. But the stability of the exchange rate reassured them that this wasn't much of a risk.

The influx of money turned Thailand into a major borrower. Thailand might be a rare case of a crisis that was actually foreseen. The head of the IMF repeatedly warned the country to "get rid of this very dangerous peg to the dollar." George Soros built up a large bet against the baht just as he had against the pound five years earlier. In July 1997, Thailand bowed to the inevitable and devalued; the baht plummeted by a sixth in a single day and went on to lose half its value over the next year. The Asian financial crisis had begun.

Thailand's problems had been well publicized; the fact that many of its neighbors shared similar problems — pegged exchange rates and excessive borrowing in foreign currencies — less so. And once savers saw that Thailand's exchange-rate peg wouldn't be defended, they concluded others wouldn't either, and fled. The Philippines devalued a week later, soon followed by Malaysia, Indonesia, and Korea.

Worried that governments and banks would default, the IMF and the United States rushed emergency loans to them, but with strict conditions: Thailand had to raise taxes, balance its budget, restructure bust finance companies, and end subsidies to state-owned companies; Korea had to allow foreigners to own bigger stakes in Korean companies and banks, halt government-directed lending to industrial conglomerates, and lower tariffs to imports. Indonesia had to submit to a particularly long list of conditions, many aimed specifically at the kleptocratic family of the president, Suharto: close many wasteful projects such as those aimed at building automobiles and airplanes headed by the family of the president; cancel infrastructure projects; eliminate monopolies in sugar, cloves, and other products that were also controlled by the Suharto family.

Many of these conditions had nothing to do with the causes of the crisis, and even those that did seek to address causes, like the demand for higher interest rates and smaller budget deficits, ended up making things worse, as the IMF itself later admitted.

Within a few years, the victims of the Asian crisis were on the mend, but the pain of the crisis and the humiliation of the bailouts left a permanent impression. Forever afterward, Koreans referred to the crisis as the "IMF crisis." Most important, all emerging countries witnessed the steep price of becoming too indebted to foreigners. Many resolved never again to be put in that position, and implemented policies aimed at preventing any buildup of foreign debt. Business investment and budget deficits, which often involve borrowing from abroad, were curtailed; exchange rates were kept low to boost exports and inhibit imports; and new rules limited how much private borrowers could borrow in foreign currencies.

The most important reaction came from a country that wasn't even hit by the crisis. China did fix its exchange rate, but because its financial markets were closed, Chinese investors couldn't rush to convert their savings to dollars and speculators couldn't attack the exchange rate. China decided it liked it that way; even as other parts of its economy opened up, over the coming decade it kept a firm hand on the exchange rate and its financial markets, ensuring that the currency remained cheap and turning China into an exporting juggernaut. The result was that whereas in 1997 East Asia was a net borrower from the rest of the world, by 2007 China had become a major net lender.

As we have seen, though, for one country to be a lender, another must be a borrower. When China exports more than it imports, it is left holding dollars that must be deployed somehow. China, like many other countries in the same situation, chose to purchase American bonds—either Treasury bonds or bonds issued by Fannie Mae and Freddie Mac, which most people treated as the same as government bonds. By 2007, China had acquired more than $800 billion of these bonds; the rest of Asia, $1.3 trillion.

This meant that even as the United States was borrowing staggering sums from the rest of the world, its long-term bond and mortgage rates remained strangely low, fueling the housing boom. Alan Greenspan called this a conundrum. His fellow governor, Ben Bernanke, had a different explanation: it was the "global saving glut." He noted that the low mortgage rates made possible by the influx of foreign savings had spurred home construction and home prices, though he didn't spot the crisis that would result.

The global saving glut is probably the least appreciated contributor to the financial crisis of 2008, and the least corrected. True, Americans curbed their appetite for borrowing, and China also embarked on an investment boom that soaked up some of its extra savings.

But numerous other countries are more determined than ever to accumulate large piles of foreign assets as insurance against the chaos of global markets and to obviate the need for politically toxic bailouts. In 2014, those collective war chests stood at $12 trillion, double the precrisis level. This excess is an important reason why interest rates remain so low many years after the crisis. Keynes's paradox of thrift has been reproduced on a global scale.

How can this be remedied? Just as Social Security saves individuals from having to save for retirement and the Federal Reserve spares banks from stockpiling cash in case all of their depositors demand their money back, the world needs a lender of last resort to reassure countries that they don't need to stockpile foreign reserves to help in an emergency. That was the original purpose of the IMF. But no country wants to subject itself to the conditions the IMF attaches to its loans, which reinforces the incentive to self-insure by saving more.

The irony is that in their efforts to protect their own economies, countries from Korea to China are pursuing strategies that subtract from the rest of the world's growth, and by holding down interest rates, they're encouraging the sorts of financial speculation that could one day produce the next crisis. It won't happen tomorrow. But as the past hundred years have demonstrated, when every country tries individually to make itself safer, the collective result is to make the world less safe.

CHAPTER 6

Unnatural Disaster: The High Cost of Taming Mother Nature

Superstorm Sandy left behind flooded subways, rivers running down Manhattan's streets, swaths of the Jersey Shore buried in sand, and millions without power, heat, or gasoline. It also carved a deep path through the economy. At $70 billion, Sandy was the second-costliest storm in American history, after Katrina. Sandy hit the world's most media-saturated city just weeks away from a hard-fought presidential election, thus guaranteeing political repercussions. Days before voters went to the polls the city's mayor, Michael Bloomberg, got off the fence to endorse Barack Obama for president. Sandy "brought the stakes of Tuesday's presidential election into sharp relief," he wrote. "Our climate is changing [which] should compel all elected leaders to take immediate action."

Bloomberg acknowledged that Sandy could not be definitively pinned on global warming, but he seemed pretty convinced of a connection, as was the public: two-thirds of voters linked Sandy to climate change.

You couldn't blame them. Science is relatively unequivocal that climate change should intensify hurricanes, worsen droughts and fires, and increase periods of intense rainfall. And as global temperatures have risen, so has the economic toll of record-breaking environmental catastrophes, from Katrina and Sandy in America to devastating wildfires in Australia in 2009 and the floods that crippled Thailand and disrupted global supply chains in the fall of 2011.

But climate change could not explain Sandy's destructive toll. After all, it wasn't even a hurricane by the time it came ashore, having been downgraded to a "post-tropical cyclone." The principal reason for Sandy's devastating impact is that millions of productive, affluent people live and work in a place that is inherently dangerous.

To understand this, you have to go back in time. Nicholas Coch, a geologist at City University of New York's Queens College, has spent his career sleuthing through history for evidence of hurricanes that have struck New England and New York. The first he could find hit in 1635 but left barely a trace, striking mostly Indian villages and uninhabited forest. More impressive was the Midnight Storm, a Category 2 storm that struck in August 1893 and, as Coch later documented, literally wiped a community off the map. Hog Island, a barrier island close to what is now JFK airport that hosted pleasure seekers and swimmers during the summer, was pushed beneath the sea and largely forgotten by New Yorkers until Coch rediscovered it. The Midnight Storm paled in comparison to the Category 3 Great New England Hurricane of 1938, at the time one of the most destructive storms in American history. Nicknamed the Long Island Express, it carved out ten new inlets between Fire Island and East Hampton, lashed New York City, and destroyed or inundated towns throughout Rhode Island and Connecticut. Yet even that storm did "just" $5 billion worth of damage (in 2014 dollars).

Coch noted that the region's geography and the nature of wind and ocean currents meant that a Category 2 storm here would have as much destructive power as a Category 4. In 2006,

with eerie foresight, he wrote, "The inevitable landfall of a northern hurricane along the most developed and populated hurricane-
prone coastal segment in America has the potential to be a
national disaster."

Sandy was not, in fact, that disaster: it wasn't powerful
enough. Compared to previous hurricanes its wind speeds were
not particularly high and it did not drop much rain. As storms go,
however, it was something of a freak. It was quite large, and as it
headed up the coast it encountered two other storm systems that
added to its energy and diverted it toward the coast. It also hit at
the daily and monthly high tide in New York Harbor, raising the
resulting storm surge. If Sandy had hit nine hours earlier, lower
Manhattan would have been spared and a lot of Queens and the
Bronx would have flooded.

But the main reason Sandy was so much more costly than its
predecessors is that in the years since 1938, the New York region
became significantly more populated. The cheap wooden cot-
tages along the shores of Long Island and New Jersey that
working-class families visited during the summer have been
replaced by year-round multimillion-dollar residences. Global
investment banks have built towering high-tech headquarters
throughout Manhattan, LaGuardia and JFK airports opened to
passengers, and the hollowed-out factories and down-at-the-heels
tenements of SoHo, Tribeca, and the Lower East Side have been
transformed into playgrounds for urban hipsters and professionals. Most either didn't know they lived in the path of a hurricane
or didn't care, since hurricanes didn't come along that often. This
insouciance virtually guaranteed that the next time New York
got hit, the price tag would be a whopper.

To those academics and risk experts who study natural disasters, neither Sandy nor its price tag was especially surprising. Just
four years earlier a team led by Roger Pielke, Jr., a political scientist, calculated that another storm just like the Long Island

Express would inflict $39 billion worth of damage. Karen Clark, a prominent catastrophe modeling expert, predicted damages of up to $100 billion. Importantly, this price tag didn't require that the storm be as intense as Katrina (a Category 5, the most powerful, when it was in the Gulf of Mexico).

Sandy is an example of a phenomenon routinely ignored in the barrage of news coverage of hurricanes, floods, wildfires, and other natural disasters. They are routinely linked to the warming climate, and indeed, climate change does play a part. For example, sea levels have risen by more than a foot around New York since 1900, adding to potential storm surges. But the main reason they are getting more destructive is because much more economic wealth stands in their way. It's another manifestation of the contest between engineers and ecologists. People are flocking to these cities because the very things that make them vulnerable to Mother Nature are the same qualities that make them productive and, usually, safe places to live. Just as the engineers' efforts to stamp out economic disasters generate different, and often bigger, financial crises later on, so their success at protecting us from nature with ever more elaborate defenses often means that the destruction will be that much more devastating when those defenses fail—as so many eventually do.

Pielke's interest in how economic development interacts with nature began when he met Chris Landsea while playing basketball during lunch hour behind the National Center for Atmospheric Research in Boulder, Colorado. In the course of their pickup games, they learned they were working on the same question—hurricane activity in the North Atlantic—and coming to seemingly contradictory conclusions. Landsea had just published a paper documenting a steady decline in the frequency of intense hurricanes in the North Atlantic; the years 1991 to 1994 were the quietest on record.

Pielke, meanwhile, was doing postdoctoral research on hurricane intensity at the request of the National Science Foundation. Hurricane Andrew in 1992 had smashed all records for the most expensive hurricane in U.S. history, just a few years after Florida had been told that its worst-case scenario was two storms costing half of what Andrew ultimately did. "It was abundantly clear the period from 1991 to 1994 was the most expensive four-year period ever for hurricane losses," Pielke told me over beer one evening in Washington. Yet after seeing Landsea's work, it was clear to Pielke that "the reason it was the most expensive period had nothing to do with it being the most active."

From those seemingly contradictory studies, Pielke and Landsea produced a new way of looking at natural disasters that married science, geography, and economics. They would study some long-ago storm, then examine how the population, wealth, and settlement patterns of the affected counties had changed since, to estimate how much damage an identical storm would cause today. They called this practice "normalizing."

Their findings were striking. The Great Miami Hurricane struck in 1926 when Miami and its surrounding county had just started to boom and the area's population had topped one hundred thousand. Today, it is the center of a sprawling metropolitan region of more than five million, with pockets of extraordinary wealth and valuable property. Houses, condominiums, and glass-walled hotels now stand on the beaches that buffered people from the storms. The 1926 hurricane cost $1 billion (in 2011 dollars). Today, the bill would be more like $188 billion.

Pielke and Landsea have done the same exercise in other countries. In February 2009 the Australian state of Victoria was sweltering through an intense heat wave when a series of bushfires, probably started by downed power lines, erupted. Driven by gale-force winds, the Black Saturday fires burned across a wide front with terrifying speed, eventually destroying 2,300 homes in the northern suburbs of Melbourne and nearby towns, and killing

173 people. As with Katrina and Sandy in America, much of the public linked the fires to global warming. Pielke disagreed. He and four Australian coauthors examined the changes in settlement and building patterns since the last intensive fires in the region, in 1967 and 1983. The 1967 fires, they estimate, destroyed half as many homes as the Black Saturday fires, but would have destroyed just as many had land been as densely populated as it was in 2009. In the two most badly damaged towns, Marysville and Kinglake, a quarter of the destroyed homes were located in or adjacent to the bushland, and between 60 and 90 percent were within ten to one hundred meters, making them much more vulnerable to flying embers when the wind changed.

Similar circumstances help explain other disasters. Bangkok has flooded so often that it was known as "the Venice of the East." Beginning in the 1960s Thailand rapidly industrialized and became a center for automotive assembly and computer parts production for multinationals from Japan, Europe, and America. The rice paddies that lined the Chao Phraya River were drained for industrial estates that were then ringed by dikes. In 2011 heavy monsoon rains overfilled the upstream reservoirs and caused the river to flood, topping the dikes and provoking battles in Bangkok, since protecting one neighborhood by stacking sandbags or breaching dikes would simply shift the water to another area. The 2011 Thai floods became the ninth-costliest natural disaster since 1970 in terms of insured losses.

Think about Pielke's findings for a minute or two, and they seem so obvious that they can scarcely be controversial. But in the charged atmosphere that surrounds climate science, everything is controversial. While the vast majority of physical and social scientists agree that man-made climate change is happening, they are split on the best way to respond. Responses encompass mitigation — doing whatever is necessary to reduce the level of greenhouse gases in the atmosphere — and adaptation, that is, accepting that climate change is going to happen and finding the most effective way of minimizing the damage. (This is of course a simplification; most experts recommend some combination of the two.) The most committed advocates of mitigation have little patience for adaptation, which they construe as fatalistic surrender to a planet-altering catastrophe. Al Gore has compared adaptation to Nazi appeasement.

Pielke has found himself the target of such criticism, regularly lumped in with climate change skeptics. Which is ironic, because he is adamant that the climate is getting warmer, and that human-caused greenhouse gas emissions are the reason. Climate change was a regular topic of dinnertime discussion in his childhood home; his father, Roger Pielke, Sr., is a meteorologist who, back in 1984, wrote an entry for the *Encyclopædia Britannica* predicting that steadily rising emissions of carbon dioxide would lead to a warmer planet.

As the planet warms, floods should become more destructive. A higher sea level, all else being equal, means a given storm surge will inundate more of a coastal city. Because moisture provides the fuel for hurricanes and warm air holds more moisture, a warmer planet is likely to produce more powerful hurricanes.

Pielke doesn't dispute the science, or that this is a reasonable conjecture about the future. What he does dispute is that climate change can explain past disasters like Sandy. He has published numerous articles pointing out that the number of hurricanes and droughts shows no long-term trend. If the toll of natural disasters is going up primarily because of human development, it is more practical to deal with climate change by making cities and settlements more resilient rather than simply trying to reverse the buildup of carbon dioxide in the air.

This is not a closed case by any means. Even if Pielke is right that storm damage, relative to GDP, isn't rising (and some scholars disagree), that may not exonerate climate change. Kerry

Emanuel, a climate scientist at the Massachusetts Institute of Technology, suggests that damage relative to GDP should actually be dropping, given society's increased ability to defend against disasters. The fact that damages aren't dropping may be due to climate change. Nor is the past necessarily a good guide to the future. If science is clear that a warming climate brings more severe storms, it makes sense to prepare accordingly, since it can take decades for rare events to leave a clearly identifiable trend. Kerry points out that if a hiker knows that the bear population in a nearby forest has doubled, he would take extra precautions immediately rather than wait until someone has been mauled. In one study, Emanuel and several coauthors estimated that global hurricane damage will about double by 2100 because of economic forces, and double again because of climate change.

The lesson of Pielke's research isn't that climate change isn't happening or doesn't have consequences; it's that human behavior explains the toll of natural disasters in ways beyond greenhouse gas emissions. And if human behavior is an important driver of why disaster damage is rising, that requires us to understand why we put ourselves in harm's way in the first place.

A good place to start is the Mississippi River, one of the most powerful, complex, and important river systems in the world. Its basin drains an area equal to a third of the continental United States. It is also the setting for an endless battle between engineers and ecologists. The river has regularly flooded since long before Europeans settled its basin and caused the river and its delta to change shape and direction. But because it is so vital to transportation, commerce, and agriculture, Americans have been fighting to tame it from the earliest days of settlement. Settlers along the Mississippi in the early 1700s built levees to contain the flooding, but these were regularly overwhelmed. Man "cannot tame that lawless stream," Mark Twain famously wrote. "The Mississippi River will always have its own way; no engineering skill can persuade it to do otherwise."

That's not the way the Army Corps of Engineers saw it. Starting in the 1850s, the Corps received ever more responsibility for management of the river. Congress had authorized two surveys of the lower Mississippi at that time, producing two competing approaches. One, led by Charles Ellet, Jr., a civil engineer, linked the flood problem to the growth of settlement on the floodplain and recommended enlarged river outlets, higher and stronger levees, and upstream reservoirs. The other, by Andrew Humphreys, an army captain, recommended building only levees. The Corps went with Humphreys's plan, which Congress formalized in 1879. After the Civil War, the demand for civil works to accelerate the commercial and industrial development of the country led to a frenzy of federally financed levee construction; canals were built to protect low-lying New Orleans from the waters of Lake Pontchartrain to the north and the Mississippi River to the south.

Until 1927, no levee built to the standard and grade of the Mississippi River Commission had failed, but that year massive floods burst the levees from Cairo in southern Illinois to the Gulf of Mexico, spreading out in a vast, yellow sea up to one hundred miles across. More than two hundred people died and seven hundred thousand — 80 percent of them black — lost their homes. The 1927 floods produced two major changes. Edgar Jadwin, the head of the Corps, recommended a radical departure from levees-only for dealing with Mississippi flooding, which we will come back to later. They also prompted Congress to make flood control an explicitly federal responsibility.

With that responsibility came the marriage of engineering

and economics known as cost–benefit analysis. It was a revolutionary step in economic planning that enabled the Corps to justify the construction of new flood control projects based in part on the increased farming, industrialization, roads, and other development such construction would make possible in the floodplain.

But this had an unintended consequence, as an obscure thirty-one-year-old government staff geographer and conscientious objector would point out a few years after the start of the Second World War. In 1942 Gilbert White, who had been pursuing his PhD at the University of Chicago while serving in various government jobs, completed his dissertation; it would drastically change thinking about floods.

White came up with what became known as the "levee effect" to describe the tendency of humanity to feel protected by levees and so build up more property in their shadows. This was a tendency the federal government actively reinforced by the enormous sums it had committed to flood control. These efforts were repeatedly foiled; people tended to assume that floods would never exceed their historical maximum, and they built to that level of protection. White compiled numerous examples of those protections being overwhelmed. An electrical generating station in Cincinnati was "constructed to operate at a flood stage one foot above the highest recorded flood of 1884, but in 1937 it was forced to halt operations by a crest that reached seven feet higher." In Brady, Texas, a masonry wall built to protect the business district after a 1930 flood was overtopped in 1935. The town built an earth levee three feet higher, which was overtopped in 1938. After Hurricane Betsy ravaged New Orleans in 1965, the Army Corps strengthened and expanded the region's levees, which led to more development, which was then exposed to Katrina forty years later.

Indeed, as fast as local and federal authorities could build new flood protection devices, economic development filled in the space, raising the level of exposure. A levee project in Dallas completed in the 1930s led to property values more than quadrupling in the protected floodplain. In the Ohio River basin, homes, factories, and stores were being built faster than the Corps could build new flood protection devices. The net result was that as the value of flood control projects rose steadily from year to year, so did the economic damage of floods.

The self-reinforcing cycle of flood protection and development assures that natural disasters will keep growing in scale. Chesterfield was a sleepy rural suburb of St. Louis that grew soybeans, wheat, and corn until, in the 1980s, it began to swell with an influx of migrating businesses and urban residents. In 1980 the county took over Spirit of Saint Louis Airport and transformed it into one of the region's busiest, catering to business and private aviation. Local farmers had built a private levee in 1947 to protect their crops. But with the influx of new business the city grew, and in the 1970s and '80s, businesses, farmers, and the county spent $2.5 million to strengthen the levee enough to withstand a hundred-year flood. Doing so qualified their airport for federal grants and relieved local business from having to buy flood insurance, normally required for anyone living inside the hundred-year floodplain. "We figured this would be high enough," Melvin Fick, a farmer who was president of the Monarch Levee District, told the *St. Louis Post-Dispatch*. "It held real well in 1973 and 1986," when record floods swelled the Missouri River.

But in 1993, raging storms caused the Missouri River to crest six feet above the record reached in 1973, smashing a seven-hundred-foot-wide breach in the levee. The airport ended up under water; planes that hadn't taken off in time floated into trees; five hundred businesses were flooded, including those in the industrial park, and 450 inmates in the nearby county jail had to be moved to other jails.

Carolyn Kousky was a teenager at the time in the St. Louis area and remembers driving downtown with her family in 1993 to watch the floodwaters rise. She is now an economist at Resources for the Future, a think tank devoted to the environment and resources, and visited Chesterfield in 2008 to record its response. It had doubled down: with federal help the town has rebuilt the levee to a five-hundred-year standard. In the following decade, development in the valley doubled to six million square feet, including America's longest strip mall. The designer of the protection system called it a virtuous circle, where more levees lead to more development, which leads to more levees.

Kousky isn't so sure. Levees are not a fail-safe; 70 percent of the levees under stress in 1993 failed, and extreme events can always overtop them. Moreover, levees do not get rid of water. Just as derivatives only shift financial risk to someone else, levees merely move water elsewhere, often upriver. St. Louis's flood protections held in 1993, but in doing so shifted more of the floodwaters to other communities. Chesterfield's increased protection will raise water levels in neighboring communities in the next flood. The result, Kousky notes, are "levee wars," in which high levees in one municipality lead to higher ones elsewhere.

The levee effect crops up in many countries that have over the centuries learned to live next to danger. The word "tsunami" first appeared in Japan in the early 1600s and was introduced to English speakers by the 1896 story "A Living God," in which a quick-thinking village headman saves his village from being destroyed by an approaching wave. The story has helped shape Japanese thinking, reflecting the mentality that although they live in an inherently dangerous place, they can protect themselves by taking enough precautions. After the Second World War the Japanese government embarked on an extensive project of building seawalls along its eastern coast to protect its industrial heartland against tsunamis. A third of Japan's coast was ultimately protected by seawalls and other flood defenses.

As a result, Japanese citizens felt safe living next to the water, and Japanese business felt confident enough to construct the Fukushima Daiichi and Daini nuclear power plants on the coasts, protected by seawalls. The Daiichi plant was originally designed to withstand a tsunami of up to ten feet high, because that was the size of the tsunami triggered by an earthquake off the coast of Chile in 1960. But much more powerful earthquakes and larger tsunamis had struck more than a thousand years earlier, and the plants didn't stand a chance against the powerful 2011 Tohoku earthquake. The thirty-three-foot-tall wave of black water washed through towns and swamped the seawalls protecting the power plants, disabling the low-lying diesel generators that maintained power for the reactors' cooling systems while they were shut down.

An even more extreme example is the Netherlands, which has long been at the mercy of nature. Dutch farmers first began building dikes around land reclaimed from the North Sea to create "polders" in the twelfth century. Over time the Dutch have built an ever more elaborate and formidable series of dikes so that today, 60 percent of the country is either below sea level or at risk of regular flooding from the North Sea or the Rhine, Meuse, and Schelt rivers and their tributaries. In 1953, a combination of a high spring tide and a severe storm over the North Sea overwhelmed dikes, flooding 9 percent of the country's farmland and killing eighteen hundred people. The Netherlands responded with a decades-long program of "delta works" to guard estuaries from storm surges, while raising and strengthening dikes. In concert with that protection, the land stretching from Amsterdam to Rotterdam has been heavily industrialized and now provides most of the country's economic output.

A few years ago I toured the polders around Rotterdam with Piet Dircke of Arcadis, a Dutch engineering firm specializing in water management. "The northern and southern parts of the Netherlands are far more safe but are economically less attractive," he told me. "People are moving to the western part of Holland because it's where the economy grows." He painted a grim portrait of the outcome if the dikes were to fail. Half of Holland would be submerged. Schiphol, the country's major international airport, would be under six or seven meters of salt water, as would the queen's home. "We'd have to rebuild our complete country," he said.

Since neither the Dutch nor anyone else is about to abandon the coasts, they are left with a dilemma: how to reconcile economic progress with the costlier disasters that result.

The pure market solution is to force people who live in harm's way to bear the price. If they won't pay, they live with the consequences or move. This means, for example, removing government subsidies for living in such places and charging insurance rates that pay for the repairs when disaster happens.

The list of policies that perversely encourage people to live in harm's way is long. America's federal government spends billions building and maintaining dams, levees, and other flood protection works through the Army Corps of Engineers. The number of federal disaster declarations—which trigger federal aid equal to 75 to 100 percent of the cleanup costs—have been rising steadily. And, of course, there are the vast sums spent rehabilitating disaster-stricken areas after the fact. Such spending is almost impossible to resist politically. Chris Christie, New Jersey's Republican governor, boosted Barack Obama's reelection prospects by praising the speed with which the federal government rushed help to the region when Sandy struck, and he lambasted his own party's leaders in Congress for "disgraceful" and "outrageous" delay in approving additional funds months later.

For a long time federal flood insurance plans charged people living on floodplains premiums that were lower than the true risk associated with where they lived. For political reasons, states such as Florida forbid insurers from charging homeowners premiums that actually reflect the risks of living there. That not only hides the true cost of living in the path of a hurricane, but has driven many insurers out of the state, leaving a state reinsurance fund as the only backstop and the taxpayer exposed to billions of dollars of claims. One brave attempt by Congress in 2012 to require homeowners in floodplains to pay a fair (i.e., higher) price for federal flood insurance was postponed just a few years later because of the political backlash.

Federal and state forestry agencies spend heavily to put out wildfires that endanger homes that are too close to the brush. More broadly, storm protection suffers from a classic market failure. Natural barriers such as sand dunes and mangrove swamps provide protection to everybody, but those benefits aren't easily priced or captured by private property owners. By contrast, the economic benefit of building mansions, condominiums, and hotels with unobstructed views of the ocean are large and readily quantified. The solution would be to end all such public subsidies, or force their beneficiaries to pay for them, preferably in the form of insurance. If the premium is too high, they'll move somewhere else. If they go without insurance, they don't get bailed out after a disaster hits.

Yet even if all the subsidized protections and insurance were removed, people would still choose to live in the path of floods, earthquakes, and other natural calamities, because they simply don't expect to need the protection. This isn't necessarily irrational; even in Oklahoma's Tornado Alley, most homeowners will never be hit by a tornado, which makes it hard to justify the cost of a basement or a tornado-proof room. The lack of personal experience with relatively infrequent events leads people to systematically underestimate their probability, and their estimates of that probability decline the longer they go without experiencing one.

Howard Kunreuther, a risk expert at the Wharton School, calls this "disaster myopia," and his colleague Robert Meyer has documented a remarkable case study. In 1969, Hurricane Camille swept the Gulf Coast and slammed into the Mississippi resort town of Pass Christian. At least eight died when the Richelieu apartment complex collapsed (although they were not, as one oft-told story had it, celebrating at a hurricane party). The land stood vacant until a developer built a shopping center on its site. That shopping center was then destroyed in 2005 by Hurricane Katrina. Just a few years later, new condominium complexes started going up within blocks of where the shopping center had stood. When I asked the mayor of Pass Christian why people would rebuild where structures and lives had been destroyed twice in the past forty-four years, he responded: "It's not like it comes every year. There ain't no guarantee that tomorrow we won't have the end of the world. Should people live in California when there's danger of an earthquake, in the east with blizzards? You tell me where the safe place is. Life is a chance. And let me tell you something else: Water sells. Water attracts more people than it will ever [scare] off."

His observation illustrates why it is so hard to break the interacting spiral between disasters and economic development: the economic logic driving people to live in places vulnerable to disaster is powerful. People have settled along floodplains since ancient times, because that's where the soil is richest and most productive. Rivers, coasts, and natural harbors facilitate trade and commerce, and thus provide the geographical underpinning for cities such as New York, Amsterdam, and London. Holland became the world's first economic superpower because its major cities are located on the Atlantic, which makes it easier to trade with other ocean-bordering cities like New York and Jakarta. The plate tectonics that produce earthquakes also produce natural harbors such as San Francisco's, which built its Marina District on the debris left by the 1906 earthquake.

The imperative of being near water for the sake of navigation and commerce has faded in the past century, but the compulsion to live near water has remained just as strong, for both economic and aesthetic reasons. Wallace J. Nichols, a marine biologist, has even argued that being close to water makes people happier and calmer.

This virtually guarantees there will be more, even costlier Sandys, not just in America but around the world. The World Bank estimates that between 2000 and 2050, the number of people in large cities exposed to tropical cyclones will rise from 310 million to 680 million, i.e., from 11 to 16 percent of the world's population. Economic exposure will grow even more, because of rising sea levels, economic growth, and urbanization. In 2005, all ten of the world's cities most economically exposed to coastal flooding were in the rich world, led by Miami, New York, New Orleans, Osaka-Kobe, and Tokyo. Those ten accounted for 5 percent of world GDP. By the 2070s, Guangzhou, Calcutta, Shanghai, Mumbai, Tianjin, Hong Kong, and Bangkok will join the list, and exposure will equal 9 percent of world GDP.

If cities are sitting ducks for a hurricane or a terrorist's bomb, why do people live there? Because, ironically, the density that makes disasters so deadly in cities also makes them, most of the time, quite safe. When so many people are clustered in one place, they can be protected far more efficiently. That was one of the founding purposes of cities. "Five centuries of violence, paralysis, and uncertainty had created in the European heart a profound desire for security," historian Lewis Mumford wrote of the origins of European cities. "Sheer necessity led to the rediscovery of an important fact...the strength and security of a fortified stronghold, perched on some impregnable rock, could be secured even for the relatively helpless people of the lowlands provided they built a wooden palisade or a stone wall around their village."

Natural disasters are also deadlier in the countryside than in cities, partly because rescuers have more trouble reaching people in remote areas than in built-up urban areas, but also because the livelihoods of people in rural areas are more precarious. In India, far more people in rural areas die in periods of extreme heat than in cities because their crops fail, destroying their livelihoods.

Abhijit Banerjee and Esther Duflo, two leading poverty researchers, visited a rural part of India with Somini Sengupta, a reporter for the *New York Times*, in 2009 to ask migrant workers how they had been affected by the slump in construction in Delhi following the global financial crisis. To their surprise, migrant workers and their families were remarkably upbeat. "There were still jobs to be had," the two economists later wrote in their book, *Poor Economics*, "jobs that paid more than twice what they could make in a day in the village. Compared to what they had endured—the routine anxiety about not getting any work at all, the seemingly interminable wait for the rains to come—life as a migrant construction worker still seemed pretty attractive."

The economic logic that draws poor peasants to cities in India does the same for highly educated professionals in the rich world. Much of the value of cities comes from "network effects," the increased productivity that each worker, manager, and professional derives from living, working, and interacting with others in close proximity. This makes it difficult to dislodge a city from a position of economic strength. One study of Japanese cities from the Stone Age to the modern era found that the built-in advantages of their location and increasing returns from their density imparted powerful staying power. Allied bombing during the Second World War destroyed more than half the buildings in the

Vulnerable Manhattan

Hurricane Sandy storm-surge areas

Outline of Manhattan Island as it was in 1609, before land reclamation

Sources: Google; TerraMetrics; NYS 2100 Commission   300 m

Much of the parts of lower Manhattan flooded by Sandy had been reclaimed from the sea, leaving them inherently vulnerable. (Illustration © The Economist Newspaper Limited, London, June 15, 2013)

sixty-six targeted cities. While the atomic bombings of Nagasaki and Hiroshima are best known, a single raid on Tokyo created an inferno that killed eighty thousand people in one night, more than Britain suffered during the entire war. Yet most of the bombed cities had fully recovered their relative size rankings within fifteen years of the end of the war. Nagasaki had returned to its prewar trend population by 1955, Hiroshima by 1975.

Compare lower Manhattan in 1609 to a present-day map and the first thing you notice is how much larger it is. Most of the buildings along the perimeter, from the World Trade Center to South Street Seaport, stand on land that has been reclaimed from the sea over the past four centuries. Not coincidentally, the areas inundated by Sandy correspond almost exactly to those parts of New York that are on reclaimed land. Thus, in some sense New Yorkers have been courting disaster virtually since the founding of the city. Yet none of this seems to have interfered with the city's prosperity.

Indeed, one might conclude just the opposite. With each passing year, New York plops more precious infrastructure in the path of destruction. Two Dutch water experts, Jeroen Aerts and Wouter Botzen, have calculated that in the past century, the value of buildings in New York's hundred-year flood zone has risen from less than $1 billion to $18 billion (in constant 2009 dollars). Today, many tunnel entrances, portions of two airports, three heliports, and 12 percent of the city's roads are all in the hundred-year flood zone. Rising sea levels alone guarantee that the hundred-year flood zone is going to grow in coming years.

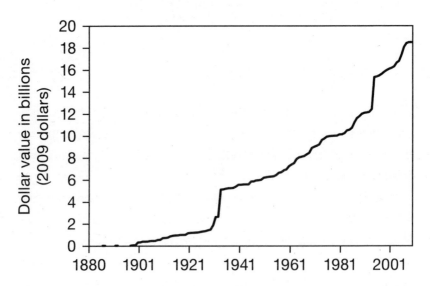

The value of structures inside the hundred-year flood zone of New York City has risen steadily. (Source: Jeroen C. J. H. Aerts and W. J. Wouter Botzen, "Managing Exposure to Flooding in New York City," *Nature Climate Change* 2 (June 2012): 377)

In the wake of Sandy, Mike Bloomberg asked Seth Pinsky, then head of the city's economic development arm, to lead a study to determine how best to protect the city against the water. Climate change was clearly a motivation, but as Pinsky later told me, the vulnerability would be there even without the changing climate.

One option Pinsky's group considered, and rejected, was to protect the entire city with gigantic, movable surge protection barriers similar to those that guard Rotterdam, London, and Saint Petersburg. That wouldn't have been cheap: Jeroen Aerts reckons four barriers, at Arthur Kill, the Verrazano Narrows, the East River, and Jamaica Bay, would cost up to $17 billion. Nor would it have been foolproof: for one thing, the water the barriers would deflect has to go somewhere, and thus unprotected neighborhoods just outside the barriers would be even harder hit. Protecting those areas would cost another $12 billion, and even then some regions would be left unprotected. Then there would be the inevitable fights between stakeholders before the barriers could be built, and the thirty years it would take—during which the city would be vulnerable.

An option they never considered was to simply abandon the waterfront. Proximity to water is what makes coastal cities like New York so productive and wealthy. When Bloomberg took office in 2002, he described New York's waterfront as its "sixth borough" and imagined reconnecting New Yorkers to the shore with parks, bike paths, and mixed-use residential and office buildings. In the years since, apartment buildings have gone up near the water in Brooklyn and Queens. Brooklyn Bridge Park, combining parks, playgrounds, and athletic fields, sprung up at the foot of the Brooklyn Bridge. Hudson Yards, a new neighborhood of parks, plazas, stores, and apartment buildings, will rise on the west side of Manhattan, while Willets Point, an industrial neighborhood in Queens, will be transformed into an entertainment, retail, and residential complex. Giving back large chunks of that space to minimize flood risk would cripple the city's productive capacity in years to come. Elevating its buildings or converting ground floors to parking garages would destroy the feel and fabric of neighborhoods where ground floors are often devoted to retail space, restaurants, and other communal spaces.

The path Pinsky chose was to consider a wide range of threats — water, wind, heat — and figure out how to make the city more resilient to all of them. "No matter how good our defenses are, from time to time nature is always going to over-come them," he told me, so "we have to make the city more resil-ient so it can bounce back faster with less damage done." Thus, some neighborhoods will have beaches and sand dunes replen-ished to create natural storm-surge barriers, while buildings will be reinforced to withstand floodwater and their electrical and mechanical systems will be moved from the basement to an upper floor. Increased bus and bicycle right-of-ways will be imple-mented when the subways are flooded.

Cities everywhere are coming to the same conclusion: rather than build ever higher defenses against inevitable flooding, they are finding ways to let the water in with as little damage as possi-ble. Many municipalities have bought up homes and businesses on riverbanks and replaced them with green space that can safely flood. One of the most ambitious is the Netherlands' "Room for the River" project. It involves demolishing some polders and either moving residents or relocating them on hills so that when the rivers flood, the original floodplain fills up, sparing down-stream cities. In Rotterdam, large storage tanks have been built below parking garages to contain floodwater; city parks have been designed to double as flood catchment areas; and the city is experimenting with putting buildings and entire neighborhoods on massive foam pontoons so they can rise and fall with the sea level.

Of course, none of this is cheap. But then, the price is small compared to what is being protected. As Pinsky notes, the potential damage a disaster can do is proportionate to how valuable the city's infrastructure is. In the 1970s, New York went into decline as infrastructure deteriorated and people left. "Those that didn't leave suffered, but the impact of that suffering was less and less with every passing year because fewer corporations were headquartered here, less economic activity was here, and it all became self-reinforcing." So while Pinsky's plan will cost $20 billion, that's a pittance next to the New York region's annual GDP of $1.4 trillion. The frenzy of real estate development in Miami might seem crazy given the city's vulnerability to a rising sea level, but Wharton's Robert Meyer thinks it might be rational because it makes the city wealthier and thus able eventually to prepare.

New York's rebound had been well under way by the time of the terrorist attacks on September 11, 2001. Pinsky, a corporate lawyer at the time, had an office across the street from the World Trade Center, but he was in Washington that day. While he watched the coverage of the attacks at a colleague's home there, someone remembered it was his birthday and brought out a cupcake with a candle in it.

The attack persuaded Pinsky to quit his firm and go into public service, working for the city; he never considered leaving New York. Many others decided similarly. If you had predicted in 2000 that New York would, in the coming twelve years, suffer a terrorist attack that killed three thousand and brought down its tallest skyscrapers, a financial crisis that toppled some of Wall Street's most powerful firms, and then a hurricane that put huge sections of the city under water, what would you have predicted would happen to the city's population? Probably not that it would grow by 5 percent, or nearly four hundred thousand people. That people keep flocking to New York despite these calamities illustrates the city's extraordinary economic pull. The economy's source of wealth creation in the past two decades has increasingly shifted from physical to intellectual capital. Intellectual capital and innovation, whether in technology, software, or filmmaking, thrive on human connections and proximity to one another, which New York offers.

Someday, New York is going to be hit by another Sandy, and chances are, it will be far more costly than the last — not because the city failed, but because it succeeded at making even more people feel safe long enough to prosper.

CHAPTER 7

Good Risk, Bad Risk: Balancing Safety with Disaster

In previous chapters, we learned how difficult it is to make ourselves truly safe, because the pursuit of safety leads to behavior that makes disaster more likely. In the remainder of this book, I'll look at what we can do about this: how to strike the right balance between safety and disaster.

At the outset, we have to ask how much safer we want the world to be. This sounds like a ridiculous question. As safe as possible, right? But what if making us safer also makes us worse off?

To answer this question, we have to examine the role of fear and risk. Fear is indispensable to survival. It's why we stay away from cliff edges, avoid angry dogs, and lock our doors at night. Yet not all of us feel fear to the same extent. Some of us would never leap off a tall bridge attached to a bungee cord, leave the Jeep during a safari to get a better photo of the lions, or cash in the life insurance policy to open a restaurant. Others, by contrast, go through life convinced that bad luck happens to other people. Not surprisingly, many of these adventurers pay a high price, whether in broken necks or empty bank accounts.

At least part of the reason for these differences is innate, as was strikingly demonstrated in an experiment at the University of Iowa led by the neuroscientist Antonio Damasio and published in 1997. Damasio had developed a roster of patients with damage to the brain's frontal cortex, which connects the decision-making part of the brain with the part that controls emotions. For this experiment he wanted to explore whether emotions helped people make better decisions. He and his colleagues assembled two groups — ten participants without brain damage and six from his roster with prefrontal damage — and gave each of them $2,000 in pretend money to play a game that involved selecting cards from one of four decks. In the two "bad" decks, turning over a card earned $100, but some cards incurred a penalty large enough to generate a net loss. In the two "good" decks, players earned smaller rewards and encountered smaller penalties, eventually yielding a net gain.

The players had no way of knowing which decks were good or bad. But after playing for a while, the players without brain damage got a hunch that there was something wrong with the bad decks and responded to them with physical symptoms of anxiety that researchers could detect through skin sensors. They naturally stopped drawing cards from those decks. The brain-damaged patients showed no such response. Even though they clearly realized that some decks were bad, they kept drawing cards from them — and losing money.

The experiment demonstrated the powerful link between emotions (or their absence) and risk taking. A sense of danger triggers an automatic, emotional response in a healthy brain that keeps the person from hurting himself. When that emotional mechanism is impaired, people take risks that put them in harm's way. But when George Loewenstein — an economist at Carnegie Mellon University who we first met in Chapter 3 and who has also studied emotions and behavior — read the results, he had a different take. Loewenstein knew that emotions generated fear, and fear interfered with risk taking. But he wondered if that was necessarily a good thing. So in the fall of 2001, he talked to some of the study's authors and together they conducted a different version of the experiment.

This time, fifteen patients with brain damage and nineteen without were offered a chance to bet on a coin toss. Each were given $20 of play money (their winnings would be converted to real money at the end) and offered two choices: accept one dollar, no strings attached, or play a coin-toss game. If he played the game and got heads, the participant earned nothing; but if he played the game and got tails, he earned $2.50. So the expected payoff of playing the game was $1.25; the expected payoff of not playing was $1. On average, playing the game would earn an additional 25 cents.

The experiment found that people with no impairment to the brain's emotional center were much more conservative. After losing money on one coin toss, only 40 percent of them agreed to invest on the next—but 85 percent of the brain-damaged patients did. By the end of the game, the brain-damaged patients had earned an average of $25.70 while the healthy players averaged $22.80.

The upshot of the two experiments is that fear is a two-edged sword. It keeps us from taking foolish risks that hurt us; but it can keep us from taking risks that could make us better off. And therein lies a dilemma. Sometimes it's easy to tell bad risks from good. But most of the time, the distinction is not obvious.

For example, most new businesses fail within the first five years. Thus, based on a dispassionate appraisal of the odds, most people would be better off going to work for a big company than trying to start a small one. So why do some people do it anyway? Partly, it's their nature.

In one experiment Lowell Busenitz, then at the University of Houston and Jay Barney, then at Ohio State, tested 124 entrepreneurs and 95 managers and found that the entrepreneurs are far more likely to suffer from a common decision-making flaw: over-confidence. Asked a series of questions, such as does cancer or heart disease kill more Americans, entrepreneurs rated far more confidence in their answers—even when they were wrong—than managers.

Being sure of yourself when you're wrong is not a recipe for success. It can make you a gambling addict, an impaired driver, or just a jerk. Yet it may be essential to entrepreneurship. As we saw earlier, people will pay to avoid uncertainty, yet uncertainty is endemic to a new business: Will the product succeed? Will customers show up? Will the employees work out—or quit? As the study's authors note, overconfidence enables the entrepreneur to neutralize this uncertainty and to persuade other stakeholders—employees, investors, suppliers, customers—to join in on the venture.

Millions of enterprises open each year, and most end up failing. Economies grow over time because the survivors succeed so well that they make up for all the losers. And while these failures may be painful for individuals, they are in aggregate good for society. The failure of a new (or even old) company seldom hurts anyone beyond its shareholders and employees while a successful one yields products and innovations that everyone enjoys.

It's a different matter if risk taking reaches a point where the entire country is exposed. This is what distinguishes routine failure from a systemic crisis, in which failures are numerous and large enough to bring the entire economy down. The best financial system nurtures good risks along with the occasional failure, but doesn't allow risk taking to get so out of hand that it creates a systemic crisis, such as the United States experienced in 2008. But here again, this is more easily said than done. Just as individuals have trouble separating good from bad risks, so do countries.

Aaron Tornell, a Mexican economist, experienced this problem firsthand. In 1989 he went to work for one of his former professors, Pedro Aspe, who had become finance minister in a government determined to liberalize the hidebound, repressed Mexican economy. For two years he was in charge of privatizing the Mexican coal and steel industries, which had become inefficient government-run behemoths. Banks, which had been mostly government owned a decade earlier, were privatized and lending was liberalized: caps on interest rates were removed, forcing them to compete for deposits, and they were relieved of a requirement to keep a certain amount of their assets in Treasury bills.

Mexican borrowing—much of it in foreign currencies—boomed, leading to a crisis in late 1994, when many banks teetered on the brink of collapse. In the wake of the crisis, it became much harder to collect on delinquent borrowers, and banks swapped bad loans for government bonds. As a result, lending to private enterprise dried up. So while the plunge in the peso in 1994 led to several years of powerful export-led growth, the parts of the economy that depended most on bank loans—small and medium-sized services-oriented businesses—suffered. Still, Mexico hasn't had another crisis.

That experience prompted Tornell to wonder: do strong growth and systemic crises go hand in hand? This is a question he has studied intensively with two colleagues, Romain Rancière at the Paris School of Economics and Frank Westermann, now at Germany's Osnabrück University.

They answer the question by contrasting the experiences of India and Thailand between 1980 and 2002. India had by far the more regulated economy. Businesses faced regulations and licenses for almost everything. Foreign investment was tightly controlled and banned in many sectors. Banks were mostly owned by the government, their deposit and lending rates were tightly controlled, they had to lend to the government on favorable terms, and faced quotas on how much to lend to particular sectors, such as agriculture and small-scale industry. The result was steady but relatively unspectacular economic growth.

By contrast, Thailand has long welcomed foreign investment, which helped turn it into a major center of automotive and electronic manufacturing. Its banks were mostly privately owned and, though pressed to allocate a certain amount of credit to agriculture and small business, largely free to borrow and lend as they wished. They were not particularly well regulated. In the early 1980s, several dozen poorly regulated finance companies and banks got into trouble; the central bank created a special "lifeboat" scheme to provide easy loans to twenty-one troubled finance companies and banks; meanwhile, their depositors were bailed out. This of course created the impression that the government would do so again.

The result was rapid growth, booming borrowing, and a catastrophic financial crisis. As we learned in Chapter 5, Thai banks had borrowed heavily from foreigners in foreign currencies while making loans in Thai baht. When Thailand devalued the baht in 1997, many of those banks went bust, cutting off the supply of credit and throwing Thailand into a deep recession.

Which country was better off? Remarkably, despite its crisis, Thailand ended the period far richer than India: its GDP per capita grew 162 percent, while India's grew only 114 percent (see charts).

Of course, Tornell and his colleagues weren't arguing that crises are good for growth, but rather that the sorts of policies that are good for growth may also lead to financial excesses and crises. Specifically, financial liberalization of the sort that Thailand pursued in the 1980s and 1990s generates more lending at lower cost and thus more investment.

Even bailouts, such as Thailand's in the early 1980s, may not be entirely bad. As the authors note, lenders who expect to be

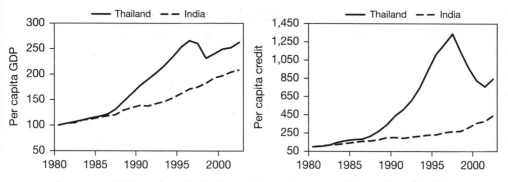

Per capita GDP and credit (adjusted for inflation) in Thailand and India. (Source: Romain Rancière, Aaron Tornell, and Frank Westermann, "Systemic Crises and Growth," *Quarterly Journal of Economics* 123, no. 1 (2008): 359–406)

bailed out in a crisis will lend more cheaply, which encourages investment. The bailout, they argue, should be seen as the bill to taxpayers for the benefits of growth that the easy finance helped generate in prior years. They're not saying bailouts and crises are good; they're merely pointing out that the benefits of easy credit are sometimes worth the crisis and bailout that follow.

Note the caveat: "sometimes." The tradeoff depends on how bad things are without financial liberalization and the severity of the subsequent bust. In many emerging countries, efficient lending is repressed, for example, because the law makes it too difficult to get your money back if the borrower defaults. In that case, the boom and the bailout help overcome that barrier to credit. If that barrier doesn't exist in the first place, the boom is less useful. The diagram on the next page illustrates this by comparing how a country fares depending on how risky and lucky it is. The key is to have few crises or mild ones, so that incomes, while more volatile, end up higher.

A disaster or crisis is such a horrifying prospect that it might seem to make sense to pay any price to avoid one. But it doesn't. Not only is the price too high, but the nature of complex systems is that if risk taking is repressed in one arena, it may migrate to

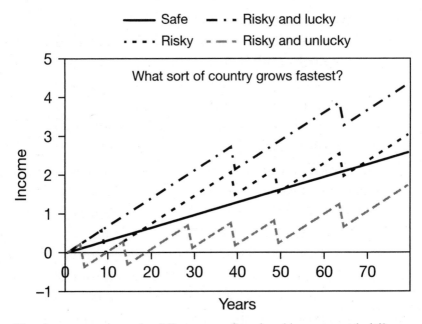

This diagram contrasts the differing growth paths of countries with different levels of risk in their economies, and different luck. (Source: Romain Rancière, Aaron Tornell, and Frank Westermann, "Systemic Crises and Growth," *Quarterly Journal of Economics* 123, no. 1 (2008): 359–406)

another, and even more costs and damage may occur through other means.

The avoidance of catastrophe is why society shuns nuclear power. The result is to indirectly cause thousands of deaths due to pollution from other sources. In response to public pressure and accidents such as the one at Three Mile Island in 1979, regulators and politicians imposed ever-stiffer conditions on the construction and operation of nuclear power plants. The price tag of a nuclear plant went from $170 million in the early 1970s to $5 billion by the late 1980s. Only a small part of this reflects increased equipment costs; most reflects the lag time, now stretching to decades, in getting a plant built due largely to the extensive permitting process and the opportunity for opponents to slow down construction. Such costs have proven prohibitive, and few nuclear power plants are now being built. Japan's Fukushima accident resulted in all of that country's nuclear power plants being taken off-line and hastened the decision by Germany to phase out nuclear power altogether. In 2011, the Swiss parliament voted not to proceed with three new nuclear reactors; those in operation would be allowed to finish their useful lives.

The burden of regulation imposed on nuclear power, and the draconian steps taken in the wake of the 2011 accident in Japan, are a direct result of the horror with which people regard the possibility of a nuclear disaster, no matter how remote.

Paul Slovic, a psychologist, has mapped risk perceptions on a diagram with two axes, as shown on the next page. On the vertical axis, the perceived risk of a technology rises the less the subject knows about it; on the horizontal axis, the perceived risk rises with the "dread" involved. Dread correlates with events and technology that are "catastrophic, fatal, uncontrollable," says Slovic. In the lower left quadrant lie familiar, mundane things such as power mowers, home swimming pools, and downhill skiing. In the upper right quadrant are unknown, horrifying risks. Near the extreme end are nuclear reactor accidents, far above fossil fuels and hydroelectric power.

The horror is linked to the potential consequences of a disaster. In an exhaustive examination of various energy sources, Peter Burgherr and Stefan Hirschberg of the Paul Scherrer Institute, a Swiss research group, show that the maximum possible fatalities are by far highest for nuclear power, followed closely by hydro (when many people live downstream from a dam), much lower for coal, oil, or gas, and lowest for new renewables such as wind. But nuclear accidents are exceedingly rare.

By contrast, oil tankers sink, natural gas pipelines explode, coal mines collapse, dams burst, and even windmills fling large

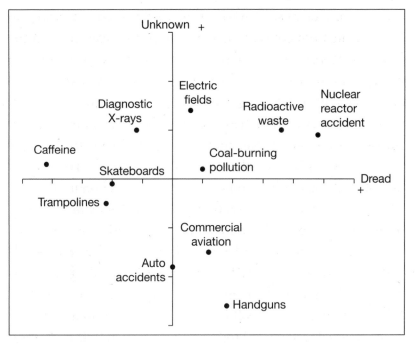

The less familiar an activity or threat and the more dread it inspires, the greater the risk it is perceived to be. (Source: data provided by Paul Slovic)

chunks of ice and pieces of fan blades at nearby homes. Between 1970 and 2008, in the thirty-four mostly rich countries that make up the Organization for Economic Cooperation and Development, accidents involving coal killed more than two thousand people, oil more than three thousand, natural gas more than one thousand, and hydroelectric power fourteen. Nuclear power? Zero. (Recall that no one died at Three Mile Island.) Indeed, the Swiss researchers conclude that by far the safest energy, by fatalities per gigawatt per year, is precisely the sort of nuclear power that could, in that rarest of accidents, kill the most people.

Although hundreds died during the evacuation following the Fukushima nuclear accident and the tsunami that caused the accident, the power plant meltdown itself has not yet been implicated in any deaths. Compare that to the litany of deaths in recent years from conventional energy sources: eleven when the Deepwater Horizon drilling rig exploded in the Gulf of Mexico; twenty-nine miners in the Big Branch coal mine explosion in 2010; eight in a natural gas pipeline explosion in San Bruno, California, in 2010; six when a gas-fired power plant exploded in Middletown, Connecticut, in 2010; forty-seven in the town of Lac-Mégantic, Quebec, when a train carrying seventy-two tank cars of crude oil crashed and set the town's center on fire.

That's only the direct toll from accidents. Far more people die indirectly, for example from pollution or radiation exposure. Researchers from Stanford University reckon that 130 people will die due to cancer caused by radiation released in the Fukushima disaster (that's their best guess in a very wide range of 15 to 1,300). The final death toll from the Chernobyl disaster by one estimate could reach 4,000 (other estimates reach 93,000), though as of 2006, only 47 deaths were conclusively linked to its radiation. Yet these figures, too, pale in comparison to the deaths attributed mainly to the pollution belched into the air each year by wood, oil, gas, and coal: more than 7,000 in the United States alone, and potentially millions worldwide.

In the wake of Three Mile Island, American regulators began cracking down on safety violations at power plants, and in 1985 the Tennessee Valley Authority, a federally operated electric utility serving the South, temporarily shut down several nuclear reactors. Edson Severnini at Carnegie Mellon University found that as a result, electricity generation from coal-fired plants operated by the TVA rose, and those plants' counties experienced more pollution and more babies with lower birth weight.

Former NASA scientist James E. Hansen, one of the loudest voices in the scientific community warning of global warming, and his colleague Pushker A. Kharecha have tried to quantify the relationship between nuclear power and mortality. They figured that between 1971 and 2009, the use of nuclear power had prevented 1.84 million deaths by avoiding the burning of coal and natural gas and the resulting air pollution. In Germany, the figure was 117,000. They then asked how many deaths would be prevented if nuclear power were not phased out. They concluded that between 2010 and 2050, if nuclear power replaced natural gas, 420,000 to 680,000 deaths would be avoided. If it replaced coal, the number of lives saved rises to between 4.4 million and 7 million. These numbers don't reflect any additional harm from climate change such as heat waves, floods, droughts, and food shortages. Without nuclear power, it would be far harder to hold carbon emissions to what they consider a safe level. Thus, the decision by Japan, Germany, and Switzerland to idle or phase out nuclear power will almost certainly cause thousands of deaths due to the ill effects of pollution and a warming climate.

Can such a decision be justified? It depends on what matters more: the maximum hypothetical deaths of a particular energy technology, or the likeliest number of deaths. The probability of a core meltdown in a modern nuclear reactor is exceedingly small. One study estimates that an existing Swiss plant would suffer a meltdown capable of killing more than two thousand about once every million years. Maximum fatalities, of course, could be much higher; it depends on the reactor type and location. So a society determined to prevent the most catastrophic accident possible would naturally avoid nuclear power, while one whose decision is based on the probability of death from different energy technologies would favor nuclear.

"While lay persons generally show an aversion toward catastrophic accidents with large consequences, they normally do not understand that such events are extremely rare in terms of probability," Burgherr says. "This is often simply due to the fact that these events are beyond our personal experience or, for politicians, beyond term of office, and thus decisions may be largely influenced by subjective risk factors (e.g., perception, aversion) and not just be based on objective, measurable risk indicators."

Switzerland's decision means it must come up with alternatives to replace the lost nuclear power. While in theory deep geothermal power has great potential, it has been set back by poor drilling results and earthquakes. Wind has a relatively limited potential, and solar power needs a lot of government support. "Then you are likely left with importing natural gas," Burgherr observes, "which people don't particularly like because it emits more carbon dioxide than the other alternatives."

These are important things to keep in mind when considering the lessons of the global financial crisis of 2008. In its wake, governments everywhere have vowed never to have another.

But is it necessary that there never be another crisis? Is it possible that preventing another crisis will suppress so much risk taking that we end up poorer as a result? And should another crisis arrive, will our fear of moral hazard stop us from doing what we can to minimize the consequences?

Consider that the United States had two bubbles in the past two decades. The first, of course, was the Nasdaq stock bubble that began in the mid-1990s and peaked in 2000. The second was the housing and mortgage bubble that began shortly afterward and ended with the financial crisis.

Both bubbles were blamed on the Federal Reserve keeping interest rates too low and bailing out the financial system every time it was on the verge of collapse. If the Fed would always intervene when markets plunged, critics said, why not pay ridiculous prices for assets? The Fed, these critics said, should prick the bubbles to prevent a bigger disaster later on.

Both times, the Fed refused.

In the case of the Nasdaq bubble, that turned out to be a good thing. In those years, more than five hundred companies listed shares on the stock market including such memorable stinkers as pets.com (known for its sock puppet) and webvan, an online grocer that went bust less than two years after going public. Then there was Amazon.com, which went public in 1997. Amazon fascinated investors, but it bled money. Much of its strategy was based on selling books at knockdown prices and zero profits. This meant that it had to constantly raise new money to invest in marketing, promotions, and infrastructure. In 1998, rather than issue shares, it decided to borrow, issuing $326 million in bonds that wouldn't pay interest for five years. The next year, it issued another $1.25 billion in bonds, convertible to shares in order to appeal to Internet-obsessed investors.

In the summer of 2000 Ravi Suria, a young, tough-minded bond analyst at Lehman Brothers, wrote a report warning of Amazon's "negative cash flow, poor working capital management, and high debt load in a hyper competitive environment," meaning the company was in serious danger of running out of cash and thus defaulting on its debts. Suria's report sent Amazon's stock skidding 20 percent in one day.

Suria's analysis was solid; Amazon's ability to stay afloat depended on its ability to keep issuing securities to Internet-crazed investors. As Suria warned, Amazon was toast unless it managed "to pull another financing rabbit out of its rather magical hat." Ordinarily, that is not a recipe for survival. But in those rarefied times, it was: the following year, though the company was still losing money and the Nasdaq bubble was deflating, Amazon borrowed $870 million in euros, also convertible to stock. In effect, Amazon exploited the irrational exuberance of the dot-com bubble to stay afloat long enough to become a colossus, revolutionizing not just retailing but book publishing and cloud computing. Between 2004 and 2008, it paid back all its bondholders, some at a premium, except those who had converted their bonds to shares.

Dot-com stocks were the most famous players during the technology bubble, but more money was lost in a different sector. A host of existing and start-up telecommunications companies persuaded investors there was a mint to be made laying the fiber-optic networks that would carry booming Internet traffic between cities and continents. To finance the high costs of laying miles of fiber, telecommunications companies such as Global Crossing, Williams Communications, Tycom, Flag, and 360 Networks raised billions of dollars issuing stock and bonds. If only a few companies had done this, things would have worked out fine. But the explosion of financing made it possible for the companies to lay far more fiber-optic capacity than was needed, causing transmission prices to plunge. Tim Stronge, who covers the industry for TeleGeography, a consulting firm, recalls warning the industry that it was building too much. Between 1997 and 2001, the capacity on just one route, between New York and London, rose one hundred–fold, and the price to lease for one month a 155-megabyte-per-second circuit fell 96 percent.

For many of the telecommunications companies who had borrowed billions, those prices proved ruinous. One after another, they went bankrupt. Though investors in the fiber-optic boom lost their shirts, the glut of fiber had an unexpected benefit: ridiculously cheap bandwidth made possible countless new business models that had been impossible when capacity was limited. Internet service providers in emerging markets could offer their customers access to the global Internet by buying cheap capacity on cables laid during the dot-com boom. Cheap bandwidth made cloud computing possible: companies could rent space at massive data processing centers thousands of miles away, giving them

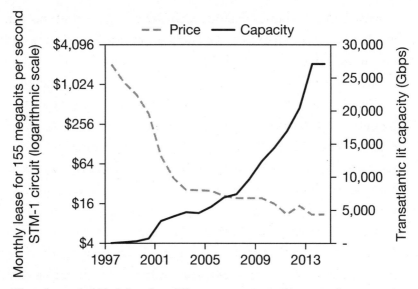

The telecom bubble left a glut of fiber-optic capacity that caused transmission prices to plummet. (Source: TeleGeography, http://www.telegeography.com)

almost unlimited processing power without costly investment in equipment of their own. Facebook members around the world communicate instantly and seamlessly with one another thanks to the long-term leases that Facebook has on these underground networks. And an astonishing share of those networks were built by now-bankrupt companies: 63 percent of transatlantic fiber-optic capacity, 35 percent of trans-Pacific, and 39 percent of the capacity between the United States and Latin America, according to Stronge.

The aftermath of the housing bubble was, of course, much nastier. The reasons the bursting of the tech bubble did so little harm while the bursting of the housing bubble had a devastating effect boil down to the different way the bubbles were financed. The investors who bought the stocks and bonds that financed the tech bubble did not, for the most part, buy them with borrowed money; that is, they were not leveraged. When the shares collapsed and the bonds defaulted, the investors were left poorer, but they were not then forced to default on the money they had borrowed. There was no chain reaction of panic and default throughout the financial system.

By contrast, as became apparent in the aftermath, the housing bubble was bankrolled by commercial and investment banks, finance companies, and funds that had themselves borrowed heavily to finance homeowners' mortgages. When those mortgages went bad, those banks and shadow banks then defaulted on what they had borrowed.

Unlike the Nasdaq bubble, the 2008 financial crisis left behind little of value other than millions of vacant homes, and the costs dragged on for years. It's the sort of catastrophe that forces you to ask whether some risk taking is so destructive that it ought to be outlawed.

Tornell and his colleagues revisited their work after the global crisis of 2008 and concluded that the benefits of the credit boom that came before did not justify the collapse that came after. Too much of the borrowing was not backed by assets of any real value.

Perhaps the Fed should have recognized the difference and popped the second bubble but not the first. After all, some people did recognize at the time that the housing and tech bubbles were qualitatively different. Yet the answer is not so simple. Knowing whether a bubble is worth its bust is seldom obvious in advance. If the Fed bought the argument for deflating the housing bubble, it would likely have done the same with the tech bubble a decade earlier. Instead, the Fed responded to both the same way: it couldn't be sure there was a bubble; even if it were sure, it might not be able to pop it; and if it popped it, the damage might be worse than if the bubble burst by itself.

Still, at times asset prices are so obviously inflated, surely the authorities should try to take some of the air out with the goal of preventing an even bigger conflagration later on. Yet assume for a moment that the Fed knows in advance that a bubble exists and that it's a bad one and that most of the risk taking is frivolous and wasteful. Should it therefore burst the bubble? The problem is precisely the same problem the ecologists have cited in their criticism of the Fed's efforts to prop up growth. The economy is a complex organism, and trying to kill off speculation is just as likely to do damage as to do good.

In 1928, this debate unfolded inside the Federal Reserve. At the time stock prices were rising rapidly, and some worried that the result was a dangerous speculative fever. Within the Fed, the leaders worried that banks were lending too heavily to finance speculative stock purchases. Benjamin Strong, the Fed's de facto leader, resisted raising rates purely to damp stock prices, fearing the damage to the economy. But Strong died in 1928, and his successors were more ecologically minded. Between January 1928 and August 1929, the New York Fed raised its discount rate from 3.5 to 6 percent. This achieved its purpose—the stock decline that would culminate in the 1929 crash began October the eighteenth. But the economy had already been slowing under the pressure of tight credit, and the combination of higher rates and the collapse in the stock market plunged it into recession. The Bank of Japan did something similar between 1989 and 1991 when, under Governor Yasushi Mieno, it was determined to stamp out the speculation that had driven stock and land prices to dangerously high levels. It succeeded in pricking both the stock and land bubbles, but the collapse ushered in a severe period of economic distress and deflation.

The Fed's antibubble campaign in 1929 can't be blamed for the Great Depression; its causes are far more complex. The source of Japan's economic stagnation during the 1990s is similarly multifaceted. But the two episodes illustrate how efforts to stamp out speculative fires are undermined by the fact that central bankers can't be certain how those effects are going to play out. Indeed, this is the challenge that all foolproofers face: there may be times when accepting the risk of a bigger conflagration later is the right choice — because trying to preempt it may be worse.

CHAPTER 8

The Rescuer's Dilemma: Chaos Today or Chaos Tomorrow?

We know more about complex systems like economies and forests today than we did a century ago. We know how to intervene to prevent a disaster, and we know that if we intervene too much, future disasters may be more likely.

Knowing that the tradeoff exists is one thing; knowing where to draw the line is quite another. Even with astonishing advances in our knowledge, the environment and the economy remain complex and unpredictable. That means that disaster, or its prevention, often rides on the judgment of those entrusted to make the decision to intervene, and they often learn whether they were right only after the fact.

Consider forests. Our understanding of the role of wildfire has changed radically in the past century; once seen as a primeval menace to be tamed, it is now considered an essential element of the ecosystem. Paradoxically, these advances in our knowledge have made the decisions of those who watch over the forests harder.

Scientists have ingenious ways of re-creating the history of fire from long before the Europeans and their written records arrived in the Americas. One is to examine the rings of very old trees for telltale scars left by fire in previous years. Another way is to drill holes into the bottom of lakes and extract tubes of sediment several meters long. That core sample is like a time capsule, preserving a record of the sediment that settled to the bottom of the lake and indicating when it was deposited. Forest fires send huge clouds of charcoal — semicombusted bits of wood — into the air that then settle onto lake bottoms. By counting the concentrations of charcoal in core samples, scientists can ascertain when fires occurred and how bad they were.

When Jennifer Marlon was pursuing graduate studies in geography at the University of Oregon in 2004, she knew friends in the Pacific Northwest who were gathering core samples from lakes to trace the history of forests in those regions. She wondered whether such samples could be stitched together to draw a portrait of the entire western United States, showing how changing climate affected forests. So she organized a "global charcoal database" to combine samples from around the country and, eventually, the world. Once she had the results, she compared them to the prevailing levels of drought and heat that other scientists had posited through separate research projects. As a result, she has been able to construct a history of fire as far back as the end of the last ice age, 21,000 years ago, and a more detailed record of the western United States of the past 1,500 years. Her data shows the level of fire rising and falling over very long cycles, closely related to drought and heat. Peaks in fires occurred during the Medieval Climate Anomaly, from 950 to 1250, when temperatures and drought were high, and again during the 1800s. The lowest level of fire, until modern times, occurred in what is known as the Little Ice Age, a period of cold, moist weather from 1400 to 1700.

Marlon and her coauthors combined these findings into a single chart with two lines; one shows the amount of burning relative to its maximum observed over the entire period, the

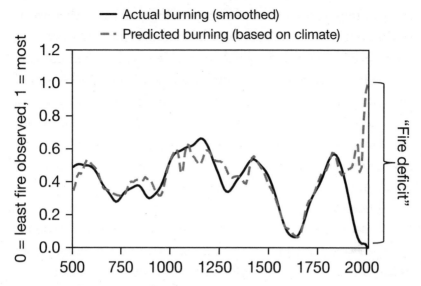

For most of the past two millennia, the amount of western U.S. forests burned by wildfire has risen and fallen with the climate, until the last century when the pattern changed. (Source: Jennifer R. Marlon, Patrick J. Bartlein, Daniel G. Gavin, et al., "Long-term Perspective on Wildfires in the Western USA," *Proceedings of the National Academy of Sciences* 109, no. 9 (2012): 3203)

other the amount predicted by drought and temperature. The two lines closely track for most of the past 2,000 years, then abruptly diverge in the past century; temperature and drought start to rise sharply, but fires fall steadily.

The message, Marlon says, is that over the course of the past century, until recently, there have been unusually few forest fires in the western United States. This is not because climate change has no impact. But the amount of fire that has actually occurred has been less than climate change would have predicted, because humans have been interfering. Marlon's data ends in the 1980s. The charcoal samples she has gathered for subsequent decades, though not directly comparable, suggest that fires have gotten bigger and more intense since then and the fire season has gotten longer. Tom Swetnam, an expert at divining the history of fire from the scars that ancient fires left in the rings of centuries-old trees, corroborates this story. The rings demonstrate that in the Southwest, "fire used to burn every five or ten years, then stopped for a hundred years. This is how the system operated until we changed it," through fire suppression, agriculture, and livestock grazing, he told me. "The problem today is fire is reasserting itself; the fuel is there, and drought and warming temperatures are driving up the areas burned."

Fire is essential to forest renewal. Surface fires race through the grasses and accumulated pine needles on the forest floor, killing off the youngest saplings and thus reducing the density of the forest, but a tree that has achieved a base diameter of four inches is highly resilient to fire. Indeed, some trees need fire: the lodgepole pine, for example, has cones that are bound together by resin. In the heat of a fire, the cone pops open, spreading its seed. Chaparral, a dense mat of shrubs such as buckthorn, evergreen oak, and lotus, drops seeds into the soil, where they germinate in the wake of fire, which in normal conditions would come every few decades.

Fire suppression changes the character of the forest, allowing some species to grow thick and choke out others. It allows more leaves, brush, and other dead tree matter to accumulate on the forest floor, providing copious fuel for when fire does start. Immature trees that might have been killed off by fire grow, creating denser forests with thinner trees interspersed with older, thicker ones. Denser forests with more abundant fuel mean that when fires are not successfully suppressed, they can quickly become bigger, hotter, and more destructive. In denser forests, fire travels up the trunks of the immature trees and into the crowns, where it rapidly leaps from tree to tree. Fire suppression is also dangerous: firefighters regularly die battling forest fires.

Fire suppression had been the default policy of the U.S. Forest Service since the fires of 1910 and of the National Park Service from its creation in 1916. By the 1950s, dissenting voices made themselves heard. Their concern was not that suppression would lead to bigger fires, but that it was upsetting the forests' natural ecological balance. Scientists and ecologists who observed how fire had been a regular—and restorative—force in Florida became evangelists for the return of fire. In the early 1960s, controversy over the culling of elk in Yellowstone National Park prompted the Kennedy administration to appoint a group of outsiders led by Starker Leopold, a prominent zoologist, to recommend changes to wildlife management in the parks. Instead of protecting animals and forests for their own sake, Leopold and his colleagues argued in their 1963 report, the parks should be restored to the way they looked before Europeans came: "A national park should represent a vignette of primitive America."

The gold seekers who crossed the Sierra Nevada into California in the 1840s "spoke almost to a man of the wide-spaced columns of mature trees that grew on the lower western slope in gigantic magnificence," the report observed. "Today much of the west slope is a dog-hair thicket of young pines, white fir, incense cedar, and mature brush—a direct function of overprotection from natural ground fires.... Animal life is meager, wildflowers are sparse, and to some at least the vegetative tangle is depressing, not uplifting." Deliberately set fire—a "prescribed burn"—was the most natural way to control the vegetation.

The Leopold report was more an expression of ecological advocacy than of science. Nonetheless, it catalyzed a radical change in the approach to fire. In 1968 the National Park Service formally repudiated the 1930s-era policy that aimed to have all fires under control by 10 a.m. the next day; in 1978, the U.S. Forest Service did the same.

But how to reintroduce fire? The forests were no longer the pristine, untouched expanses of the pre-European era; people lived, worked, fished, hunted, and camped in them. They were vital to the livelihoods of countless loggers, fishermen, and hoteliers. Letting a fire burn that threatened to kill or displace people or do broad economic damage wasn't an option. Forest managers would have to judge whether to let a fire burn or even when to deliberately set a fire.

In the summer of 1988, when fire broke out in Yellowstone, that decision would fall to Superintendent Bob Barbee. One August day in 2014, I went to Bozeman, Montana, to visit Barbee. He retired from the Park Service in 2000, and at seventy-eight years old was ruddy-faced, with a sweep of thinning gray hair and a gruff but steady voice. We chatted in his sitting room, which was filled with artifacts from his tenures in Yellowstone, Alaska, and North Carolina, and furniture draped with Navajo blankets. Barbee's love of the outdoors was readily apparent, from his hiking pants to his stunning photographs of forests, lakes, and mountains decorating the walls.

Barbee discovered this love while working summers as a ranger shortly after graduating with a degree in natural resources from Colorado State University. So when the National Park Service gave him the opportunity to work full-time in the parks, he jumped at it. In 1968 he became a natural resources specialist at Yosemite National Park in California. Shortly afterward, he paid a visit to Harold Biswell, an ecologist at the University of California at Berkeley and an evangelist for reintroducing fire to the parks. Biswell, decked out in field clothes, suggested they head out right away, and they spent the next three days setting fires.

At Yosemite, Barbee was tasked with adapting Leopold's recommendations. He already knew that California owed its majestic sequoia trees to the fires that would periodically thin out the faster-growing white firs and allow the sequoias to thrive. At Yosemite, though, years of fire suppression had allowed the white firs to become dense. Barbee put together a plan for prescribed burning in Yosemite. Much of the public greeted it as barbaric; Biswell was nicknamed Harry the Torch, while Barbee was the "Midnight Ecologist," a "Neanderthal running through the forest with his drip torch," as he paraphrased it. But he pressed ahead, and one summer set a prescribed burn in the beautiful, famous El Capitan Meadow. The meadow's hydrogeography had been altered years earlier by road building, which caused it to dry up and become a seedbed for pines; the Park Service was constantly cutting down those pines to keep the meadow intact. Barbee's fire raced through the meadow for forty-five minutes and killed every pine. The results were apparent by the following year: strawberries and azaleas were growing back where the pines had once choked them.

Barbee became superintendent of Yellowstone in 1983. Park policy since 1972 had allowed some natural fires to burn in limited areas that were then allowed to expand. Whether a fire was left to burn or was suppressed was based on a scientific analysis of fuel load, weather conditions, moisture content, and the proximity of valuable structures. Over the next fifteen years, there were 235 fires ignited by lightning that consumed 34,000 acres (of a 2.2-million-acre park), 1981 being the worst year, with 20,240 acres burned. It helped that those years were relatively moist, reinforcing the belief that rain would in reasonable time extinguish almost all naturally ignited fires.

On June 14, 1988, a lightning strike started a fire in Montana, just outside the park's northern border. In the following weeks, lightning started other small fires. In keeping with Park Service policy, Barbee decided to let the fires burn while monitoring them. But the fires' behavior took Barbee and his staff by surprise. The moisture they expected didn't materialize; the summer became one of the driest on record in the park, and powerful winds blew all summer long. Fires usually die down at night, but that summer they burned fiercely after the sun went down.

Then there was the fuel factor. The park's ecological staff had studied the rings of the park's oldest trees and knew that the area had seen massive fires in 1705 and 1850. The evidence was visible from the air, as the trees that had grown back after those events looked different from the surrounding trees. Fires had been routinely suppressed since the late 1800s. In the 1960s Yellowstone began prescribed burning and allowing natural fires to burn. Nonetheless, the forests had grown thick with fuel that could potentially permit fire to reach the crowns and burn with particular intensity.

By mid-July, Barbee changed tactics: all fires would be suppressed. Some of his scientific staff, anxious to study the effects of the fire on the forest's ecology, resisted, but by then the fires had grown beyond their control. Forest staff had bulldozed firebreaks or set backfires to stop the flames from spreading, but high winds were blowing embers across roads, streams, and firebreaks. Fires spread by as much as five to ten miles per day. By August 20, 165,000 acres were burning and the black clouds of smoke resembled a nuclear mushroom cloud. By early September, fire was approaching the Old Faithful Inn, the largest log structure in the world. Barbee sat down with the fire commander and said, "We've got the Sistine Chapel here. Losing the Old Faithful Inn is not an option. If we lose it I'm dead meat, and so are you." Three days before the fire arrived, firefighters soaked and foamed the building. The fire destroyed seventeen nearby buildings and exploded a fuel truck, but the inn survived.

Barbee's staff had predicted that natural fire would consume at most 40,000 acres that year; a total of 248 fires in Yellowstone and environs eventually burned more than 1 million acres, a public relations nightmare for the National Park Service. "I kept hoping maybe Qaddafi would do something outrageous" to draw the media's attention, Barbee later recalled, "but he didn't. So they all came to Yellowstone."

The public and politicians had never understood why the Park Service would welcome fire, especially in Yellowstone, the nation's oldest and most beloved national park. In August, NPS director William Mott declared a freeze on all prescribed burning in national parks. That September, a group of congressmen petitioned Ronald Reagan to force the NPS to forsake prescribed burning, or what they derisively called "Let it burn." The park had become a vital source of tourist revenue for western states, and in addition, many saw the policy of prescribed burning as endangering the economic vitality of the logging and tourism industries. Some scientists were also critical; one compared the policy to "making incantations to the Greek God Zeus."

The science behind prescribed burning is sound; what can't be changed is the inherent complexity and unpredictability of fire. This became searingly apparent in 2000 in the Frijoles Canyon that cuts through Bandelier National Monument, just south of the town of Los Alamos, New Mexico. Park officials fretted that the worst drought in sixty years had made the region ripe for a massive wildfire. An arsonist was on the loose and had already started one major fire in 1998. And everyone worried that a massive fire might damage the nuclear weapons laboratory in Los Alamos. So, intent on reducing the fuel load and avoiding such an event, the Park Service began a prescribed burn on May 4 on the slopes of Cerro Grande Peak above the canyon by igniting grass with gasoline spilled from drip torches.

Within a few hours, the fire had begun to spread beyond its prescribed boundaries. By the next day, it had changed from a prescribed burn to a wildfire. To contain the blaze, firefighters built backfires along its western boundary to keep the flames from spreading to the heavily wooded areas farther down in the canyon.

When winds began to strengthen, pushing the flames from that backfire into the thickly wooded areas of the canyon, the

Park Service called in helicopters to drop retardant on the spreading blaze. That fire, too, got out of control; flying embers ignited spot fires to the east, closer to Los Alamos. Flames were soon racing toward the town at nearly a mile per hour. On May 10, New Mexico governor Gary Johnson ordered the town's 11,000 residents to evacuate. Blowing embers lit spot fires on the forty-three-square-mile lab complex, prompting the Department of Energy to send teams to monitor for radiation leaks from the nuclear weapons laboratory (none occurred). Eventually, 1,400 firefighters and sixteen tanker aircraft and helicopters were called in to battle a blaze originally intended to consume 900 acres. It burned 48,000 and destroyed more than 200 homes.

Investigations began almost instantly. Bruce Babbitt, the interior secretary, blamed "seriously flawed" calculations by the National Park Service. That and subsequent reports faulted park personnel for inadequate attention to changes in wind forecasts and failing to have adequate firefighters and tankers on hand to contain the fire should it get out of control. They also, according to some critics, had too little experience managing prescribed burns.

For the people charged with managing forests, deciding whether to let a fire burn or to suppress it carries enormous personal conse-quences. In Yellowstone in 1988, outraged residents and business owners nicknamed Barbee "Barbee-Que Bob," and a cartoon fea-turing burning teddy bears labeled "Barbee Dolls" appeared in a Montana newspaper. Barbee was used to making unpopular deci-sions, from the prescribed burns in Yosemite to blocking motel development in Cape Hatteras. It was not, he recalls, a job for some-one who worried a lot about how his decisions would be viewed.

After the Cerro Grande fire, Roy Weaver, the superintendent at Bandelier, was vilified and threatened with the loss of his pen-sion, though a board of inquiry recommended against any disci-plinary action. Weaver, who retired shortly afterward, later said,

"Things happened that we couldn't or didn't anticipate. And that we couldn't control." Barbee sent him a sympathetic letter of support. Many other park personnel had been in the same position, he said, and "there but for the grace of God go I."

Today, Barbee is convinced that nothing could have prevented the fires that summer, even if they had tried to suppress them earlier. There was a confluence of events that made a repeat of the fires of 1705 and 1850 inevitable.

Officially, natural fire and prescribed burns remain central parts of federal forest management. But the Yellowstone and Cerro Grande episodes illustrate the extremely high risks that the people tasked with carrying out those policies must run. The same complexity that makes management by fire suppression dangerous in the long run also makes the use of fire unpredictable in the short run. Countless things can cause fire to get out of control, from unexpected wind changes, lack of precipitation, and lightning to the underlying characteristics of the terrain.

The ferocity of the Yellowstone and Cerro Grande fires was due at least in part to the lack of fire in preceding decades. Yellowstone was established as the first national park in 1872, and in 1886 the army took over responsibility for fighting fire there. Suppression remained the default policy until the 1970s. "In 1988, you burned off a century's worth of buildup," says Stephen Pyne, the fire historian. Swetnam believes large fires occurred roughly every six years in the eighteenth and nineteenth centuries around Los Alamos, but there had been no large fire since 1881.

If Swetnam's and Marlon's calculations are right, and the past century has been unusually quiescent in terms of fires, then the frightening implication is that there will be many more megafires ahead. Experience seems to bear that out: the past decade has witnessed more fires topping half a million acres than in previous decades. This is not simply the consequence of climate change, but the legacy of fire suppression.

Unfortunately, knowing this doesn't tell us what to do. Should we encourage more fires to eliminate the fire deficit? Or be more alert and faster at putting out fires to prevent a megafire from erupting? Science supports the former course of action; day-to-day reality, the latter. For those whose job it is to manage the forests, the consequences are highly asymmetric. If letting a fire burn accomplishes the desired goal, the result will be a healthier forest and fewer megafires many years later. Few people will notice the healthier forests, fewer still the absence of fires. If the fire gets out of control, the consequences are millions of dollars' worth of damage, lives potentially lost, and a gauntlet of television cameras and outraged congressmen demanding answers. Add to that the fact that prescribed burns and mechanical thinning of forests, both natural ways to reduce fuel and encourage natural growth, are expensive, and the temptation to suppress rather than burn becomes overwhelming.

Suppression in turn induces behavior that makes the choices harder. The temporary moratorium on prescribed burns in western national parks following the Yellowstone fires led to increased land development nearby compared to areas where prescribed burns continued. Such development makes it more costly to let fires burn. Pyne attests to this, saying that for most forest managers, there's a strong default in favor of suppression: "If you set a prescribed fire or let a natural fire burn, and that escapes, that could be a career-ending move. If you attack a fire and it escapes, you'll be applauded as a hero." He quotes a forester he met at Sequoia National Park saying, "I go to work every day knowing that a wind shift could land me in jail."

Forests are not the only systems that adapt to humanity's efforts to control them. Many ecological and social systems share this trait. Bacteria are similar to forests. For a while the advent of antibiotics raised the prospect that humans could control and even defeat countless deadly and crippling pestilences, from war wounds and sore throats to venereal diseases and urinary tract infections. But as with forests, microorganisms adapted and in some instances became even deadlier.

Alexander Fleming famously discovered penicillin in 1928 through an act of sloppy serendipity. He had left a plate of bacterial culture in his lab sink and later came back to find a mold, penicillum, growing on the plate. The bacteria had also grown everywhere on the plate, except around the mold. Fleming, however, never figured out how to isolate pure penicillin; that task fell to three other British scientists at Oxford University in 1940, and in 1941 they were able to manufacture penicillin for administering to people.

British scientists visited the United States in 1941 to tout the drug's miraculous properties in an effort to persuade the U.S. government to begin mass production. But the government did not make the drug publicly available, reserving it instead for military use. Then, in 1942, a fire gutted the popular Cocoanut Grove nightclub in Boston, killing 492 people. Many of the survivors were treated at Massachusetts General Hospital for severe, extensive burns. *Staphylococcus aureus* often infects skin wounds, in particular on burn victims and skin graft recipients; at the time, infected victims usually died. But in the wake of the fire, Merck & Co. rushed a supply of penicillin from its plant in New Jersey to the hospital, where it was used to successfully treat burn victims.

Penicillin's success at treating the fire's burn victims earned it the label "miracle drug." And it was miraculous. Penicillin works by binding to an enzyme in the bacteria that it needs to make its cell wall, without which it dies. Since human cells don't have cell walls, pencillin is harmless to people, which makes it an extremely safe drug.

The use of antibiotics rapidly spread, and soon age-old scourges such as gonorrhea and tuberculosis were being vanquished. In 1962 Sir Frank MacFarlane Burnet, an immunologist who shared the 1960 Nobel Prize for medicine, declared, "One can think of the middle of the twentieth century as the end of one of the most important social revolutions in history, the virtual elimination of the infectious disease as a significant factor in social life."

But the embrace of penicillin as a miracle drug sowed the seeds for its demise. Fleming had warned in 1945 that bacterial mutation could lead to resistance to penicillin, a simple expression of Darwin's process of natural selection. And bacteria evolve far more rapidly than other species because they replicate several times per hour. Fleming had induced this process directly by subjecting bacteria to ever-greater doses of penicillin until the only survivors were strains that had developed cell walls that penicillin could not penetrate. In 1945 Fleming warned that resistant strains would become much more prevalent if penicillin became available in a pill, allowing patients to self-medicate rather than receive the drug intravenously in a hospital.

Though Fleming was right about the possibility of resistance, he underestimated its potency. Fleming assumed that resistance would develop through natural selection. Suppose a strain of bacteria contained a mutation on its chromosome — the "double helix" of DNA that acts as a blueprint for the entire organism — that made it resistant to penicillin. Treating the patient with penicillin would kill off all the microbes except the resistant strain, enabling it to thrive and spread. Imagine a change in climate that kills all of a species of rabbit except some with unusually thick fur; the thick-furred species would thereafter become dominant because it was better adapted to this new climate.

Bacteria acquire resistance through much more ingenious, and potent, means than mutation. Bacteria are home to thousands of plasmids, essentially free-floating chunks of DNA, separate from the chromosome, that perform supplemental functions. Plasmids may contain a gene to produce an enzyme that shuts down the antibiotic or protects the part of the host bacteria that the antibiotic targets. In 1959, Japanese doctors were stunned to encounter a strain of bacterial dysentery that was resistant to four different antibiotics. They estimated that a bacteria would need to double 10^{28} times (that's 1 followed by 28 zeros) for that to happen through the normal process of mutation, which was impossibly improbable. Scientists concluded that bacteria carrying resistant genes on their plasmids were exchanging them with other bacteria, enabling them to acquire more than one form of resistance. It would be as if thin-furred rabbits learned how to grow thicker fur instead of simply dying off in the cold.

Bacteria can even harbor genes that "turn on" their resistant properties only when an antibiotic is encountered; in effect, susceptible bacteria suddenly become resistant. Resistance appears with astonishing speed—in as little as two weeks after a patient starts an antibiotic. Penicillin-resistant strains of staphylococci appeared in London hospitals within a few years of the drug's introduction and spread to the broader community in the following decades. In the 1970s American soldiers contracted a penicillin-resistant gonorrhea that was traced back to Vietnamese prostitutes who were regularly given the drug to remain disease free.

Scientists responded to resistant strains by developing new antibiotics to target different parts of the infectious agent. Derivatives of penicillin such as methicillin, oxacillin, and nafcillin entered use in the early 1960s. Within a few years, methicillin-resistant *Staphylococcus aureus* (MRSA) appeared, and by the 1990s, it was widespread in hospitals. In the 2000s, it spread to the wider community. MRSA may now cause ninety thousand infections and twenty thousand deaths per year in the United States.

Resistant bacteria don't owe their existence to antibiotics; many existed centuries, even millennia, before antibiotics appeared. But natural selection dictates that antibiotics increase the prevalence of resistant strains. As the microbiologist and physician Stuart Levy says, "Antibiotics select for the kinds of bacteria that they can no longer kill." They are, he says, "societal drugs. They are the only drug where one person's use interferes with the success of another." One person's decision to take an anticholesterol drug, for example, has no impact on whether someone else with high cholesterol will suffer. By contrast, each individual's decision to take an antibiotic exposes the rest of society to a slightly greater risk of resistant bacteria. They aren't quite zero-sum drugs, but they come close. This perverse property is apparent from the fact that antibiotics are least effective in countries where they are used the most.

Levy is seventy-six years old, with bow tie, spectacles, and a gentle smile. He works out of an office at Tufts University's medical school in Boston's Chinatown. Levy got interested in antibiotic resistance while on sabbatical in France, where he met Tsutomu Watanabe, a Japanese scientist who had done pioneering work on antibiotic resistance. In 1981, Levy created the Alliance for the Prudent Use of Antibiotics (APUA), which campaigns around the world against their overuse. He has scoured the globe in search of the sources of antibiotic resistance. He has photographed pills for sale over the counter in hole-in-the-wall pharmacies in Bangladesh, trekked through villages in Nepal to trace the incidence of resistance, and hung out on French farms to see how far afield the antibiotics that chickens receive can travel.

Antibiotics are routinely prescribed for conditions in which the infectious agent is probably not bacterial; for example, colds,

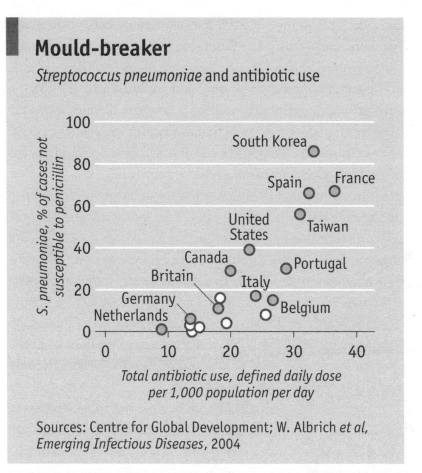

Mould-breaker

Streptococcus pneumoniae and antibiotic use

Y-axis: *S. pneumoniae*, % of cases not susceptible to penicillin

Data points:
- South Korea
- Spain
- France
- United States
- Taiwan
- Canada
- Portugal
- Britain
- Italy
- Germany
- Belgium
- Netherlands

X-axis: Total antibiotic use, defined daily dose per 1,000 population per day

Sources: Centre for Global Development; W. Albrich *et al*, *Emerging Infectious Diseases*, 2004

In countries with greater use of antibiotics, resistant strains of bacteria are more widespread. (Chart © The Economist Newspaper Limited, London, March 31, 2011)

which are caused by a virus and therefore will not respond to an antibiotic.

There are many causes of antibiotic resistance, from widespread use in farm animals, self-medication, especially in countries where antibiotics are sold without prescription (or patients are taking unused pills from an earlier prescription), pharmaceutical companies' abandonment of developing new antibiotics in favor of more lucrative treatments for chronic illnesses, and plain ignorance: one survey by APUA found that 45 percent of antibiotic users think they can kill viruses.

Steps have been taken against all these problems, such as restrictions on antibiotic use on livestock — Denmark banned it outright — to prescription requirements. But regulatory restrictions do not address one of the most prevalent sources of resistance: excessive prescribing by physicians. Their overuse is rooted not in economics or ignorance but in the tension between physicians' private and societal duties. Doctors seldom know with certainty what ails a patient. An upper respiratory infection may be viral and thus unresponsive to antibiotics, or bacterial. The condition may get better on its own or, for reasons specific to the individual, dramatically worse. This uncertainty alone motivates physicians to prescribe more powerful antibiotics, though this is more likely to encourage resistance. One study of American hospitals from 1997 to 2010 found that doctors prescribed antibiotics for 60 percent of patients complaining of sore throats, even though only 10 percent of sore throats respond to antibiotics.

A physician weighing the benefits of prescribing an antibiotic is much like the forest manager deciding whether to suppress a fire: the benefits are immediate and visible, while the costs are distant, intangible, and borne by someone else. A survey of doctors in Wales found that awareness of resistance was widespread yet seldom entered into doctors' decisions: "The consequences of not prescribing antibiotics, especially in situations where patients might go on to develop more serious problems, worried them more than the theoretical, 'downstream' complication of antimicrobial resistance." One doctor told the researchers that "resistance is probably...tenth out of ten of issues that come into whether you prescribe an agent or not...not wishing to miss an infection that may get very much worse is pretty high up there."

"We as treating physicians do not know what our patients have, with certainty," says Brad Spellberg, chief medical officer of the Los Angeles County+University of Southern California Medical Center, who, like Levy, has campaigned for years to curb the overuse of antibiotics. "We make our best guess and that guess is haunted by the fear it might be wrong."

Spellberg tells the story of a twenty-eight-year-old woman who came to a community hospital in Los Angeles with flu-like symptoms: sore throat, fever, and malaise. The hospital had adopted protocols to avoid overuse of antibiotics, and, following those protocols, sent her away with chicken soup and Tylenol. She returned several days later, sicker, and was again told that her illness was not bacterial. Several days after being sent away, she was diagnosed with Lemierre's syndrome, in which a bacterial infection in the throat spreads to the jugular vein, producing a blood clot that then breaks apart and spreads throughout the body, in particular to the capillaries of the lung. She soon died.

The situation is highly unusual. By Spellberg's reckoning, the odds of an adverse reaction to an antibiotic, such as an allergic reaction, are about 1 in 10, whereas the odds that someone will suffer because antibiotics were wrongly withheld are about 1 in 10,000. Nonetheless, most physicians do not want to run the risk of letting a patient suffer when an antibiotic could help. In the decades Levy has been fighting antibiotic overuse, resistance rates have gone up, and he despairs that he is losing the battle. He has made headway educating doctors about overuse, but at the same time antibiotic overuse is rampant in agriculture and in emerging markets. His research in Nepal produced the depressing finding that antibiotic resistance was highest in communities with the most doctors.

Spellberg thinks trying to persuade doctors not to prescribe antibiotics is a doomed strategy. Better, he says, to develop tests that rapidly identify what bug a patient has and thus whether an antibiotic is needed. And since much of an infection's harm comes from the body's response, it might be better to train the body not to respond to infection. The bottom line, he says, is that "we are not going to win a war against a species that outnumber us by 10 to the power of 22, outweigh us by 100 million, replicate 500,000 times faster than we do, and have been doing this for 10,000 times longer than our species has existed. We need to achieve peaceful coexistence."

The dilemmas raised by forest fires and bacterial infections are similar to those raised by financial crises. Should the government intervene to save a bank, a hedge fund, or a country from failing, knowing that this would create expectations that future banks, hedge funds, or countries might be saved?

This is a quandary that Jay Powell knows intimately. Trim, plainspoken, and silver haired, he looks and sounds like the senior Treasury official he was in the early 1990s. He subsequently pursued a career in private equity and investment banking before returning to public life as a Fed governor. I met Powell in 2010, between those two stints in government. He was ensconced at the Bipartisan Policy Center, a think tank that, as its name suggests, nobly tries to find solutions to the country's pressing problems that both parties can agree to. Powell and I, at the time working for *The Economist* magazine, were working on financial "war games": we'd recruit a bunch of real-life former policy makers to confront a simulated financial crisis on the stage at one of *The Economist*'s conferences. One year, the challenge was to handle a megabank on the verge of failing.

We asked policy makers to wrestle with the intricacies of Dodd-Frank, the massive financial law passed in 2010 that was supposed to make bailouts a thing of the past. We wanted the simulation to be as politically agonizing as possible. Let the bank fail and witness the 2008 crisis all over again — or bail it out and reverse everything we'd done to extinguish moral hazard? In the process, I learned to my surprise that this stuff was not abstract to Powell: he had faced these dilemmas himself.

In January 1991, the country was gripped by recession and banks were falling like dominoes, particularly in Texas and New England. The governor of Rhode Island had just closed forty-five credit unions, and because the state's deposit insurance fund was insolvent, depositors' funds were frozen. Bank of New England, one of the country's largest regional banks, had grown rapidly thanks to acquisitions and the booming New England economy but was now buckling under the weight of bad loans linked to collapsing real estate values. On Friday, January 4, it announced that it had just lost $450 million, wiping out its remaining capital and rendering it essentially insolvent. Depositors mobbed branches in Massachusetts, Rhode Island, and Connecticut to withdraw their money.

On the morning of Sunday, January 6, Powell and his colleagues at Treasury met with officials from the FDIC and the Federal Reserve. Of the $19.1 billion on deposit at Bank of New England and its two sister banks, more than $2 billion were in accounts exceeding the $100,000 insured by the FDIC. What would become of them? Bank of New England was not particularly big; it was only the thirty-third largest bank in the country. The problem was that so many other banks also relied on uninsured deposits.

Powell and his fellow Treasury officials objected to protecting uninsured depositors. It would, they worried, create moral hazard— the expectation that they would bail out uninsured depositors again, thereby guaranteeing that the risky activity would increase. "This is the classic too-big-to-fail problem: you have a bailout now to avoid the worst outcome, but you create moral hazard and in a way kick the can down the road, and maybe you ultimately face an even worse problem," Powell told me years later.

John LaWare, the Federal Reserve governor responsible for bank supervision, told Powell and his colleagues that it was a raw time, with the credit union closures and the weak regional economy: "We'll tell you what will happen if we haircut the uninsured depositors. What we think will happen is that there will be runs on a lot of the banks in Europe and the U.S. when the U.S. opens on Monday morning." Pretty quickly, the others came around to the idea that that should not be allowed to happen, and voted without dissent to bail the uninsured depositors out.

The tensions of 1991 were repeated on a much larger scale in 2008, when big firms, one after another, teetered on the brink of collapse. The Fed and Treasury were in agreement that March that Bear Stearns should be saved; there was just too much dry kindling around waiting to go up in flames if the firm went down. Similarly with Fannie Mae and Freddie Mac: the consequences of the fall of these firms, long considered equivalent to the federal government itself, were intolerable. But by that September moral hazard concerns had taken precedence, and Henry Paulson, the Treasury secretary, insisted that no public money be used to save Lehman. It was the most controversial decision of the crisis. Lehman's failure ignited a forest fire of mammoth proportions and forced the authorities to backstop AIG, money market funds, commercial paper, Citigroup, and Bank of America. Paulson, roundly attacked for breeding moral hazard with the bailout of Bear Stearns, now faced even more scathing criticism for letting a big bank fail in the midst of the worst systemic crisis in memory. One prominent columnist labeled Paulson "the most incompetent economic policy maker in U.S. history."

Future Treasury secretaries will see the aftermath of Lehman the way future forest managers will see the aftermath of the Cerro Grande or Yellowstone fires: as proof of deeply unpleasant, asymmetric rewards: if you don't intervene, you risk a catastrophe for which you are personally held responsible. It's easy to see why the temptation will always be to intervene.

This is the sort of dilemma that divides engineers and ecologists. Engineers will always be tempted to intervene, trusting in their ability to make it right; ecologists will always fear the unintended consequences of that intervention. As the experiences described in this chapter show, the right choice changes with the circumstances, and it may not be obvious, even in hindsight. One broad lesson is that ecologists are right about micro-level risk: systems benefit from the lessons and resistance that small-scale disasters nurture. Engineers are most valuable at staving off macro-level risk — that is, preventing large-scale catastrophe.

Stuart Levy offers a personal template for precisely this approach. He himself has never taken an antibiotic, for fear of contributing to the problem of resistance. If a doctor were foolish enough to suggest one, his response is: "No way, I'll fight this on my own." This obviously isn't because he doesn't trust antibiotics; just the opposite. He'd certainly accept an antibiotic if his life were threatened: "I'm not stupid. It's not like I'm holding on for some record." That's the point: he so reveres their potency that he wants antibiotics reserved for when they are truly needed. Overuse of antibiotics for minor infections renders them ineffective for deadly infections.

In their own chaotic way, American policy makers have tried to do something similar with the financial system. The Dodd-Frank Act did two seemingly contradictory things. First, it made it much tougher for the government to bail out any entity that gets into trouble. The promise of a bailout, the argument goes, has been a consistent source of crises in the past and will create crises in the future. Indeed, since the government bailed out so many big companies in 2008, the expectation that it will do so again is even greater. To neutralize this, rules have been written to force regulators to let big banks go bust in all but the most extreme cases, and new limits have been imposed to forbid the Federal Reserve from lending to a single company as it did to Bear Stearns and AIG.

Second, the law gives regulators new powers to take over a failing firm and manage its collapse in a way that minimizes the risk of a Lehman-like conflagration. Powell wishes he'd had that power in 1991. With Bank of New England, he and his colleagues were offered "two bad choices ... and we get to make the less horrible one." Dodd-Frank offers a third choice: to "resolve" the failing institution cleanly, by protecting depositors and some creditors while forcing stock- and bondholders to absorb losses: "It was the missing tool in our regulatory tool kit," says Powell.

To work, the law must persuade everyone that these banks really can fail, and that will make an actual collapse much less damaging. In the war game that Powell and I developed back in 2011, the former officials playing actual officials onstage used Dodd-Frank to successfully close down a failing megabank without a crisis. It was a happy ending but a fictitious one. In real life, could the private markets absorb the loss of one of their own? Could they do so without causing panic? Would the government be content to stay out of the picture, willing to trade some chaos today in hopes of avoiding even more chaos tomorrow? No one knows. But it's a start.

The Price of Peace of Mind: Why Insurance Protects Us from Small Disasters but Not Big Ones

Few financial innovations have improved human happiness as much as insurance. Through the mathematics of risk pooling, society can, at only minor cost to each member, spare any one of them the financial catastrophe of death, disaster, or illness.

Insurers like to think of this as God's work—quite literally, in the case of those that started life as mutual assistance societies united by religion or ethnicity. Their mission was not to make money but to combine resources to support those members of the community struck by misfortune. As one early industry handbook put it: "while the aggregate of human suffering and calamity remains undiminished...human ingenuity and cooperation equalize the distribution of this fearful aggregate, and alleviate the terrors of uncertainty."

From its earliest days, the insurance industry has marketed to its customers' feelings. Indeed, insurance ads seldom mention probabilities or money; instead, they tap into the emotional satisfaction of protecting one's loved ones from misfortune. In 2014, Thai Life Insurance brought Southeast Asia to tears with a maudlin television commercial in which a young man performs random acts of kindness—giving money to a beggar girl, feeding a dog, moving a potted plant to a spot where it can receive water—with no expectation of payback. Why, the viewer is asked? Because "He witnesses happiness. Reaches a deeper understanding. Feels the love. Receives what money can't buy. A world made more beautiful."

To be profitable, though, insurance depends on the bloodless logic of statistics. First, what is the probability of the risk that's being insured: How likely is that person to die? That house to burn down? Second, how correlated are those risks: If he dies, does this make it more likely that his neighbor will die? If his house burns down, does it mean that others are more likely to burn down, too?

Beyond the arithmetic, insurers must also consider several aspects of human behavior. The first is adverse selection: people who buy insurance may be more likely to need it. For example, someone with terminal cancer is more likely to want life insurance, but this is a poor risk for an insurer to cover. The other is moral hazard: the tendency of someone to be more careless about the risks he has insured against. Insurers, for instance, do not want people to burn their own houses down to collect the fire insurance or drive faster because they have car insurance.

References to insurance have been found as far back as Hammurabi's Code, written around 1790 BC, which stipulates that a man whose crops are destroyed by flood or drought "shall not pay corn to his creditor. He shall dip his tablet in water, and the interest of that year he shall not pay." The earliest known commercial contracts date from the 1300s.

Incorporating human behavior such as moral hazard and adverse selection into insurance policies took longer. The process was hampered both by lack of statistical tools and theological objections; since accidents, disasters, and hazards were seen as acts of divine will, humans had little ability to affect their occurrence.

In the 1800s, with better statistical tools, insurers began to differentiate risks, for example, requiring medical exams for life insurance. The term "moral hazard" first appears in the 1860s, in *The Practice of Fire Underwriting*, wherein it was defined as: "the danger proceeding from motives to destroy property by fire, or permit its destruction."

As the term suggests, moral hazard has long been linked to debates about right and wrong. In the nineteenth century, parents, who benefited from their children's labor, sometimes bought life insurance policies on their children. Children's advocates thought the practice repellent and warned it was incentive to parents to neglect or even murder their children.

When economists in the 1960s began studying moral hazard, they gave it a more neutral, even positive character: it was simply the product of incentives. If insurance reduced the cost of risky activity, people did more of it. If this sounds a lot like the Peltzman effect we encountered in Chapter 4, there's a good reason; moral hazard and the Peltzman effect are essentially the same thing. Proving moral hazard in real life is tricky, though. Car insurance does seem to lead to more accidents, while health insurance does not lead to less healthy lifestyles. Part of the challenge is that insurance is supposed to enable people to do things they otherwise might not. Sometimes, this is by law: you can't drive without liability insurance. And sometimes this is by choice: financial innovation has enabled many to take risks they otherwise would not.

The insurance industry has come up with many ways to deal with both moral hazard and adverse selection. The use of deductibles, copays, and insured maximums ensure that customers bear some of the cost of a peril. Customers are screened for characteristics likely to lead to higher claims—serious illness, for example, in the case of life insurance, or previous traffic offenses in the case of automobile insurance.

This model works extremely well. Insurance is a gargantuan industry, by some measures the world's biggest; Americans spend $1 trillion each year to insure against fire, flood, disease, death, car accidents, robbery, disability, and every other imaginable setback, and that doesn't include the hundreds of billions of dollars they contribute toward Social Security, Medicare, and other government-sponsored insurance. In the financial realm, insurance on financial events, such as a default or a decline in stock prices, runs to the trillions of dollars. The peace of mind industry is, in other words, huge.

Yet there are times when insurance, an industry built on probabilities, conservatism, and protection, becomes a source not of safety but of danger. This tends to happen in the case of extreme events—devastating floods, earthquakes, and financial crises—when insurance must cope with two problems: emotional consumers, and emotional insurance companies.

Recall that Howard Kunreuther, a risk expert at the Wharton School, says that consumers suffer from "disaster myopia": they are simply incapable of evaluating risk when probabilities are small. Kunreuther, Nathan Novemsky, and Daniel Kahneman demonstrated this incisively in an experiment they reported on in 2001. They asked several hundred participants to consider a scenario that described a chemical plant in an urban New Jersey area that used a dangerous chemical called Syntox (in fact, a fictitious agent). An accidental release of the chemical could produce a deadly toxic plume. They then showed three separate groups of participants three different probabilities that someone living near the plant might die in any given year from a toxic discharge: 1 in 100,000, 1 in 1 million, or 1 in 10 million. To help put those numbers in context, all were told that the risk of dying in a car accident was 1 in 6,000. Then they were asked to evaluate how much they agreed with statements such as the "plant poses serious health and safety risks for those currently living in the community." Their answers were then converted to a scale of perceived risk from 1 to 5. Remarkably, participants shown the highest probability did not assess the risk any differently from those shown the lowest probability; they simply couldn't differentiate.

So the researchers approached the question differently. They assembled another three groups of participants, and showed each a different insurance premium the chemical plant must pay in case a resident dies from a discharge of Syntox: either 15 cents, $1.50, or $15 per year per death. The researchers surmised that because most people pay insurance premiums regularly, they would easily relate premiums to risk. But they were wrong: again, higher premiums did not evoke higher assessments of risk.

To help respondents understand accident probabilities and insurance premiums, some were given the example of how accident risk and insurance premiums differed between snowy Colorado and sunny Arizona. These subjects were better able to properly judge the differences in risk posed by the chemical plant scenarios. From this finding, the researchers concluded that people can better evaluate risk when they have a strong, narrative context. Knowing the probabilities, or premiums, of events with which they had little personal experience was no help. Indeed, Kunreuther has found that with rare events, people often won't even expend the time or effort needed to figure out the probabilities and the cost of insuring against them.

If people are so bad with probabilities, what induces them to buy insurance? Often it's emotions. Insurers know this. Car rental companies push the loss damage waiver on customers at the check-in counter when the image of a car crash is most vivid in drivers' minds; retailers sell extended warranties on electronics at the point of sale when the buyer is most protective of his brand-new television. And Kunreuther and his colleagues have demonstrated that people are far more likely to purchase flood insurance right after a flood, then cancel their policies after just three or four years; even Katrina didn't change this short horizon.

If the problem were just the consumers, insurance should still work. It's a competitive market, so companies have an incentive to price their policies correctly. But the people who sell insurance for a living care about more than just raw arithmetic in deciding whether to insure against low-probability events.

That became crystal clear in the wake of the 1994 Northridge earthquake, which delivered two big surprises. The first was geological. California may be one of the most seismically studied regions in the world, but the quake happened on a previously unknown fault, and did damage no one thought possible: on thousands of buildings with steel frames designed to withstand the lateral shaking of an earthquake, welded joints failed.

The second surprise was financial. Despite California's known earthquake risk, insurers had routinely sold quake insurance as a rider on homeowner policies, with premiums calculated based on "benchmark" earthquakes and exposure to various earthquake zones. Northridge hit them with claims they didn't imagine possible: $12.5 billion, which was four times all the premiums collected for earthquake coverage between 1969 and 1994. Since insurers had to sell earthquake policies in order to offer property insurance in California, many simply pulled out. Those that remained dramatically jacked up premiums and deductibles.

This may seem logical given the losses insurers had just suffered, but it isn't. In theory, insurance premiums should equal the expected loss, plus administrative costs and a reasonable profit. For example, if a $1 million loss has a 1 percent chance of occurring over one year, the expected loss is $10,000 and the premium should reflect that. That's not what happened after Northridge. Kenneth Froot, a retired economist at Harvard, found that after Hurricane Andrew in 1992 and the Northridge quake in 1994, the average premium skyrocketed, from under two times the expected loss in 1989 to more than seven times by 1994.

Moreover, when he dissected the data further, he found that price increases were most dramatic for the lowest-probability events, where premiums exceeded expected losses by a factor of more than 25. The increases could not be explained by insurers raising the probability of another disaster just like the one that

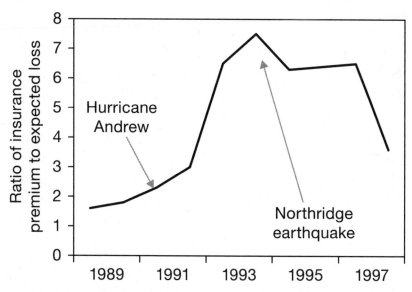

After two major disasters in the 1990s, insurance premiums rose to levels many times the expected loss. (Source: Kenneth Froot, "The Market for Catastrophe Risk: A Clinical Examination," *Journal of Financial Economics* 60 (2001): 529–571)

had occurred: when they raised premiums in certain counties for perils that had occurred, such as hurricanes, they also raised them for perils that hadn't, such as earthquakes. Nor could demand explain increased prices; homeowners bought fewer policies, not more.

Froot's work points up a glaring weakness in the insurance market that explains why an industry so efficient at dealing with *individual* catastrophes such as death, medical bills, and car accidents so often fails at dealing with *systemic* catastrophes such as earthquakes, terrorist attacks, and financial meltdowns. Indeed, as we will see, insurance that protects one person or one company can have the perverse effect of putting everyone else at greater risk.

Insurers may pride themselves on being ruthlessly numbers-driven people, but when faced with the prospect of bankruptcy, they are as susceptible to fear as everyone else. Northridge woke up many insurers to the possibility of losses they could not survive. This meant that they would only sell coverage at a price that looked irrational—so irrational, in fact, that only one company seemed willing to buck the trend, a company that belonged to the celebrated investor Warren Buffett.

The exodus of insurers after the Northridge quake threatened to tank the state's housing industry for lack of coverage, so the state stepped in and created the California Earthquake Authority. Private insurers would write and service the policies and contribute capital, but the authority would issue the policies and assume the risk. To allow it to continue to pay claims even if it ran out of capital, the authority bought $2 billion in reinsurance— that is, insurance that kicks in when claims exceed an initial level—and then planned on $1 billion or more by issuing "catastrophe bonds." At the time, these were a new idea. The buyer of a catastrophe bond collects interest each year but doesn't get his principal back in the event of an earthquake. Thus, the interest rate on the bond is determined by how likely investors think an occurrence will be. The rate the authority would have paid would have been expensive: perhaps 11 to 14 percent.

That's when National Indemnity, a unit of Buffett's holding company, Berkshire Hathaway, swooped in. Buffett is best known as a canny picker of stocks and undervalued companies, yet a great deal of his wealth comes from selling insurance. His philosophy of insurance is similar to his philosophy of stock picking: predicting the future is less important than assessing risks dispassionately and making sure he is paid to bear them. That's why Buffett buys companies likely to generate significant cash soon enough to pay back what he paid, and why he decided to sell $1 billion worth of reinsurance to California for an annual premium of $113 million. The reaction: the stock market value of Berkshire Hathaway jumped by $300 million.

When Froot analyzed the deal, he quickly deduced why. The best estimate that the reinsurance would be triggered (i.e., that an earthquake big enough to eat up all the authority's other coverage) was 1.7 percent per year, while National Indemnity's premium was 10.75 percent of the coverage amount. The gamble, he reckoned, was equivalent to Berkshire collecting $400 million in premiums in return for a 6.6 percent chance of losing $600 million over the four-year life of the contract.

How could Berkshire sell reinsurance so profitably? If premiums were so much higher than any plausible loss, why didn't other insurers undercut Berkshire? True, catastrophes by their nature are unpredictable, and losses may well exceed the estimated maximum. But dealing with such uncertainty is, after all, what reinsurers do for a living. Economists have a number of theories for the unusual gap between what premiums should be and what insurers actually charge, from tax considerations to inefficient capital markets, but none seemed adequate. The real reason was advanced by Buffett himself after he closed the earthquake deal. Some companies would be crippled by $600 million in losses, but not Berkshire; that sum represented a mere 3 percent of book value. As he explained: "Were a truly cataclysmic disaster to occur, it is not impossible that a financial panic would quickly follow…there could well be respected reinsurers that would have difficulty paying at just the moment that their clients faced extraordinary needs.…When it's Berkshire promising, insured know with certainty that they can collect promptly."

In other words, insurers weren't just afraid of losing money by selling earthquake insurance: they were afraid of going out of business. The prospect of bankruptcy is most vivid, and premiums highest, in the wake of a catastrophe that depletes insurers' capital. As time goes on and capital rebuilds, the fear subsides and premiums drop. This is not how it should work; premiums ought to be based on the risk of a future catastrophe, not on the time elapsed since the last one. But apparently it's not just individuals who have trouble coping with catastrophe; so do insurers. They seem incapable of imagining events that can wipe them out until they happen, and then they can imagine little else. Two scholars recall interviewing an insurance executive in Vancouver in the late 1990s. They noted that an earthquake could cause $10 billion in damage, while the industry had the capacity to pay only $4 billion. The executive, whose company sold a lot of commercial earthquake insurance, said, "Well, if I really thought we were going to have [an earthquake], I wouldn't live here."

Not all insurers suffer from that lack of imagination. A few years after the California earthquake insurance deal, Buffett declared that too many investors had rushed to buy catastrophe bonds, driving down their yields and thus the implied price of insuring against catastrophe. As a result, he declared, he would sell less insurance.

The fact that insurers' herd mentality is driven by fear does not mean it's irrational. Carolyn Kousky and Roger Cooke prove that with an elegant bit of math. We have already met Kousky; she showed us how levees encourage development that leads to bigger losses. Cooke is a risk management expert and a colleague of Kousky at Resources for the Future. They start with the assumption that an insurer needs to know that it will be solvent for all but the 1 percent worst possible losses. Then they assume that losses are independent—one customer suffering a loss doesn't make it more likely that another will—and that they are "normally distributed"—that is, losses follow the familiar bell-curve-shaped distribution, with lots of disasters around an average and a tiny number at the extremes. Under those assumptions, the insurer would have to charge premiums only 50 percent higher than the expected loss. In other words, if there's a one-in-a-million chance of a $1 million loss, the expected loss is $1 and the correct premium is $1.50.

Kousky and Cooke then tweaked their assumptions: suppose losses are "fat tailed," that is, really big losses (called "tail events") occur more often than a normal distribution would imply; suppose, furthermore, that losses aren't independent, that is, the odds of two occurring together are more than random; and finally, suppose that tail events tend to occur together. To be confident that it will not face insolvency, the insurer will have to charge premiums that exceed expected losses by four to eight times. This seemed to explain what actually happens in the market for catastrophe insurance. More important, it suggests that consumers are perfectly rational not to buy insurance against catastrophes such as earthquakes in California: the prices far exceed the expected loss.

The inability of insurance to cope with natural disasters also goes a long way toward explaining how financial disasters happen. Insurance and finance have a lot in common. They are both about risk management. A bank is a form of risk pooling: a saver would be foolish to lend all his money to one person. A bank gathers up the savings of many depositors to make many loans. If a few loans go bad, that won't endanger the savings of any other depositors. Capital markets perform the same job more broadly. A company that funds itself by issuing stocks or bonds spreads the risk of the enterprise to others; if it fails, the loss is spread among all bond- and stockholders, not just the founders. All these innovations enable companies and entrepreneurs to take bigger risks, which is great for society as a whole: we all benefit from the innovations and products that result from their risk taking.

But with this ability comes a different problem: the fallacy of composition. This fallacy occurs when what benefits an individual is wrongly assumed to benefit an entire group. For example, if one moviegoer stands, he can see the show better. But if everyone in the audience stands, no one sees better, and everyone is uncomfortable.

Financial innovations like mortgage-backed securities and derivatives allow an individual or a bank or company to do something risky, then transfer the risk to someone else. The investor's or bank's belief that it is now safer encourages it to take more risk—so the level of aggregate risk in the system goes up. This is not a problem so long as the risks are uncorrelated; life insurance works because policyholders don't all die at once, which would bankrupt life insurers. But in finance, risks often are correlated, and that correlation may become apparent only in extreme situations. This means that an innovation designed to redistribute risk can make the broader system less rather than more stable.

Starting in the 1970s, financial derivatives made it possible to insure a much more dazzling range of risks than simple stocks and bonds could. The first important innovation was the "forward": this is a contract in which buyer and seller agreed to exchange something at a future date at a price agreed upon today. For example, a farmer may agree to sell corn to a food processor at $5 a bushel in three months' time. If, when that time comes, corn is trading at $4, the farmer wins: he sells his corn for more than he otherwise could. If it's trading at $6, the processor wins: it buys corn for less than it otherwise would. That such a trade has a winner or loser does not make it a zero-sum game, because both farmer and food processor get something valuable: the certainty of what corn will cost in three months' time. This makes it easier, and less stressful, to plan. Swaps are similar to forwards, and futures are forwards traded on a public exchange. There is evidence of forward-like arrangements dating back three thousand years. The forerunners of listed futures date to the 1840s, which, starting in the 1970s, became the basis for a vast new financial market for managing risks related to currencies and interest rates.

The next big innovation was the option. This is a contract that gives the holder the right, but not the obligation, to buy or sell some underlying asset or commodity at a particular "strike" price. For example, a farmer may buy an option giving him the right to sell corn at $5 per bushel anytime in the next three months. If corn drops to $4, he's protected. If it rises to $6, he can still sell at that higher price. Options function much like traditional insurance. The option seller acts just like an insurance company, taking on the risk of an adverse move in the markets in return for a premium. Options date to the 1500s, and in the 1970s listed options on stocks, stock indexes, interest rates, and currencies took off.

Futures, swaps, and options make it possible for an investor or a market participant to manage a vast array of market movements. Since financial markets are by their nature quite volatile, this has potentially endless applications. These instruments also make possible things that ordinary insurance doesn't allow. For example, you can't buy insurance against someone else's house burning down. But you can buy financial insurance against the decline in value of a stock you don't own. Moreover, with ordinary insurance, you can't generally get back more than you put at risk. But finance doesn't require deductibles or copays. You can get back everything you've insured, and more.

Hayne Leland, a professor at the University of California at Berkeley, was among the first to hit upon the potential use of options as a form of insurance. In the mid-1970s his brother, who worked in the investment business, told him that many pension funds that had dumped equities during the bear market of 1973–74 and then missed the subsequent rally might be tempted to return to stocks if they could protect their holdings against another drop. Financial options were new at the time, and it occurred to Leland that they could be used to provide that sort of insurance. But whereas regular insurance generally worked for uncorrelated risks, such as fire and death, stocks were highly correlated: they tended to go up and down together. This meant that the seller of that sort of insurance couldn't rely on the premiums earned on stocks that didn't go down to make up for losses on those that did. He needed a way to protect against the entire market going up or down.

Around this time, Myron Scholes and Fischer Black, two academic economists, had devised a formula for valuing options. The formula contains several principal elements: the asset's current price, the option's strike price, the time until the option expires, interest rates, and volatility. These conditions help determine the premium you must pay an option seller. The formula can also be reversed: if you know the premium, you can figure out how volatile the stock is assumed to be.

Options dealers use this formula to "dynamically" hedge themselves. If they promise to buy a stock at a set price no matter how low the price goes, they then sell a bit of the stock short. (A short position goes up in value as the stock goes down.) As the stock falls further, raising the odds of them having to pay up, they short more stock. That negative bet against the stock protects against the cost of making good on the contract.

Leland didn't know much about options, but his colleague at Berkeley, Mark Rubinstein—a finance professor who also traded options on the floor of the Pacific Stock Exchange—did. Together, the two deduced that the owner of a portfolio of stocks could dynamically hedge by switching from stocks to Treasury bills as the market declined, and back as it rose. In 1980 they were joined by John O'Brien to market the technique, and the three formed LOR in February 1981.

As portfolio insurance caught on, they switched from using Treasury bills and stocks to stock index futures, which are contracts that track all the stocks in a popular index such as the S&P 500. One of the early criticisms was that portfolio insurance didn't just limit losses; it reduced gains as well, much as buying traditional insurance entailed a costly premium. LOR's response: shift more of your money out of lower-returning cash and bonds to more "aggressive" investments such as equities. Leland and Rubinstein argued this would enable pension, educational, and endowment funds to boost their returns by as much as two percentage points.

The pitch caught on. The Brady Commission later found that funds using portfolio insurance invested more of their portfolio in stocks than those without such insurance: "Many investors felt they had a safety net that enabled them to take greater risks and have a higher equity exposure than they may have normally accepted." By the eve of the October 1987 crash, $60 billion to $90 billion in stock assets were covered by portfolio insurance. Eleven of eighty pension funds surveyed used portfolio insurance. The popularity of this insurance thus made investors more comfortable about owning stocks, which contributed to the 44 percent run-up in stocks in the first seven months of 1987.

Portfolio insurance—indeed, all financial options—contained a potentially perverse feedback mechanism. As a stock's price falls, anyone who has sold insurance against such a fall sells some of the stock. As long as his selling is a small part of overall volume, the strategy works. It is thus dependent on abundant liquidity, that is, many buyers and sellers willing to trade at a given price. The illusion of infinite illiquidity is an example of the fallacy of composition, which Keynes had identified in *The General Theory of Employment, Interest and Money:* "There is no such thing as liquidity of investment for the community as a whole." When the selling is large, it exceeds available liquidity and forces the price down, which exacerbates the initial decline. Portfolio insurance thus worked when it was small. As it grew, it collided with the fallacy of composition. Many investors trying to use portfolio insurance could not avoid moving the market, as they did in dramatic fashion on October 19, 1987.

There are multiple explanations for what precipitated the crash, ranging from news of a growing trade deficit to proposed tax legislation to penalize leveraged buyouts. But once the market began to fall, portfolio insurance required investors to sell stock index futures, steepening the drop.

Portfolio insurers accounted for more than 40 percent of stock index futures selling. Stock indexes and stock index futures are supposed to be tightly coupled. Arbitrageurs can buy the future, sell the stocks, and capture a tidy, riskless profit while bringing the two markets back together, but the systems used to execute stock orders couldn't keep up with the order volume, causing the two markets to disconnect. Moreover, nosediving futures acted as a "billboard," signaling to any potential buyer that the entire market might be about to follow the futures down. And so they stayed out. In other words, because many investors were taking their cues from the level of prices themselves, the selling of portfolio insurers had an effect far beyond their immediate, direct impact on prices.

The result was a huge disconnect between futures and stocks themselves; at one point on October 20, the futures indicated that the Dow should be 19 percent lower than the actual market reached that day. The precise contribution of portfolio insurance to the 1987 crash remains in dispute, by Leland and Rubinstein, for example. Nonetheless, the crash taught an important lesson about insurance against financial catastrophes. It works when only a few people buy it; when everyone does, it not only makes the catastrophe more likely, it threatens the survival of the system.

This became apparent when, twenty years later, an almost identical problem erupted over the use of another financial innovation: credit default swaps, or CDSs. J.P. Morgan hit upon the idea of the credit default swap in 1994. As Gillian Tett recounts in her book *Fool's Gold*, Exxon (now Exxon Mobil) had asked for a $4.8 billion credit line to handle an expected fine for the *Exxon Valdez* oil spill. This was more than J.P. Morgan was comfortable committing to a single client, but it didn't want to say no, so it asked the European Bank for Reconstruction and Development to take on the credit risk of the loan in exchange for a fee. The loan remained on J.P. Morgan's books, but the firm now had an insurance policy against default. (The instrument gets its name from the fact that the two parties swap the risk of default and a premium.)

The popularity of CDSs grew, largely through J.P. Morgan's marketing prowess. Banks and their regulators saw potentially great value. If banks could use CDSs to reduce the risk of defaults, this would make them safer—and increase their lending capacity. In the 1990s, European regulators formalized this by permitting their banks to hold less capital if they reduced the risk of their loans by buying insurance that shared the risk of default with others. And here is where AIG saw its natural role. It already had plenty of experience insuring against all manner of other disasters; now it would insure European banks against the default of their clients. From their original role financing corporate loans, CDSs grew in popularity as a way of insuring mortgage-backed securities, and then as a way of making bets on such securities irrespective of whether the buyer owned any.

Just as flood and earthquake insurance enable more people to live in flood- or earthquake-prone regions, insurance against market disruptions enables more investors to pile into those markets and perversely make the event more likely and more severe. Portfolio insurance had enabled this with stocks in 1987, and now CDSs did the same with mortgages. As we learned earlier, AIG believed that the risk of selling insurance against default of mortgage-backed securities with the highest credit ratings was extremely small. However, because so many people could now take on additional risk thanks to the insurance that AIG (and others) were selling, those prior assumptions were wrong.

As with catastrophe risk, a long period without a housing or mortgage market collapse had made insurers willing to sell insurance against such an event for a very low price. In turn, the availability of this insurance emboldened more people to dive into the subprime-mortgage game. They could do this by actually owning mortgage-backed securities or simply betting on their direction by buying or selling a CDS that would pay out if an MBS defaulted (the owner of a CDS did not have to own the underlying asset). By mid-2007, there were CDS contracts in place covering $45 trillion worth of debt. AIG itself had sold more than $500 billion worth of CDSs. It was as if it sold a lot of earthquake insurance. And because it (and other insurers) didn't think an earthquake would happen, it sold that insurance too cheaply — which encouraged more people to buy it.

How do you protect yourself against catastrophe? Nassim Nicholas Taleb, a former derivatives trader, philosopher, and author, has argued that we should strive to be "antifragile," a word he came up with to describe people or things that "thrive and grow when exposed to volatility, randomness, disorder, and stressors." Many financial contracts "are antifragile: they are explicitly designed to benefit from market volatility." Options and credit default swaps, for example, go up in value when the underlying market becomes more volatile or default becomes more likely.

The catch, of course, is that the gain to the holder of the option, or the credit default swap, or the insurance policy, is a loss to the seller. If enough people buy such policies, a catastrophic loss will wipe out the insurers. And the more people who buy such insurance, the fewer will actually be protected in the event of a catastrophe. Idiosyncratic, or "micro," risks, are insurable, Taleb told me; systemic, "macro" risks are not: "As you go from micro to macro, you have the problem of having to buy insurance on the *Titanic* from someone on the *Titanic*." Not everyone, in other words, can be antifragile.

Goldman Sachs is a company that seems to embody antifragility. It has, over the years, earned a reputation for astute risk management and thrives when others are flailing, both in the financial and the nonfinancial realm. During a scare over the swine flu in 2009, eyebrows were raised when the firm's name appeared among the companies that had secured a supply of vaccine at the same time as major hospitals (only for high-risk employees, the company insisted). When Superstorm Sandy flooded most of lower Manhattan in 2012, the entrance to Goldman's downtown headquarters remained dry thanks to a wall of sandbags stockpiled several days ahead of the storm.

But much of what Goldman does to protect itself indirectly makes others less safe. This isn't a criticism of Goldman: it is merely acting in its shareholders' best interests. During the 1987 stock market crash, Goldman had advanced hundreds of millions of dollars to the Chicago Mercantile Exchange on behalf of customers to pay for losses on futures contracts, then waited with growing alarm as those customers' banks had yet to deliver the necessary funds to Goldman. The money did eventually come through, but some at Goldman felt it had erred by paying out to some customers' creditors before being paid by those customers, and that if the same situation rose again, it should not pay until it was paid. Naturally, such a policy would have made Goldman safer, but it would make everyone else a little bit less safe by forcing them to wait longer to get the money Goldman owed them. (It is not clear such a policy would have been practical; in any event, reforms to trade processing made it unnecessary.)

Goldman also resolved to survive any financial storm that would sink an ordinary bank. As the Bear Stearns collapse later showed, an otherwise healthy firm can implode if lenders pull their loans and clients withdraw their money en masse. Years before, Goldman made sure that it could not suffer such a fate. Burrow deep into Goldman's balance sheet and you will find an entry called "global core excess." This is a stash of highly liquid, supersafe securities such as government bonds and overnight cash deposits that can be instantly sold to meet immediate needs. Goldman prepares for worst-case scenarios such as "financial and political instability ... reputational damage, litigation, executive departure ... [and] no support from government funding facilities." As the firm explains: "The first days or weeks of a liquidity crisis are the most critical to a company's survival. . . . As a result of our policy to pre-fund liquidity that we estimate may be needed in a crisis, we hold more unencumbered securities and have larger debt balances than our businesses would otherwise require."

That stash amounted to $61 billion in 2007, and it was a key reason Goldman did not succumb, like Bear Stearns, to a run on its cash. By 2014 Goldman's emergency fund had grown to a staggering $183 billion. This is impeccable risk management from the point of view of Goldman but a problem from the point of view of the entire system. It poses the same problem as sovereign nations racking up trade surpluses and plowing the proceeds into government bonds of other countries. The supply of such supersafe, liquid securities is finite. By walling off some of that supply, Goldman indirectly forces everyone else to hold less, and to hold riskier paper instead. This strategy, in other words, works if only Goldman follows it, but not if everyone does.

Goldman protected itself from the subprime collapse in a similar way. It was a major player in the subprime frenzy, originating $100 billion in mortgage-backed securities and related collateralized debt obligations in 2006 and 2007. But at the end of 2006 it became nervous and decided to cut its exposure, and in early 2007 it switched to a short position, in other words a position that would go up in value if mortgage-backed securities fell.

A few years earlier, Goldman and several other banks spotted a problem in the mortgage market. If you held a big position in stocks, you could protect yourself against a drop with an option or a futures contract. No such instruments existed in subprime mortgages; the only way to protect yourself was to sell them. So in early 2006, Goldman and these other banks teamed up with a company called Markit to create the ABX, a series of indexes that tracked credit default swaps on groups of mortgages.

The ABX helped Goldman to shift its position in mortgages. Knowing how events unfolded, it's hard not to admire the firm's foresight in buying insurance against the coming catastrophe and pity those who sold it the insurance. By February 2007, as the ABX plunged, a Goldman executive wrote, "our profitable year was underway." But that profit came at the expense of those unfortunate enough to have sold it the insurance, among them AIG.

There was a wrinkle with the ABX. Just as stock index futures are a proxy for the underlying stocks, the ABX is a proxy for the actual mortgages. Mortgage-backed securities don't change hands very often, and as conditions got worse in 2007 and 2008 they changed hands even less. Thus, the principal indicator of their value was not the mortgages themselves, but the ABX — it was much like judging someone's looks based not on actually seeing him, but on someone's description of him. While in theory the derivative and the actual security should track each other, in practice the two could diverge. In the stock market crash of 1987, stock index futures fell far below the actual value of stocks because of heavy selling by portfolio insurers. In 2007 and 2008, the ABX disconnected from the underlying mortgages.

Goldman had bought insurance from AIG on $23 billion worth of mortgage-backed securities and collateralized debt obligations. In 2007 and again in 2008, it felt their value had declined enough to require AIG to pony up collateral, just as your broker can demand that you deposit cash in your margin account if your stocks go down. Goldman's demands were based in large part on the ABX. AIG thought Goldman put too low a value on the underlying securities and paid only part of the collateral that Goldman demanded.

Goldman's use of the ABX was logical, but that didn't mean the ABX was correct. In 2011, Nancy Wallace and Richard Stanton, two professors at the University of California, Berkeley, studied whether ABX was in fact a faithful representation of reality. By examining its price, they could back out of the defaults that investors supposedly expected on the underlying mortgages. They found that in June 2009, the index price was implying that 100 percent of the underlying loans would default; actual defaults turned out to be around 20 percent. They blamed this phenomenon on the same reason that earthquake insurance became so prohibitively expensive in 1996: it was based not on the likelihood of the event, but on the fear among insurers that they would be wiped out if that event were to happen.

By June 2008, AIG was in desperate straits. It was besieged by Goldman and other counterparties demanding cash to compensate for possible defaults on MBSs. The fact that it didn't think those defaults would happen didn't really matter. Customers could point to the ABX and demand that AIG post cash collateral to ensure that they would still get their money in the event that AIG went bankrupt. As the year progressed, the cash calls became bigger and bigger, and by September 16, AIG was no longer able to meet them and had to sell 79.9 percent of itself to the U.S. Treasury in exchange for a bailout.

Goldman realized that AIG could get into trouble, and as befits its culture decided to purchase insurance against such an eventuality: it had bought CDSs that would pay off if AIG defaulted. This is why it later claimed that it would have been fine even if the Fed had not rescued AIG. A glance at who sold Goldman the insurance suggests that those claims are questionable. On September 15, 2008, the day before AIG was rescued, Goldman had a net $1.7 billion of insurance against a default by AIG. But $170 million of that protection was provided by Lehman Brothers, which declared bankruptcy that day, and $402 million was from Citigroup, which itself would need a bailout two months later. Whether Goldman could have collected in a world struck by the financial equivalent of an earthquake was doubtful.

Goldman's astute risk management in 2007 and 2008, then, has a sobering message. It worked as long as only Goldman did it. Once enough firms did the same, the profits earned (or the losses avoided), thanks to their insurance, would bankrupt the insurers, which is what would have happened that fall if the federal government had not intervened.

The basic message of the Northridge earthquake, the 1987 stock market crash, and the 2008 subprime mortgage meltdown is that no system can insure itself against collapse.

In the past few decades, we have seen a growing number of natural and man-made events fall into this category. Even the deepest-pocketed insurers have their limits, as Warren Buffett discovered after 9/11.

Prior to 9/11, terrorist attacks were so rare that insurers didn't calculate their probability and simply included coverage for them with general property and liability coverage. After 9/11 insurers ended up paying out $32.5 billion in claims. As they did after the Northridge earthquake, insurers either withdrew or repriced policies in terms that put them out of reach. Prior to 9/11, the City of Chicago paid $125,000 for $750 million of war- and terrorism-related insurance for its two major airports, O'Hare and Midway. After 9/11, its policy was canceled and the city was told it would have to pay $7 million for just $150 million of coverage.

One of the most exposed insurers was General Re, one of Warren Buffett's companies. General Re, Buffett later said, broke one of his cardinal rules: it took on risks for which it was not paid. The entire industry had considered only the costs of known threats such as windstorm, fire, explosion, and earthquake. "All of us in the industry made a fundamental underwriting mistake," Buffett confessed, "by focusing on experience, rather than exposure, thereby assuming a huge terrorism risk for which we received no premium."

Buffett went on to predict that there were some terrorism risks the insurance industry could not absorb. "No one knows the probability of a nuclear detonation in a major metropolis this year ... [or] the probability in this year, or another, of deadly biological or chemical agents being introduced simultaneously (say, through ventilation systems) into multiple office buildings and manufacturing plants." Moreover, "the war against terrorism can never be won." A "close to worst case" scenario, he said, could do $1 trillion in damage: "Only the U.S. Government has the resources to absorb such a blow."

He certainly wasn't alone; one survey found that people put the likely number of terrorism-related deaths at anywhere from 33 to 35,000. And thus in 2002, the federal government became the official reinsurer against terrorism risk. In France, Germany, Britain, and Israel the government is also the reinsurers of terrorism risk. States too have stepped into the breach: in Florida, the state is the reinsurer for hurricane risk, as California is for earthquake risk.

The federal government's role as insurer of last resort is not a new one. Since the 1930s, it has assumed an ever greater role insuring its people not just against major catastrophes but smaller ones as well. Social Security was launched in 1935. Franklin Roosevelt, signing it into law, declared, "We can never insure one hundred percent of the population against one hundred percent of the hazards and vicissitudes of life, but we have tried to frame a law which will give some measure of protection to the average citizen and to his family against the loss of a job and against poverty-ridden old age."

Unemployment insurance came shortly afterward, disability insurance in 1956. In 1965 the federal government became the public health insurance backstop for the elderly and poor with Medicare and Medicaid, and in 2010 for the near-poor with the Affordable Care Act. Today, federal insurance extends to private pensions, crop losses, floods, mortgage defaults, and bank deposits. And this doesn't even include unofficial insurance: the prospect of federal disaster aid pouring into a county struck by floods, blizzards, or earthquakes, or the implicit promise of the federal government to dive in, as it did in 2008, to bail out the financial system rather than see it collapse.

What do Americans get in return for all that insurance? It is certainly not free. Someone, ultimately, must pay for the claims: the young, the healthy, the affluent, the solvent must subsidize the elderly, the sick and the poor, the bankrupt. And of course there's moral hazard: the tendency of insurance to dull the policyholder's incentive to avoid the peril he's insured against. This has emerged as the biggest preoccupation of governments around the world in the wake of the financial crisis: trying to find a way to expunge the moral hazard that multiple rescues of financial companies and even sovereign governments have created among investors.

Governments worry that with their bailouts, they have only encouraged the very activity that brought on the crisis—and will bring on the next. And thus they have put enormous effort into ensuring that no one gets insurance without paying a steep and debilitating price. Banks, for example, must hold more highly liquid securities so that the next time lenders yank their funds, they don't have to come to the Fed to borrow, as so many did, to the tune of more than $400 billion, in 2008 and 2009. In effect, banks must look more like Goldman Sachs with its "global core excess."

This may sound sensible at first, but think about it for a moment. Imagine arriving late one night at the train station and finding just one taxi left. You breathe a sigh of relief—until the taxi driver tells you that government regulations require that there always be at least one taxi at the station. What happens when the game across town lets out?

Similarly, if the government requires banks to hold gobs of liquid assets, they won't be available in a panic, when everyone really needs them. Requiring banks to have this liquidity is meant to make crises less likely. But when a crisis happens, the requirement could make it worse, if companies suddenly scramble for safety and find less of it available.

It would make more sense for the federal government to

acknowledge that it is the insurer against some catastrophes and to arrange to be paid appropriately for it. To be sure, it will lose money if politicians insist that the insurance be sold for less than its actuarial value—as it does with flood insurance and health insurance. But absent that, the government should be able to make money insuring against catastrophes, since, as we've seen, the private market so often gets the price wrong. In the late 1960s, riots in many big American cities prompted insurers to stop selling property insurance. So the federal government introduced the "riot reinsurance" program to offer reinsurance to property owners facing debilitating private premiums. Civil disturbances, however, never reached the expected levels, and the program turned a modest profit for the Treasury before eventually being discontinued for lack of private insurer participation. The federal government has yet to pay a claim on terrorism insurance. The Treasury reported a profit of $15 billion on its widely loathed Troubled Asset Relief Program. The Fed's profits were comparable. None of this means that the federal government should want to be in the insurance business; as Buffett says, in insurance, it can be years before you know whether you set the price correctly, and all surprises are unpleasant.

Still, insurance has benefits that go beyond money: it creates peace of mind. Freedom from fear may not have a price, but who would doubt it has value? A famous experiment involving government-funded health insurance made this point. At first glance, the experiment seemed to suggest that such insurance was a failure. In 2008 Oregon decided to reopen enrollment to an extended Medicaid program for adults below the poverty line, but since it had only enough money for ten thousand enrollees, it decided to hold a lottery for the slots among the ninety thousand who applied.

Amy Finkelstein, an economist at MIT, first heard about the plan on late night television: Stephen Colbert had labeled the lottery "Pick Sicks." But Finkelstein, a slim, intense woman with curly hair and spectacles, saw the natural experiment of a lifetime: an opportunity to compare the health of people with insurance to that of people without. She and her teammates tracked about twelve thousand lottery entrants—half winners, half losers—for the next two years. To their surprise, insurance appeared to make little difference to health: people on Medicaid went to the doctor more often and ran up bigger health bills, but Medicaid had no impact on their blood pressure, cholesterol, or glycated hemoglobin (an indicator of diabetes). With one exception: the incidence of depression dropped sharply for people on Medicaid, and by more than the use of antidepressants could explain.

The finding was a surprise, and Finkelstein was unsure how to account for it. She is an empiricist who wants the numbers to speak, but in this case she resorted to anecdotes from focus groups. The newly insured claim to be "less anxious, less stressed." Anxiety and depression, she notes, are not the same thing. But, I asked Finkelstein, could simply knowing that the next illness would not ruin them explain the reduced depression? "It's hard to quantify that. But that's a perfectly reasonable interpretation."

Can insurance make people happier? It's not as strange as it sounds. In a series of fascinating experiments, Orit E. Tykocinski, a psychologist in Israel, investigated the effect of insurance on people's perception of danger. In one experiment, commuters on a train were asked to estimate how likely they were to suffer a variety of misfortunes in the next five years. Half were asked beforehand if they had medical insurance; half were asked afterward. In fact, all of the respondents had insurance (Israel makes it available to everyone), but those reminded of the fact thought themselves less likely to suffer an illness in the next five years. In another experiment, respondents to a telephone interview were asked to rate the odds that Iran would attack Israel in the next three years, and that the attack would be with unconventional weapons. Before answering, half the respondents were asked if they had a gas mask; the other half were asked afterward. In fact, all of them had gas masks; the Israeli ministry of defense had distributed them in 2010. But those reminded of the fact rated both the probability of an attack, and the probability that it would involve unconventional weapons, as significantly lower. As Tykocinski pointed out, whether an individual possessed a gas mask could not have affected the odds of an attack, but the thought of the gas mask, like the presence of medical insurance, seemed to affect the respondent's mental state in a way that made the world seem less scary.

Unfortunately, comparable evidence of the effect of deposit insurance on the happiness of bank customers doesn't exist. And it's hard to find anyone happy, much less feeling safer, because the federal government bailed out a bunch of bankers in 2008 to save the country from another depression. The benefits of the government's role as insurer of last resort are hard to quantify, but they still matter. There is no question that in that role the federal government creates moral hazard and encourages some foolish risk taking. But by shielding businesses and individuals from the worst of riots, terrorist attacks, and financial crises, it also makes it possible for them to take some good risks, without which we'd all be worse off.

CHAPTER 10

"If you think you are dangerous, you are safe": Why Airplanes Hardly Ever Crash

If you regularly fly or read the news, you are aware of at least two things about aviation. First, disaster always lurks. A mechanical malfunction, a pilot's error, bad weather, or a terrorist can knock an airplane out of the sky and kill everyone aboard. Second, these things almost never happen. Flying is incredibly safe.

As Don Arendt, a veteran safety expert with the Federal Aviation Administration, told me: "Roaming around in the ozone layer in an aluminum tube in air you can't breathe that's sixty degrees below zero is not a safe thing to do. Yet we reliably do it millions of times around the world every day and bring everyone back to the ground in one piece."

This is, to say the least, remarkable. We have seen how hard it is to foolproof ourselves in so many other walks of life, from finance to football. If aviation can do it, can the rest of us? That depends on whether we are willing to respond to disaster the same way aviation does. A good place to start would be the terrifying voyage of British Airways Flight 9.

On June 24, 1982, Flight 9 took off from Kuala Lumpur at

around 8 p.m. local time. It was en route from London to Auckland, New Zealand, with 263 passengers and crew aboard. A few hours later, as the Boeing 747 approached the Indonesian island of Java, passengers and crew noticed something unusual. A sulfurous-smelling smoke had begun to fill the passenger cabin. First one, then in quick succession all four, engines surged, then flamed out. Seven miles above the Indian Ocean, Flight 9 was utterly without power. "Mayday, mayday, mayday," the crew radioed to air traffic control in Jakarta. "We have lost all four engines."

In the cabin, passengers prayed, cried, consoled one another, prepared to evacuate or prepared to die, as passenger Betty Tootell later recalled in an entertaining memoir. As the plane fell to thirteen thousand feet, the crew readied themselves to ditch in the Indian Ocean.

And then, abruptly, one of the engines restarted, and soon so did the other three. The plane resumed course for Jakarta. As it prepared to land, the crew realized that the windshield had been badly scratched by whatever they had encountered in the air. They guided the plane down by peering at the runway lights through a small clear strip of the windshield and manually checking their altitude.

In Jakarta, investigators examined the airplane and concluded that Flight 9 had flown into a cloud of ash spewed by Mount Galunggung, a volcano that had erupted the same night. Volcanic ash consists of sharp, tiny fragments of volcanic glass including feldspar, pyroxene, and quartz that can scratch windscreens, light covers, and fuselage and wing edges. It can also become heated in the superhot gases of jet engines and coat the fuel nozzles, combustors, and turbine blades, restricting the passage of air through the engine and causing it to surge, flame out, then stall.

Flight 9's miraculous survival garnered massive publicity, a medal of honor for its crew, and a television documentary. It also set in motion an urgent effort to prevent a repeat. Global regulators began putting together a series of recommendations on dealing with volcanic ash, spurred on by further incidents following eruptions of Alaska's Mount Redoubt in 1989 and the Philippines' Mount Pinatubo in 1992.

In 2001 aviation's global governing body, the International Civil Aviation Organization (ICAO), declared: "At present there are no agreed values of ash concentration which constitute a hazard to jet aircraft engines.... In view of this, the recommended procedure in the case of volcanic ash is...regardless of ash concentration—AVOID AVOID AVOID."

That zero-tolerance advice was in effect on April 14, 2010, when Iceland's Eyjafjallajokull erupted. It was not a particularly big eruption. But its location meant that its ash cloud would spread through some of the world's busiest airspace: the North Atlantic and all of Europe. Taking the ICAO's decade-old advice to heart, regulators in more than twenty countries closed three hundred airports and canceled one hundred thousand flights; ten million passengers were grounded.

The costs of the biggest disruption to European aviation since the Second World War were staggering. Tourists and business travelers canceled, altered, or postponed travel. BMW and Nissan temporarily suspended auto production at plants in Germany, Japan, and the United States because of a shortage of airfreighted parts. Three-quarters of Europe's imports of fresh-cut flowers come by air; the shutdown cost thousands of flower growers in Latin America and Africa jobs or wages. Stranded passengers spent an aggregate eight thousand years away from home and work. All told, a study commissioned by Airbus put the total cost to the global economy at $4.7 billion.

The shutdown achieved its goal: no plane crashed and no one died. Indeed, to date, there have been no deaths due to an encounter between a commercial jetliner and a volcanic ash cloud. The cost the aviation industry and its overseers were willing to shoulder to maintain that record flows directly from the fear that events such as Flight 9's incident over the Indian Ocean inspires. Shutting down swaths of the European economy to prevent the small possibility of an aircraft crashing because of volcanic ash may seem excessive. But not if that's what it takes to persuade people to fly. "The obsession with safety is part of the reason it's so phenomenally safe," says Arnold Barnett. "In that sense it's rational."

Barnett should know. He's probably the world's leading authority on the statistics of aviation safety. And for a long time, he was one of the roughly one-third of adults who is afraid of flying. I met Barnett one blustery March day at Boston's Logan Airport. Sixty-seven years old, he is tall with unkempt, thinning reddish-brown hair. Together we walked to the airport's outskirts, to the 9/11 Memorial, a striking glass cube etched with the names of the passengers and crew on the two airplanes that the terrorists hijacked after takeoff from Logan. The terrorist attacks created a lot of demand for Barnett's services, for example, calculating the probability of a bomb being smuggled on as luggage, and the most efficient way to minimize that risk. On the way, Barnett told me how he ended up in his unusual specialty. It wasn't, he assured me, from any childhood fascination with flight. He grew up in Brooklyn, and, like most people in the 1960s, seldom flew: the only time he heard about airplanes was when they crashed. He didn't fly for the first time until 1967, at age nineteen, and his maiden flight was not auspicious. There was an article in the *New York Times* that morning about a midair collision in Indiana. As the plane taxied away from the gate, he thought, "This isn't so bad." Only when the plane accelerated for takeoff did anxiety grip him. Barnett never stayed home out of fear of flying, but for years it was an unpleasant experience. Two days ahead of a planned flight, he would feel the anxiety build; on the day of departure, if the weather was bad, so was his anxiety.

Barnett studied math and eventually joined the faculty at MIT as an "applied probabilist," applying the rules of math and probability to public policy problems. He found probability both challenging and relaxing, forcing him to think logically and clearly about how events could happen. His interest in probability also provided a way to cope with his fear of flying by giving him a reason to investigate just how dangerous it was. Probability is cited all the time in aviation safety, but in Barnett's view, often incorrectly. For example, if one airline has two crashes and another has one, the first is often described as twice as dangerous. But they had three crashes between them, and it was impossible for each to have 1.5; one had to have twice as many as the other. This revealed nothing about their intrinsic safety: "It's as if you tossed a coin three times and got two heads and one tail, and said, 'It's not a fair coin because you got two heads for one tail.'" This matters, because the public tends to read enormous significance into the number of crashes in a given year or by a given airline, as if this represents a trend, when it really represents the random workings of probability.

He was also bothered by the use of death rate statistics. The death rate when a full airplane crashes is double that of a half-empty plane, yet the intrinsic safety of the two is the same. A good year for the industry, when more planes fly full, would have a higher death rate, even if the crash rate was the same. Then there's the oft-repeated maxim that it's safer per mile to fly than to drive. That, he notes, overlooks the fact that not every mile of a flight is equally safe: crashes occur more often around takeoff and landing, and seldom while cruising. So on shorter flights, when the plane spends more of its time ascending or descending, per-mile crash rates are higher. By contrast, crash rates don't vary much with the length of a car trip. That means, he concluded, that there must be some point at which a car trip becomes more dangerous than a flight. That point, when last he calculated it, falls at 150 miles. Trips less than that length are safer by car.

He was also initially suspicious of some of the comforting numbers the industry tossed around. Early on he read that the odds of dying on a flight were 1 in 200,000. But suppose, he says, you're a consultant who takes a round-trip per week. After thirty years, your odds of dying have risen to 1 in 67. "What looks like a very comforting statistic, if you think about it more carefully, is not all that comforting."

So, out of nothing more than personal interest and with no outside funding or encouragement, Barnett began the painstaking process of accumulating as much information as he could on flights, miles flown, passenger loads, and so on to come up with authoritative statistics. And he was pleasantly surprised by what he found: flying really is quite safe. And it has gotten steadily more so. Here are a few ways he has found of expressing that:

1. Over a lifetime, an average American is 1,330 times as likely to die in an auto accident as to die in a plane crash, based on the number of automobile fatalities and the risk of flying.

2. An American who flies to another city for hospital treatment is 20,000 times as likely to die because of a mistake at the hospital as on the flight there.

3. Even for the safest drivers, intercity travel is much safer by air than by car. For every hour that a safe driver saves because she flies rather than drives, there is a bonus: a seventy-eight-second increase in life expectancy tied to choosing the safer form of travel. (On a trip from Boston to Chicago, for example, a safe driver gains fifteen minutes in life expectancy by flying as well as saving twelve hours.)

4. A Massachusetts resident is 2.5 times as likely to win the jackpot in Megabucks as to perish on the next flight.
5. An American kid at the airport is as likely to grow up to be president as to perish on today's flight.

Barnett eventually lost his fear of flying. After a while, anxiety became boring. And the numbers were persuasive. Barnett would use his findings to calm nervous friends, colleagues, and even fellow passengers. He would experiment with different ways to convey his findings. Comparing the odds of dying to winning the lottery was not comforting: "When people buy lottery tickets, they hope to win the lottery. Here you are, juxtaposing their best hopes and worst fears." He came up with a better one: "If you could take a flight every single day, Saturday, Sunday, and holidays, you could fly for 28,000 years before succumbing to a crash. That surprises people. They think, 'I'm not going to live 28,000 years.' And people would start to be comforted. The funny thing is that, even if it's 28,000 years, for you it could be tomorrow. That taught me how people's reactions to statistics depend on how you present them."

Westerners also tend to think that stepping onto a plane operated by a developing country's airline is more dangerous. But except for truly poor countries, such as in much of Africa, it is not. Barnett has crunched the numbers and can tell you that you have a 1 in 16 million chance of dying if you board a plane from a middle-income country such as the Czech Republic, China, or Brazil, almost as low as boarding an affluent-country airliner, where the odds are just 1 in 18.3 million. The avalanche of media coverage that greeted the crash landing of an Asiana Airlines jet in San Francisco in 2013, which killed three people, dwelt on whether Korean culture interferes with communication in the cockpit. But, Barnett notes, Korean airlines had experienced no fatalities in the preceding four years. Even when the Asiana Airlines accident was included, that yielded odds of just 1 in 75 million of dying each time you boarded a Korean airliner.

As a traveler, I find this remarkable, and comforting. As an economist, I find it confounding. This is, after all, a fiercely competitive industry in which profit is a perpetually endangered species, bankruptcy routine, and pressure to cut costs relentless. How can aviation resist the temptation to cut corners on safety, overcome the Peltzman effect, and foolproof itself, where finance, sports, and automobile transport fail?

As I delved into the paradox of how something so dangerous can be so safe, I learned that it is not a paradox at all. If people are abnormally afraid of doing something, they will go to abnormal lengths to make themselves feel safe. One day Barnett got a call from a reporter writing about parents who take separate planes for fear of orphaning their children in a crash. Based on probability, Barnett knew the exercise was largely pointless. But, he told the reporter, "If it gives them peace of mind, let them do it. You shouldn't ridicule them." The reporter confessed that she was such a person.

Public wariness about flying was well founded in aviation's early days when it really was dangerous. In the 1920s, a pilot had a 1 to 2 percent chance of dying within a three-year span. After the First World War, a surplus of military airplanes found their way into the hands of gypsy fliers and barnstormers, who would tour the country performing stunts that often ended with the plane crashing and the pilot dying. In one memorable week in 1922, an aircraft buzzed a road in Long Island, causing a driver to lose control of his car and die in the subsequent crash; another plane, performing stunts over Far Rockaway Beach, crashed; and an army officer who had previously buzzed the crowd while Warren Harding dedicated the Lincoln Memorial crashed in Washington, killing a passenger.

Public perception that flying was only for the reckless was a serious impediment to the industry's development, as was the prohibitively expensive insurance caused by frequent accidents. "One of the severest handicaps to the normal development of transportation by air is the belief that it is extremely dangerous," the Manufacturers' Aircraft Association told Congress in 1921. Godfrey Cabot, president of the National Aeronautic Association, thought fear of flying was the chief deterrent to development, which he blamed on "ever-recurring accidents due to defective airplanes and incompetent pilots."

The industry could also observe an alternative model with a far superior safety record: the U.S. mail service, which used government-owned planes, government-employed pilots, strict criteria for pilot selection including medical exams, and regular aircraft overhauls that required employing four mechanics per plane. The postal service suffered one fatality per 789,000 miles flown compared to one per 13,500 miles for commercial fliers.

The result was something unusual in business history. As Herbert Hoover, then secretary of commerce, wrote to a congressman in 1921, "It is interesting to note that this is the only industry that favors having itself regulated by government." When a Senate committee held hearings on one air regulation measure, it was surprised that no one showed up to oppose it.

Federal oversight began in 1926 with the creation of the Aeronautics Branch of the Department of Commerce. It was replaced in 1938 by the Civil Aeronautics Authority, which regulated the airlines, and the Air Safety Board, which investigated accidents. The Federal Aviation Administration replaced the CAA in 1959, and in 1966 the National Transportation Safety Board took over accident investigations.

Fatalities steadily declined throughout this period. Even so, this was not enough to fully assuage the public's fear of flying. In 1969 Chauncey Starr, a nuclear scientist and dean of engineering at UCLA, sought to explain why people were more afraid of some activities than others. He compared the benefit of participating in an activity (in money or time saved) to how many people participated and estimated that between two activities with similar risk of death and similar benefit, far fewer people participated when they perceived the risk as involuntary, or beyond their control. He concluded that the public was willing to accept voluntary risks roughly 1,000 times greater than involuntary risks.

Starr compared commercial aviation directly to car travel and found that by the mid-1960s they had become similarly risky in terms of deaths per hour of exposure and yielded similar benefits, yet twenty times as many people drove as flew. He concluded that the perceived riskiness of air travel was holding back participation, and increased participation would "increase the pressure to reduce the risk," given the public's low regard for the benefits. He was right: airline fatality rates since the 1960s have fallen much further than automobile fatality rates.

It's not just absence of control that makes people afraid to fly. Recall the two axes of risk that Paul Slovic introduced us to. On that diagram, commercial aviation is less familiar and induces more dread than auto accidents. As flight has become routine, the fear of the unknown has receded. Nonetheless, flying still combines "all kinds of underlying complaints," Lucas van Gerwen, a Dutch psychotherapist specializing in fear of flying, told me: "Fear of heights. Claustrophobia. Loss of control. Social phobia. Fear of dying." News of a crash arouses dread in a person predisposed to think of flying as dangerous in the first place. "The year of 9/11," he said, "was a bad year for those who wanted to overcome fear of flying."

The economic harm of even an isolated accident makes aviation behave in ways that other businesses don't. Automakers routinely tout their performance on crash tests to sell cars, but airlines do not compete on safety or exploit one another's acci-

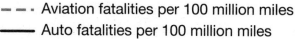

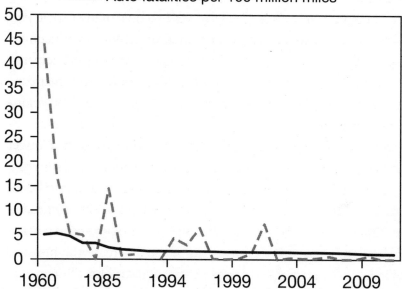

Since the 1960s, accident rates have fallen much further for aviation than for automobiles. (Source: U.S. Department of Transportation, Bureau of Transportation Statistics)

dents to improve their sales, for fear that calling attention to an accident will hurt all of them, not just the one airline. Indeed, insurers find it prohibitive to insure airlines against terrorism because of the risk that one airline's negligence (for example, handling baggage) causes another's airplane to blow up. Regulators use this mutual vulnerability to force other countries' airlines to shape up. After a string of accidents by foreign carriers in 2005 killed several hundred Europeans, the European Union created a blacklist of foreign carriers banned from European airspace because of noncompliance with international safety standards.

Aviation is a prototypical "high reliability organization," a term popularized by the organizational behavior experts Karl Weick and Kathleen Sutcliffe to describe organizations such as nuclear power plants, in which a mistake can lead to catastrophe.

One of the characteristics of a successful high reliability organization is "preoccupation with failure," which means being attentive to subtle signs of something going wrong and is sometimes described as "being a little bit scared all the time."

Aviation has practically institutionalized preoccupation with failure. For example, one evening in November 2013, a commercial airliner took off from Burlington, Vermont. As it ascended, the tower instructed it to turn left to get out of the way of two fighter jets taking off directly behind it. A trainee in the regional traffic control center then took over and told the airliner to set a course due south for a point designated HANAA, one of the five-letter codes controllers use for the thousands of invisible intersections in the sky. That should have steered it well away from the fighter jets. The airliner did not respond; it continued on a collision course with the fighters, even after the trainee again told the crew to proceed to HANAA. The plane was now less than four miles from the fighters and distance was closing rapidly; soon they would be just a few hundred feet apart. At that point the controllers ordered the crew to switch from instrument to visual control; they soon spotted the fighters. The airplane's captain and first officer then realized their error: instead of entering HANAA into their flight management system they had entered HANNA, which is near Australia, causing the plane to follow the wrong course.

The incident drew no public attention at the time. The reason it came to light was that the controllers and pilots, alarmed by the near miss, reported it themselves. Every day, more than two hundred of these self-reported incidents flow into a nondescript office building at Moffett Field, California, down the road from Google's headquarters. The office is leased by Booz Allen Hamilton, a consulting company on contract to the Aviation Safety Reporting System, a branch of NASA and probably the most important contributor to aviation safety you've never heard of.

ASRS traces its origins to a tragic accident in 1974, when a TWA jet approaching Dulles airport near Washington descended too quickly in cloudy weather and hit a mountaintop in Virginia. In the subsequent investigation, it emerged that just six weeks earlier, a United Airlines jet nearly crashed on the same approach to the same airport. The United pilots had shared the information with their colleagues, but not with the wider world. "Industry and government came together and said, 'We have to quit going to the scene of the accident to find out how it had happened,'" says Linda Connell, head of ASRS. "That was the first step towards the 'We're in this together' culture."

Connell trained as a psychologist and ended up specializing in human factors—the way the interaction between humans and technology causes mishaps. She is also a pilot. She passionately believes that the culture of how mistakes are dealt with is critical to safety. In aviation, the fear of disaster is a powerful motivator, she says, quoting a Japanese peer: "If you think you are safe, you are dangerous. If you think you are dangerous, you are safe."

Near-miss reporting is qualitatively different from accident reporting. Since by definition no accident occurred, it is free of "hindsight bias," the tendency to assume a certain explanation since you already know the outcome. Near misses also occur much more frequently than accidents and thus are more likely to generate patterns worthy of action.

Anonymity is central to the system; incident reporters need to know their candor will not get them disciplined or sued. Thus, every report that comes into ASRS is examined by at least two investigators, who are usually retired pilots or controllers. If necessary, they may phone the reporter on a confidential line for more information. After the reports are taken, all identifying information is destroyed. In the middle of the office stands a padlocked garbage can marked "Secure burn only." In describing an incident, staff deliberately blur details to limit their usefulness in litigation.

When a report suggests that remedial action is necessary, Connell sends a memo to the FAA or any other entity with an interest in a recommended course of action. That's all she can do: the recipients can accept or ignore the advice. ASRS has received several reports of five-letter destination codes being entered incorrectly because of their similarity and has alerted the air traffic control centers in question. Some have agreed to change them; others have not.

In this age of big data, ASRS is defiantly analog; all incidents are reported in narrative form so that readers get a real sense of what happened and why. ASRS highlights the most interesting reports in a monthly newsletter, "Callback," available to anyone on the Internet. If you are afraid of flying, don't read them. The reports can be hair-raising, all the more so for their candor: "When you consider the congested airspace in that area, it's critical that you don't turn the wrong way after takeoff, but that's exactly what we did. Why we did that, I don't know," reads one. Another pilot described how he was showing his iPad to another pilot and taxied past the spot where he was supposed to stop on the runway "until Ground said, 'Stop. Stop!' I would never dream of texting on my phone while driving, but wasn't this sort of the same thing?"

Most companies are reluctant to admit to mistakes that compromise safety for fear of driving away customers, inviting regulatory punishment, triggering a lawsuit, or helping their competitors. Airlines share all these concerns, but they are trumped by an even bigger concern: that an accident will scare the flying public and hurt them all. They have thus found unique ways to cooperate, and one is to constantly remind each other of how accidents can happen by voluntarily reporting them.

Other industries have sought to emulate aviation's system of blameless incident reporting. Hospitals and other health care providers have for decades toyed with systems for reporting medical errors. They have had only limited success. Errors are much harder to classify in medical settings, the sheer volume entails more time and cost in collecting and analyzing the data, and the sources of most medical errors are actually known: the bigger problem is preventing knowable errors. Charles Billings, the creator of ASRS, has argued that the biggest obstacle an industry faces in adopting such a system is the extent to which it thinks the problems merit attention. There is more consensus on the origins of many medical errors than on whether they happen frequently enough to merit the attention needed to eliminate them entirely. Finally, ASRS works because pilots really believe, and have seen, that it is used to make aviation safer, not to apportion blame or discipline pilots. In medicine, as in so many other fields, confessions of error often lead to litigation or even prosecution, which chills any inclination to fess up.

For airlines, bracing for cancellations in the wake of any well-publicized accident became over time a fact of life, known as the "book-away" phenomenon. Studies have indeed found that airline share prices, profits, and traffic decline after accidents, though the impact is usually transitory. In the weeks after a United Airlines DC-10 crashed in Sioux City, Iowa, in 1989, killing 111 people, bookings on other flights using DC-10s fell about 30 percent, Barnett and his coauthors found in one study. Within a few months booking was almost back to normal. More intriguingly, a study of twenty-six accidents involving domestic Taiwanese airlines between 1981 and 2000 found that the airline involved in the accident suffered a 22 percent drop in monthly traffic right after the accident, while all other airlines' traffic fell 6 percent.

Whether or not the collective damage of an accident is sufficient to change airlines' behavior, regulators do not hesitate to exploit it to justify increased safety measures. Arnold Barnett has helped them. A few years ago international regulators became concerned that aircraft flying over the North Atlantic were too far from any air traffic control tower to be visible on radar. Tracking their location required reliance on pilots reporting their location. To minimize the risk of collision, they proposed that all aircraft flying the North Atlantic install equipment to report their location in real time, with the goal of reducing a midair collision. Airlines blanched at the cost: $1.5 billion over eighteen years, or $1.1 billion in discounted current dollars.

To help make the case, ICAO asked Barnett to conduct a cost-benefit analysis. Barnett calculated that a collision between two jets that killed 417 people would incur costs of $1.7 billion in fatalities (assigning a value of $6.2 million per life) and $50 million for the aircraft. The odds of such a collision were minuscule, amounting to one fatality per 10 million flight hours, or half a collision from 2014 to 2028. The data link would cut those odds even further, to just 0.05 collisions over the same time frame. Thus, savings from avoiding half a collision amounted to some $900 million — still not enough to justify the cost.

"But then we said, 'What if there were a midair collision over the mid-Atlantic with two wide-bodied airplanes?' It's hard to imagine that would have no effect on flying. Someone thinking about flying to Paris, and told there was no air traffic control over the North Atlantic, maybe they'll say, Why don't we go to Montreal instead to have the French meal?"

Barnett reckoned that in the event of such a collision, revenue would drop $1 billion, or 2 percent, which, he told the airlines, was conservative, because it assumed that the collision wouldn't hurt traffic on domestic flights, and the impact would last only a year. With that revenue loss added in, the technology's benefits now exceeded its costs. "The airlines were willing to buy that argument," Barnett says. He sounds almost sheepish in describing the assumptions he made to get his results. Of course, the loss wasn't zero; still, "coming up with a dollar value is equally speculative."

Stalin supposedly said that one death is a tragedy, a million is a statistic. That's not a bad analogy for our attitude toward accidents involving airplanes versus cars. Though airplanes crash much less often, the publicity they attract elevates each to the status of a disaster. Cars crash daily, and the sheer number numbs the mind. The same distinction carries over to accidents investigations. Aviation regulators have a morbid joke: "We regulate by counting tombstones." It takes an accident to advance the cause of safety. To be sure, it would be better to figure out how to prevent accidents before they happen, but you can accomplish a lot by examining every accident. This becomes readily apparent when you compare aviation to driving.

The National Highway Transportation Safety Administration receives some fifty thousand complaints a year. It can't investigate them all. Instead, it looks for trends in the mass of data. For example, NHTSA learned in 2005 that a woman had died when her Chevrolet Cobalt crashed and the air bag did not deploy. In 2007 the agency took a closer look; it found many reports of air bags in small General Motors cars failing to deploy; it also found that the same thing often happened in other manufacturers' models. Indeed, the agency concluded that nondeployment of air bags didn't happen in GM cars any more often than in vehicles made by GM's competition, so it declined to open a formal investigation. Only later did the agency learn that in the GM models the ignition had a tendency to shut off too easily if, for example, there were heavy objects attached to the key ring. That would deactivate the air bags, leaving the passenger vulnerable in the event of an accident.

By contrast, airplane accidents have always drawn intense public attention and corresponding demands for a government response. When a plane crashed in 1931 killing all its passengers, including the famed football coach Knute Rockne, the accident aroused widespread public demand for tougher regulation; football fans argued that air carriers should carry parachutes.

By law, the National Transportation Safety Board must investigate every commercial aviation accident, a mandate not extended to automobiles, rail, or any other mode of transport. There is no preset limit to how long, or how involved, an investigation will be. While airline regulators do not officially aim for zero accidents, that is how they behave, given the intensive attention given to every accident. This is one reason why aviation's success is difficult to replicate in other realms. Financial regulators, for example, not only accept that some banks fail; they consider it necessary. Bank regulators do not conduct post mortems of every failed bank to figure out how to avoid a repetition. And bankers generally do not share notes with their competitors on how to avoid making bad loans or otherwise endangering the survival of the bank. Doing so may only help their competitors, or, worse, invite a lawsuit or a fine.

As Alan Greenspan was fond of saying, "The optimal failure rate in banking is not zero. If we did not permit risk-taking, and therefore the possibility of failure, the banking system would not be in a position to foster economic growth." Aviation regulators suffer no such ambivalence about the optimal number of plane crashes: it's zero.

The people who operate and fly airplanes are not inherently more cautious than those who drive cars or manage banks. What sets them apart is the environment in which they operate. Pilots take more chances when they fly by themselves than when they fly with hundreds of passengers. One morning in 1986, William Bain, a commercial pilot for Eastern Airlines, was flying his own plane, a twin-engine Piper Apache, to Tampa in order to board a commercial flight that he would then pilot to New Jersey. It was foggy that morning and air traffic control advised him not to land. Bain aborted one landing, then returned for a second attempt and somehow landed on a taxiway instead of a runway. He collided head-on with a 727 waiting to take off. He died, and several passengers on the 727 were injured during the evacuation. Quite simply, he would not have been permitted to take those chances had he been flying his commercial jet.

Larry D'Oench, a retired pilot and aviation consultant, neatly explains what a driver would experience if held to the same standards as commercial pilots:

> To emulate the airline industry drivers would need to have a physical every six months from a designated examiner, attend a one- to three-day ground school every six to nine months and at the same time successfully complete simulator training in normal, abnormal and emergency procedures, put up with an in-car checkride annually from their company or designated sponsor, and be at risk for a random driving exam from the state police. Furthermore, all drivers would be banned starting at age 65. Cars would have a vehicle proximity warning device, intersections would generally be controlled by a human coordinator backed up by state of the art electronic tracking equipment, speed limits (yes, airplanes have speed limits) would be strictly enforced, and violating any of the above could mean loss of your job.

General aviation, a category that includes private pilots who don't carry paying passengers, operates under much more relaxed criteria, so it's not surprising that such aircraft crash much more often and kill more people. Indeed, general aviation accounts for 91 percent of the fatalities in aviation in the past decade, and the death rate per hour flown is about sixteen times higher in general than in commercial aviation. The stunning improvement in commercial aviation safety is largely absent in general aviation, where the number of fatalities has declined by less than that for automobiles since the early 1990s.

Aircraft manufacturers, meanwhile, have used technology to eliminate bad luck and human error as threats to flight. Aircraft at risk of colliding talk to one another to prompt evasive action. Computers that detect wind shear, a dangerous weather formation, automatically fly the aircraft around it. Until the 1970s, pilots usually used controls that were mechanically or hydraulically linked to surfaces such as flaps and ailerons. Thereafter, pilot instructions were routed by wires to computers that relayed those instructions to the control surfaces. Fly-by-wire, as this became known, enables the plane's computer to notice if the pilot is entering a command that could endanger the aircraft, and either alert or override him.

In 1984 Airbus launched the A320, the first aircraft to fully incorporate fly-by-wire. Airbus engineers had designed into it "flight envelope" protection. The envelope is the overall range of positions in which the aircraft can operate safely. An aircraft that banks too hard, dives too sharply, or climbs too steeply has left its flight envelope. The A320 contained several new protections to prevent a pilot from leaving that envelope. If the pilot pushed the stick to one side, the A320 would limit how much it banked to stop it from rolling over. If the pilot tried to pull the nose up too sharply, risking a stall, the computer would also intervene, either pushing the nose down to recover speed and thus lift, or adding thrust. In sum, the A320 was designed to neutralize the human factor.

Pilots have not always welcomed these advances, sometimes complaining that flying may be more dangerous if pilots are focused on adhering to rules rather than on flying the airplane. Indeed, there have been echoes of the Peltzman effect in aviation: pilots become complacent when they think their plane can't crash. On the evening of Sunday, May 31, 2009, an Airbus A330 with 228 passengers took off from Rio de Janeiro for Paris. A few hours into the flight (it was now early in the morning of June 1), it encountered thick clouds and thunderstorms, then abruptly disappeared. For two years, the plane remained missing and the cause of its crash a mystery. Investigators knew, for example, that icing on the plane may have interfered with the airspeed indicators, but this should not have caused it to crash.

Finally, with the help of robotic submarines, French investigators found the wreckage and retrieved the black box, and what they learned was sobering. As they suspected, ice had accumulated on the exterior of the aircraft, causing the tubes that track airspeed to ice up, meaning that the crew did not have accurate readings of the aircraft's speed. Loss of the airspeed indicators made it more difficult for the autopilot to fly the aircraft, so it shut off — leaving the pilots in charge. Shortly after the autopilot shut off, the crew took manual control and the copilot, for reasons that are still unclear, pulled back on the control stick to make the aircraft climb. Soon the computer began issuing loud warnings that the airplane was about to stall.

Under normal conditions the A330 would have ignored the copilot's command to climb so steeply, because that would stall the airplane. Indeed, the pilots had never trained for a stall at such high altitude. However, with the airspeed indicators not operating, the airplane's computer had lifted those restrictions (dubbed "alternate law"), permitting the pilot more discretion. If the copilot flying the aircraft didn't realize he was now operating under alternate law or understand its implications, he may have ignored the stall warning in the mistaken belief that the plane was not allowed to stall, and thus that the warning must have been spurious. "Airbus said their aircraft could never stall, so clearly pilots were not trained for this situation," a spokesman for the Air France pilots' union said.

The Air France accident raises a more fundamental challenge for aviation. Flying is now so safe that there are fewer opportunities for pilots, regulators, and others in the industry to learn from accidents. Aviation experts call this "the curse of ubiquitous normalcy." Since aviation safety advanced by counting tombstones, the lack of tombstones interferes with learning. Clearly, it's better to have fewer tombstones and less learning. But it means that efforts to increase safety are also, in some sense, flying blind. "Mistakes are cognitively useful," writes René Amalberti, a French doctor and former air force general. "An incident free system becomes mute." It is almost impossible to improve a system that never has an accident. In 2001 he noted there were about twenty million departures per year worldwide and an accident rate of one per million, i.e., on average twenty accidents per year. Suppose someone proposes an innovation that should cut accident risk by 50 percent, down to ten per year. Evaluating the innovation carries two risks: that it actually works, but a fluky spate of accidents will lead you to conclude that it doesn't; or that it doesn't work, but a fluky safe spell will lead you to conclude that it does. Amalberti reckons that you would have to wait just 2.3 years to correctly conclude that it does work. In reality, no imaginable innovation could cut the accident rate that much. So consider a more modest innovation that cuts the accident rate by 15 percent. It would now take thirty-two years to conclude, correctly, that the innovation worked.

This means that regulators are unlikely to know whether anything they propose now will have provable benefits; it also means that accidents will increasingly be of the truly mysterious, unimaginable variety—such as 9/11, and the disappearance of Malaysia Airlines 370 in 2014. A similar challenge faces those who wish to prevent another global financial crisis: such events happen rarely enough that solutions cannot be tested with any confidence. The solutions we think will work can be imposed, perhaps at enormous cost, and we will still be taken by surprise when something we didn't imagine arises.

Because changes in safety are harder to justify with empirical data, the industry also pushes back more, as the Eyjafjallajokull eruption demonstrated. By day four of the groundings, passenger patience was running out and airlines began pestering regulators to reopen the skies. Several airlines sent test flights into the cloud and regulators concluded that it was safe to fly at relatively low concentrations of ash. Soon airports were reopening across Europe. In the aftermath, airlines and national regulators gained more flexibility in how they respond to volcanic ash.

Aviation also has a more compelling argument against tightening safety even further: just as raising the cost of nuclear power in pursuit of total safety condemns more people to death from fossil fuels, raising the cost or inconvenience of flight puts more lives at risk on the highways. In 1989 United Airlines Flight 232 had just taken off from Denver when an engine exploded, severing the hydraulic lines that enabled the pilots to control the aircraft. Jan Brown Lohr, the chief flight attendant, later told Congress the heartbreaking story of how, while preparing passengers for a crash landing, she instructed parents with children on their laps to place them on the cabin floor, to give them more time to brace themselves and their children against impact. The plane stayed aloft for forty more minutes before crash-landing in Sioux City, Iowa. It skidded into a cornfield, broke into four pieces, and caught fire. One mother tried to return to retrieve her twenty-two-month-old son from the burning wreckage; Lohr blocked her. The mother "looked up at me and said, 'You told me to put my baby on the floor, and I did, and he's gone.' My first thought was, 'I'll have to live with this for the rest of my life.' I then replied, 'That was the best thing to do.' That was all we had. Evan [the child] was killed."

Lohr became a vocal and impassioned campaigner for requiring all children on airplanes to have their own seats. She had a powerful ally: in 1990 the National Transportation Safety Board recommended that child restraints be mandatory. Many in Congress agreed. The American Academy of Pediatrics in 2001 decided to endorse the infant seat proposal. That drew the attention of Thomas Newman, a pediatrician and specialist in biostatistics at the University of California at San Francisco. Newman wanted the academy to base its positions on evidence, and he hadn't seen any to support the regulation. So he and two colleagues sat down to calculate the proposal's costs. When he read Lohr's testimony, "I was close to tears," he later wrote. "I began to wonder whether to continue writing my scientific paper on the costs and benefits of the proposed regulation." As Newman later told me, "When someone tells a story like that, you want to be on their side. You want to help. These are actual human beings. The statistical ones who might waste their money on a plane ticket or end up driving? I'm never going to meet them." But he pressed ahead, and concluded that the cost per death prevented was a staggering $1.3 billion.

Is a child's life worth $1.3 billion? That's the wrong question. The life of any child is priceless. The right question is, If society is to devote $1.3 billion to saving lives, what is the most efficient way to do it? And there are countless ways to spend such a sum and save far more lives, as David Bishai, an expert in public health economics at Johns Hopkins University, noted in an editorial accompanying Newman's article. They include reducing the risk of death by drowning, suffocating, choking, poisoning, or riding in a car, all of which empirically pose greater risks to children than does flying on an airplane. If society chooses not to spend that money, then its insistence on spending it to save one life in aviation reflects emotion, not rational calculation.

There was another cost. When the FAA studied the proposal, it concluded that the measure would prevent five aviation deaths over a decade. But raising the cost of a flight would prompt many families to drive rather than fly, causing an additional eighty-two road deaths. One congressman took the FAA to task for its "ghoulish cost/benefit ratio." So did Ralph Nader. The FAA's decision, he and a coauthor wrote, "protects theoretical children driving in cars at the expense of real flesh-and-blood infants whose safety is unquestionably compromised when flown as a lap-baby." To date, the FAA has remained steadfast in its refusal to require child seats, even while recommending that parents use them. How long it will hold out is anyone's guess; advocates, including the NTSB and Lohr, continue to press for the change.

While cost-benefit analysis won in that instance, it has not in another. After 9/11, a new federal agency, the Transportation Security Administration, was created to take over airport security screening from private companies. Passengers must submit to full body scans, surrender their pocket knives, remove their shoes, surrender liquids, and sometimes miss their flight if they're unfortunate enough to share the name of someone on the terrorist watch list. The cost is staggering. Beyond the $5.60 per trip direct fee, one study put the value of added travel time due to security at $25 billion in 2005. Another study put the cost of the federal air marshal program at $180 million per life saved. Even that may not be a comprehensive accounting. The increased cost, inconvenience, and fear induced by the attacks encouraged some people to drive rather than fly. One researcher found that increased traffic following 9/11 could explain 353 additional road deaths, more than the 266 who died on the hijacked airplanes.

No one knows how many, if any, terrorist attacks the added procedures may have averted. This makes it impossible to say with confidence that the price is too high, as the TSA discovered when in 2013 it proposed an ever-so-modest relaxation of the procedures: permitting passengers to take pocket knives with blades less than two inches long onto aircraft. As the agency's administrator, John Pistole, pointed out, hardened cockpit doors, watch lists, and passengers' readiness to tackle a would-be terrorist all meant that "a small pocket knife is simply not going to result in the catastrophic failure of an aircraft." Allowing the knives, he noted, would allow screeners to focus on more serious threats. But he ran into a wall of opposition from pilot, flight attendant and air marshal unions, and sympathetic legislators. One congressman perfectly captured the intolerance of risk in aviation by noting that there had been zero hijackings and violent attacks with sharp objects on airplanes since 9/11. "That begs the question, can that number get better? And the answer is no. It also begs the question of can that number get worse. And to my mind, the answer is yes." The TSA relented and postponed the change.

CHAPTER 11

A Foolproofer's Handbook: How to Make the Most of Our Best Instincts

Stability and safety have long been a central preoccupation of civilization; they are why our lives have gotten longer, healthier, and more prosperous. Yet we still periodically suffer devastating financial crises, costly natural disasters, and deadly accidents. When we look closely at the behavior that precedes these calamities, we discover that they are often the unintended consequence of our pursuit of safety. "Stability is destabilizing," is what Hyman Minsky concluded about the tendency of stability in the financial system and economy to breed complacency and, ultimately, instability. But it is true of much more than that. Everything we do to make ourselves feel safer brings with it the inherent danger of amplifying our appetite for risk taking, the possibility that we'll treat something dangerous as less dangerous, and the potential for panic when we discover we are wrong.

The world's twin financial crises were the product of this pursuit of safety. By defeating inflation, the Federal Reserve ushered in the Great Moderation, an era of subdued business cycles that made it safer to buy homes and take on debt with the help of financial innovations that made risk more manageable. Europe's leaders sought to abolish the currency crises and political tensions that threatened their unity by introducing a single currency. Both the United States and Europe were so successful that they unleashed massive booms in borrowing that ended in financial catastrophe.

The high cost of many of the natural disasters in recent years, so often blamed on climate change, are in fact more the product of our efforts to put cities, people, civilization, and wealth in nature's path, where they can be destroyed.

The pursuit of safety is usually effective. Most of what we do to stay safe works because it doesn't cause offsetting behavior. Washing our hands with ordinary soap does not cause germs to develop resistance, and teaching your child to look both ways before crossing the street does not increase the volume or speed of traffic. The challenge arises when making an activity safer changes people's behavior, offsetting some or all of the benefit. Sometimes this is because making an activity seem safer leads us to do more of it or do it more dangerously, the way antilock brakes and studded snow tires encourage us to drive in conditions when we might have stayed home or driven more slowly. Financial innovations such as mortgage-backed securities and derivatives allow an individual or a bank or a company to do something risky, then transfer some of the risk to someone else. The belief that they are now safer encourages them to take more risk, and so the level of aggregate risk in the system goes up.

Or it might cause the risky activity to migrate elsewhere. In the 1980s, fear of another banking crisis led to rules on banks being tightened. But that didn't change the demand for credit or the desire by investors and borrowers to buy houses or take on riskier investments. Consequently, lending and risk migrated to less regulated shadow banks. Public concern curtailed construction of new nuclear power plants in the 1970s and 1980s but not the need for electricity. So alternative generating sources had to be found, and many, such as natural gas and coal, are more dangerous for our health.

As individuals we are not expected to evaluate how others' behavior will change if everyone does what we do. We're hardwired to be selfish, to take the action that benefits us as individuals; we seldom have the foresight or the incentive to put ourselves at risk for the sake of making society safer. This is why antibiotic resistance has become a global scourge: a single doctor or parent is hard-pressed to compromise a patient's or child's health for the sake of people he or she has never met.

Insurance is a classic expression of this dilemma. It reduces risk for the person who buys the insurance policy while raising it for the person selling it. Insurance is usually a dull, profitable business because most risks are uncorrelated. Life insurance policyholders don't all die at once, and car insurance customers don't all crash at once. This axiom of risk pooling breaks down when risks are correlated, as they are for the worst disasters: when home prices fall in every part of the country at the same time or thousands of homeowners are hit by a hurricane or an earthquake simultaneously. That's when the survival of the insurance company is endangered and the protection the insurance buyers thought they had is illusory.

Saving is a form of insurance. Individuals save to guard against economic setbacks. Countries do the same by accumulating hoards of foreign currency reserves. But for one person to save, someone else must borrow. If a country as a whole saves too much, it pushes down interest rates and encourages another country to borrow more, producing debt-driven asset bubbles and financial crises. If interest rates are already as low as they can go, a decision by everybody to save more and spend less simply reduces everyone else's income and makes the country poorer. This is the paradox of thrift.

In the face of this irony, what should we do? Can we truly foolproof our surroundings if we so often cause more mischief in doing so? Or should we be ecologists and allow natural systems to take their course? At the end of this journey, I concluded that the answer is neither: we must reconcile the engineers with the ecologists. But how?

In praise of moral hazard

In search of an answer, I traveled to Cambridge, Massachusetts, one March morning in 2014 to meet with Larry Summers. Serving Bill Clinton in the 1990s and Barack Obama in the 2000s, Summers has dealt with some of the worst financial crises of the past quarter century. But because he favored less regulation of derivatives and banks in the 1990s, his adversaries lay some of the blame for the excesses that produced the crisis on him. They lobbied successfully to prevent him from being nominated to head the Federal Reserve.

Summers had now returned to teaching at Harvard, and I took a seat at the back of a lecture hall off Harvard Yard to hear him teach a class on the economics of crises. Though it was spring, it felt like winter, and many of the graduate students wore hats and jackets in the drafty lecture hall. Summers apologized for the weather, then turned to that day's topic: the International Monetary Fund and international crises, a subject he had been steeped in since the 1990s, when first Mexico, then East Asia, then Russia melted down. "Financial systems enable the mediation of capital between those who have put aside something for consumption in the future and people who have a productive use of those resources," Summers explained. "Those principles apply between individuals, companies, and countries. Sometimes, countries have difficulty paying the money back, and it becomes a panic, just like the game we played describing a bank run. Everyone wants to take their money out at once, and everybody can't take their money out at once. So there is a need to provide confidence."

Confidence is central to Summers's thinking about crises. We regard confidence as good and moral hazard as bad, but, he likes to note, they are two sides of the same coin. Moral hazard means encouraging us to take risks by protecting us from their consequences. We assume that's reprehensible, but it's not. By providing confidence, moral hazard enables society to do things and take risks that it otherwise wouldn't, many of which make us better off. To take a very basic example: money is central to a market economy because it makes it possible for people who don't know one another to do business. It can perform this function only so long as it commands confidence. If people do not believe money can be redeemed at face value, it becomes worthless and commerce grinds to a halt.

The evaporation of confidence can be immensely destructive. Financial panics begin when something people came to believe was 100 percent safe turns out not to be. In the nineteenth century, this happened when banks could no longer redeem their currencies with gold. In the twenty-first century, it happens when money market mutual funds can't redeem their shares for one dollar each, or top-rated mortgage-backed securities that are collateral for various IOUs default, or a too-big-to-fail bank fails, or a risk-free sovereign European government can't repay its debts. People who crave certainty cannot tolerate even a slight increase in uncertainty, and so they flee not just the bad banks, the bad paper, and the bad country, but everything that resembles them, just as in food panics, millions of pounds of safe food are discarded along with the tainted.

In the wake of the twenty-first century's twin crises, many reformers argue that the mistake was to let our sense of safety develop in the first place. With an ecologist's logic, they say that governments created moral hazard by bailing out bad banks and bad countries in the past; get rid of moral hazard, and you get rid of crises. This remedy has enormous intuitive appeal. It assigns us responsibility for our own safety and relieves society of having to pay for others' delusions. Yet it has a couple of problems. The first is that safety is a state of mind, not a statute. You can write laws that tell people their bank can fail, their money market fund may not pay back a dollar per share, their home is not insured if a nearby levee fails, or their uncooked food might carry dangerous pathogens. Yet this won't change their behavior if their experience tells them that banks never fail, money market funds always pay back a dollar, the levee always holds, and uncooked food never makes them sick. The second problem is that expunging moral hazard would also expunge confidence and all the beneficial risk taking that confidence enables.

The twin crises have caused us to learn some lessons too well and others not well enough. Even as central banks try to revive growth with zero interest rates and feed new financial bubbles in the process, there remains a shortage of confidence and thus borrowing by households and businesses. The German obsession with saving has gone global. Governments everywhere are trying to cut their deficits, corporations are accumulating huge amounts of cash, and emerging markets are stockpiling foreign reserves as protection against the next crisis.

Regulators have forced lenders to toughen their lending standards, hold more capital and highly liquid assets such as Treasury bills that could be sold in an emergency, and reduce their involvement in risky things like proprietary trading and derivatives. It's hard to feel sorry for banks, whose propensity for bad behavior, from mishandling foreclosures to manipulating interest rates, seems limitless. Still, the wave of regulation and litigation made banks more reluctant to lend at a time when the economy badly needed more credit.

Of course, we cannot endure a crisis and recession that cost the United States from $6 trillion to $14 trillion and do nothing. The question is, what can we do that won't make matters worse? That's what I wanted to ask Summers. Summers is an engineer: he is a vocal advocate of using the macroeconomic levers of government to control inflation and raise employment, yet his appreciation for how markets misbehave in ways economists can't explain resonates with ecologists.

In his office, we discussed the conference held some twenty-five years earlier at which he and Minsky both spoke on financial crises. He didn't recall meeting Minsky; still, he is philosophically on the same plane. In late 2006, on the eve of the crisis, he said, "We have nothing to fear but lack of fear itself." In spirit, this was the same as Minsky's aphorism that "stability is destabilizing." Years earlier, when he was Bill Clinton's Treasury secretary, he would make the same point from the opposite direction: "Complacency is a self-denying prophecy." If everyone worried about complacency, no one would succumb to it.

Doesn't this mean, I asked, that any system that succeeds in making us more confident and willing to take risks is also more likely to breed complacency, dampen fear, and eventually lead to disaster? Summers thought about this. "The jet makes things better, it connects things in better ways, but the crashes are more dramatic. If you never invented the jumbo jet, you could never have a crash that killed more than two hundred people. If you didn't have electricity, you couldn't have power failures. There's no question that having anything that has more connections creates more vulnerability."

That, he told me, is no "excuse for fatalism." To put it in economic terms: we must find a way to reduce the ratio of crisis to innovation.

The price of life and freedom

Economics is quite helpful in suggesting how to reduce that ratio because it displaces emotion with rational calculation. Decades ago, when the federal government was contemplating flood control projects, it would work out how much a new dam cost and what economic benefits would result. This practice gave birth to the discipline of cost-benefit analysis, which is now routinely applied to health, safety, and environmental regulation. For example, when fuel economy standards on cars are raised, the government must calculate both what consumers must pay for more efficient cars and the benefits of less fuel burned, less pollution, less greenhouse gases, and less time spent filling the gas tank.

When it comes to saving lives or preventing the occasional catastrophe, this gets tricky. Some costs, such as adding a new scrubber to a smokestack or hiring more bank supervisors, are easy to calculate. Some are more difficult: how much more do people drive—and thus how much more pollution do they create—when their cars get better mileage? Even harder to assess are the benefits. How many injuries, illnesses, or deaths are prevented? How much rarer have we made the next financial crisis or terrorist attack? How do we value those benefits?

Though it seems repugnant to put a price on human life, it happens all the time, when juries award damages for negligence resulting in death, when we decide how much life insurance to buy, when we consider whether to pay for that added safety feature on a car. Federal agencies, for example, typically put the value of a statistical life at $9 million. Would you pay $9 million to save your own life (assuming you had $9 million)? Of course you would. Now let me ask the question slightly differently: would you pay $9 to reduce the chance of death by one in one million? Quite possibly not. That's not surprising; though the economic value of both choices is the same, the first offers certainty and the second does not. Yet in real life you are much more likely to confront the second. Seldom are we offered a choice that, with 100 percent certainty, will save a life. Far more often our choices involve slight differences in tiny probabilities.

Cost-benefit analysis brings clarity and discipline to rule making, especially in subjects fraught with emotion. Bioethicists refer to the "rule of rescue," the urge to help those we see are in distress, even when the help might better be devoted to serving a larger, less visible population. The rule of rescue can lead to very bad decisions.

We have seen how aviation owes its safety to the extraordinary costs it is willing to impose on airlines and travelers—costs that might not pass a cost-benefit test, such as the $4.7 billion in lost commerce sustained to avoid volcanic ash over the North Atlantic. Yet even the aviation industry has its limits, as regulators have shown in their refusal to require that infants ride in seats—and rightly so. We owe it to ourselves to decide how safe we want to be through analysis, not emotion. Putting a price on human life helps us do that. It demonstrates, for example, how dangerous for our health it was to shut down nuclear power in the wake of the Fukushima accident.

There is another cost that foolproofers must consider when trying to make us safer: our loss of freedom. We really can limit danger and risk if we are willing to use rules, prohibitions, and jail time. This is one way around the Peltzman effect. If we worry that making an activity safer encourages more risk, ban the activity altogether. But then you have to weigh truly effective rules against our freedom to do things we want to do. We have seen, for example, how ineffective driver's education is at reducing accidents among novices. On the other hand, graduated driver licensing laws, which curtail the rights of young drivers to use cell phones, drive at night, or drive with more than a certain number of passengers, are very effective.

People are usually happier to limit the freedom of others, such as children, than they are to limit their own. Opponents of seat-belt laws often base their arguments on freedom, not health. Despite overwhelming evidence that they reduce deaths and injuries, mandatory motorcycle helmet laws have been repealed in many states, often in response to litigation branding such laws an infringement on motorcyclists' liberty and an unconstitutional exercise of police power. As one senator declared, "I have a hard time, philosophically, accepting that the role of the government is to tell us how to lead our lives."

The same tradeoff between safety and freedom applies to finance. The decades after 1934 are sometimes called "the quiet period" because they had no financial crises. The quiet period was quiet in part because financial freedom was tightly circumscribed. For years after the Second World War, many countries limited how much money residents could take in or out of the country or invest in another country's stocks and bonds. The purpose of these capital controls was to tamp down the big flows of money that made it harder to keep currencies pegged to one another, as the postwar monetary system required. They were also intended to force savers to fund investments at home by making it harder to seek better returns abroad. The strategy worked, but it was burdensome: for a while Britons couldn't take more than £100 when they traveled abroad, and Americans paid a tax when they bought foreign stocks and Treasury bills.

There were other restrictions. American banks had ceilings on the interest rates they could pay depositors and charge borrowers. Banks didn't mind, because they didn't have many competitors. They operated by the 3-6-3 rule: pay depositors 3 percent, lend at 6 percent, hit the golf course by 3 p.m. The heavy hand of government also routinely limited speculation. From the 1940s to the 1970s, the Federal Reserve, Congress, and the White House intermittently rationed credit to dampen demand for autos and other big-ticket items, and used higher down-payment require-ments to cool off the housing market.

Inflation, deregulation, and financial innovation brought the quiet period to an end. Savers chafed against the limits and econ-omists said they hurt growth. Capital controls force savers to accept inferior returns at home and deprive worthy investment projects of capital from abroad. They are also unfair: people with the right connections can usually find their way around them. And if legal detours aren't available, illegal ones, such as the black market, are.

By the 1970s, in wealthy countries, international capital con-trols had largely been dismantled and domestic controls on credit were heading the same way. As far back as 1952 bankers were vilifying credit controls as "a long step in the direction of Gov-ernment planning." By the 1970s, inflation was drawing savings from bank deposits to money market funds and eroding banks' comfortable monopoly over people's financial lives. In short, the era of repressed finance came to an end because we concluded that whatever benefits it was delivering in terms of reduced crises were not worth the loss of freedom.

We could have that financial system back again. All forms of lending and borrowing outside of regulated banks could be banned or severely restricted. Financial innovations such as money market funds and derivatives could be outlawed or taxed so heavily that no one would use them. Capital controls could be reintroduced. Down-payment requirements could be raised dra-matically for anyone interested in buying stocks or a house. Some economists have proposed the radical idea of forbidding banks to make loans at all; depositors' money would instead be invested in government bonds or cash.

Assume for a moment that this would work and that finan-ciers could not find a way around these new rules. Would we accept these limitations? The jury is in, and the answer is no.

Americans are content to slap controls on bankers but not on themselves. Consider, for example, that after the crisis, regulators considered requiring a 20 percent down payment for most mortgages. This would have guaranteed less severe housing busts, because home prices would have to fall 20 percent before the home was no longer worth more than the mortgage. But bankers, home builders, and consumer advocates, who are normally at one another's throats, united against the idea, complaining (correctly) that it would lock millions of potential buyers out of the housing market. The regulators backed down. For many aspiring homeowners, leverage equals freedom.

How space saves us

If we are going to erect rules and barriers, they should limit the damage of risk taking with as few unintended consequences as possible. As I explored our efforts to create safety, I discovered one remedy that seems to work everywhere: space.

For example, when I asked Adrian Lund of the Insurance Institute for Highway Safety why aviation has had more success reducing accidents than automobiles have, his answer surprised me: "In aviation . . . it's an easier problem to deal with. Most of the time you are flying in open air and need basic rules that you're not impinging on other aircraft. But when you're driving a car, almost all the time you're at some risk, unless you're stopped still, at a stop sign or a traffic light, and even then at risk to someone hitting from behind."

Think about it: when you're driving on an undivided highway, you will frequently pass other cars and trucks at a combined speed of one hundred miles per hour, separated by ten feet. One minor error—you hit ice, an animal runs onto the road, you're distracted by your cell phone—and within seconds you drive off the road or into the path of an oncoming car.

Fatal Accidents and Onboard Fatalities by Phase of Flight
Worldwide Commercial Jet Feet | 2004 through 2013

Percentage of fatal accidents and onboard fatalities

	Taxi, load/ unload, parked, tow	Takeoff	Initial climb	Climb (flaps up)	Cruise	Descent	Initial approach	Final approach	Landing
							14%		47%
Fatal accidents	10%	8%	6%	8%	10%	3%	8%	22%	25%
Onboard fatalities	0%	7%	3%	12%	20%	3%	15%	22%	18%
Exposure (Percentage of flight time estimated for a 1.5 hour flight)		1%	1%	14%	57%	11%	12%	3%	1%

Note: Percentages may not sum precisely due to numerical rounding.

Aircraft are least likely to crash when they are at their highest altitude. (Diagram © 2014 Boeing)

The most dangerous part of a flight is when the aircraft is close to the ground. Takeoff, initial climb, the final approach and landing represent just 6 percent of a 1.5-hour flight but account for 61 percent of accidents (see the chart). Air traffic controllers call this the "big sky, little airplanes" principle: once at cruising altitude, aircraft are surrounded by space that provides a margin of error against the unexpected. Aircraft pilots and controllers observe strict rules of separation: aircraft are to remain a thousand feet apart vertically and three miles laterally. Think about this the next time you're at cruising altitude and are suddenly tossed about violently by turbulence: you might crack your skull against the ceiling if you're not belted in, but you're not going to crash. Because the ground is so far away, pilots can trade altitude for control by descending and reducing airspeed.

My wife is a stickler for space. Early in her driving career, she learned that keeping space around your car is one of the easiest ways to avoid a collision. I sometimes find her insistence on keeping as much distance as possible between us and the other cars on the road to be overkill. But there's no disputing her logic.

While driving next to a truck is sometimes unavoidable on a crowded highway, it leaves no margin for error if something goes wrong. While driving through France, I saw a sign posted on a freeway: *"La vitesse aggrave tout"* (*"Speed makes everything worse"*). The faster you're traveling, the quicker you'll use up your protective buffer of space (and the more violent will be your impact). I repeat that line to myself whenever I find myself exceeding the speed limit.

The rule of space translates to the natural world as well. In natural disaster management, space wins hands down as the most reliable protector of lives and property. In Australia homes that border the bush are supposed to maintain a perimeter of "defensible space" to keep nearby fires from burning houses. This leaves homeowners less dependent on fire suppression, which can take the lives of firefighters and lead to more dangerous conflagrations later.

Levees protect cities, farms, and factories from floodwater, but levees need constant maintenance, can fail, and can be overtopped. After the devastating Mississippi floods of 1927, Edgar Jadwin, chief engineer of the Army Corps, with the backing of Calvin Coolidge, undertook an examination of the causes. Jadwin had made his reputation building railways, docks, barracks, and hospitals in France for the U.S. Army in the First World War. He was also "pompous and aloof," as one historian put it, with little patience for his political overseers. Nonetheless, his diagnosis of the flooding problem was spot-on. Jadwin wrote in his report:

> The loss of life and property in the recent great flood in the alluvial valley followed the breaking of the levees which reclaimed the land for the use of man. This reclamation had been pushed so far that insufficient room was left in the river for the passage of the unprecedented vol-

ume of flood water. The levees must be strengthened, but a halt must be called on further material increase in their heights and the consequent threat to the inhabitants of the areas they are built to protect. Man must not try to restrict the Mississippi River too much in extreme floods. The river will break any plan which does this. It must have the room it needs.

Jadwin recommended the creation of a series of floodways—normally habitable land that would be allowed to flood to relieve pressure on the river. When floodwaters once again reached heights that threatened to top the levees, the Corps would blast holes in the levees and send the extra water into nearby flood-ways such as the Atchafalaya River Basin, bypassing New Orleans to the Gulf of Mexico. By deliberately flooding less populated farmland, the Jadwin plan would protect the cities and more pop-ulated centers along the river.

Jadwin's plan wasn't exactly a capitulation to the ecologists; it didn't renounce the Corps' responsibility for protecting human habitation on the floodplains. Yet it was still a radical break from the approach engineers had thus far favored, which involved meeting every challenge from the water with more and higher levees.

The Jadwin plan has helped reshape floodplain thinking ever since. The Dutch have been building levees for a millennium, and that long history has given rise to the expression "There are two types of levees: those that have failed, and those that will." That may be too fatalistic, and even the Dutch don't take it liter-ally; their gigantic dikes have been built to withstand "10,000-year" floods.

Still, after devastating floods in 1993 and 1995, the Dutch also rethought their commitment to levees and began to design their cities and countryside to let the floodwater in where it does the least harm. Room for the River is a nine-year project that involves demolishing dikes built decades, even centuries, ago so as to restore the natural floodplain in less populated areas upstream, relieving pressure on cities downstream. Throughout the United States, many cities are building parks and other green space next to rivers as foolproof flood defenses.

In the record floods of 2011, Jadwin's plan was tested; it passed. In the middle of a May night the Corps dynamited breaches in the levees in Missouri, flooding thousands of acres of farms but saving the town of Cairo, Illinois. Later that month it opened massive sluice gates and flooded huge swaths of Louisiana countryside, saving New Orleans from a repeat of the Katrina disaster.

The importance of space speaks to a more general principle: foolproof safety should work no matter the threat. Relying on the ability to anticipate and adjust to threats as they arise is a strategy prone to failure if the threats are by nature unexpected or unprecedented.

The financial and economic worlds have their equivalent of space: it's called capital. This is essentially the cushion of shareholder capital that is available to absorb losses. The higher the capital ratio, the more losses a bank or financial company can sustain without becoming insolvent. Unlike lenders or depositors, shareholders know their investment isn't safe and they don't panic if its value declines.

The beauty of capital is that it works no matter what causes the loss. Banks' risk management seeks to protect against adverse movements in financial prices, excessive exposure to particular borrowers, a counterparty reneging on a deal, rogue traders and criminals. Yet it regularly fails. In 2012, J.P. Morgan Chase & Co. learned that a trader nicknamed "the London whale" had taken on huge derivatives positions in what seemed to be a flawed attempt to hedge the bank's positions. The loss eventually grew to a staggering $6.2 billion. Yet the loss never threatened J.P. Morgan's survival, thanks to the billions of dollars in capital it already had, some of it raised under pressure by regulators.

Capital has, correctly, become the central tool in regulators' drive to reinforce the financial system against another crisis. Indeed, given enough capital, almost nothing else matters. Moreover, one bank having more capital does not make another less safe; there's no theoretical limit to how much capital banks can have. Of course, it's not flawless. More capital makes banks less profitable, because the same profit must be shared among more shareholders. This can put banks at a disadvantage and shift lending, and risk, to the shadows, as happened during the Great Moderation. Preventing such slippage requires constant vigilance.

Make the most of memory

That leads us to the final lesson of how to foolproof ourselves. As we have seen throughout this book, we often seek safety in response to fear, and fear is rooted in experience. The experience of crisis or disaster makes survivors more conscientious and risk averse. Houses built immediately after a hurricane are less likely to suffer damage in the next one.

Fear can be overrated; a life lived in fear is not a pleasant one. As Gordon Tullock, an economist, once remarked, you could make people drive quite safely by having a sharp dagger protrude from the center of the steering wheel. Moreover, experience is of limited help when disasters are rare. "One can be a particularly poor driver and never become involved in an auto accident," note Donald MacGregor and Paul Slovic.

Yet if applied systematically instead of spastically, fear and experience can be potent foolproofing tools. This is incisively illustrated by contrasting two oil companies: BP and Exxon

Mobil. The Deepwater Horizon had one of the best performance and safety records in BP's fleet of drilling rigs, a feat that several executives were studying on the rig the evening of April 20, 2010. That safety record was deceptive. Subsequent inquiries found that BP had a culture of cutting corners and sacrificing safety for speed. Engineers knew that the Macondo well was difficult to control but they kept trying rather than abandon it. That evening the well suffered a blowout and the escaping gas exploded, destroying the rig, killing eleven, and causing one of the worst oil spills in history.

In 1989, the supertanker *Exxon Valdez* ran aground in Prince William Sound, Alaska, spilling eleven million gallons of crude oil, soiling more than a thousand miles of coastline, and killing thousands of birds, otters, seals, and whales. The reputational and financial damage caused by that catastrophe was enormous. For years afterward the first word that people in focus groups thought of when they heard "Exxon" was "Valdez."

Exxon Mobil, as the company is now known, could have cleaned up, moved on, and allowed the bad memories to fade, but it didn't. It used the disaster to institute a culture of safety that is encapsulated in its Operations Integrity Management System, or OIMS, an eleven-point framework that governs every aspect of life at the massive company, from the accountability of managers to the construction of oil rigs and simulation of emergency drills.

Glenn Murray helped with the cleanup at Valdez and then was tasked with working on and teaching OIMS. OIMS is designed to maintain the culture of safety and risk management even as memories of Valdez fade. Sometimes at training sessions he will ask how many attendees were present when Valdez happened; each year fewer hands go up: "They weren't there through Valdez, and we don't want them to have to experience the emotional shock that something like that brings about."

Operating and maintenance procedures from the start until

the end of the day are governed by OIMS, from issuance of work permits to the type of clothing worn. Accidents are the focus of relentless postevent analysis, and employees are encouraged to report near misses so that, much as with ASRS in aviation, lessons can be learned before disaster occurs. Some sites have a "near miss of the month" contest, where the employee reporting the incident is acknowledged for praise. OIMS extends to the office: bee stings, paper cuts, and a finger prick from a stapler are all candidates for investigation. Employees admonish one another for taking stairs without using a handrail.

To outsiders, this borders on the ridiculous. Why waste time ensuring that employees use handrails? To Exxon Mobil, however, it's not ridiculous. People do get injured when not using handrails. More important, the program changes underlying attitudes about risk. Exxon Mobil employees won't tolerate things that many ordinary people will. They are encouraged to apply the lessons of OIMS at home, for example, to take more care when mowing the lawn, and to apply lessons at home to their work. One employee noted that he had phoned in to report an incorrect sign on a freeway ramp as a potential safety hazard. The company studies others' disasters; an entire team analyzed the breakup of the Columbia space shuttle in 2003 for lessons that could be applied to Exxon Mobil.

Drilling for oil, of course, is a dangerous business, and Exxon Mobil would not survive without taking some risks. It seeks, rather, to know what risks it is taking on and whether they can be managed. In 2005, it began to drill a well called Blackbeard, at the time the deepest in the Gulf of Mexico. The company had studied the risk of a blowout and how it could be mitigated. As drilling progressed, OIMS required that Exxon Mobil reassess risks with new data from the well. Its engineers became alarmed when they encountered immense pressure and temperature and a "kick"—a sudden surge of liquids and natural gas. Worried that such a surge could exceed its ability to contain a blowout, Exxon Mobil abandoned the well and the $187 million invested in it.

Many in the industry asked, in the wake of that decision, whether Exxon Mobil lacked guts. After the Deepwater Horizon disaster, the company's culture of caution looked much wiser. No one knows whether Exxon Mobil would have had a different experience with Macondo; what is clear is that Exxon Mobil's safety record is one of the industry's best and it remains immensely profitable. Exxon Mobil's approach to safety costs no one else anything, and the company happily shares its knowledge with its competitors.

A country can change its attitude toward risk just as a company can. Canada drew praise in the wake of the global financial crisis for the fact that none of its banks failed or needed bailouts; indeed, they emerged stronger than they had been, an important reason Canada's recession was much milder than that of the United States. This is often attributed to culture: the stereotype is that Canadians are more risk averse, less swashbuckling than Americans. There's some truth to this. I began my journalism career in Canada, and one reason I moved to the United States is that business and finance are more exciting here. There are spectacular successes and failures that can be brutal for companies' shareholders and employees, and that also make for amazing stories.

Yet the different experiences during the crisis are not all due to culture. Canadians are as susceptible to bubbles, fraudsters, and charlatans as Americans. Two small Canadian banks collapsed during the 1980s, and a crippling real estate depression laid many banks low in the early 1990s. Importantly, this left an imprint on both bankers and regulators.

In 1984 Ed Clark left a career in government to work in finance and in 1988 was hired to run a troubled trust company, which is similar to a bank. Its deposits were evaporating, and regulators were breathing down its neck. He soon sold the company to another trust company. That company collapsed a few years later under the weight of real estate loans gone bad and was sold to Toronto Dominion Bank for almost nothing. In the early 2000s Clark found himself running Toronto Dominion. The early 1990s "left a scar," Clark told me shortly after he retired in 2014. In the world of real estate, attitudes of both banks and clients changed. "Even the borrowers didn't ask the banks to do stupid things." To this day TD will not finance speculative construction, i.e., buildings with no tenants signed in advance.

TD had also joined the rush by banks around the world to buy or build securities dealers that made money from stocks, bonds, and derivatives rather than old-fashioned lending. By the early 2000s it was relatively successful; it was a major derivatives dealer in the United States. Clark learned that the securities business didn't just affect how banks made money, it affected their culture. Securities dealers have "a very entrepreneurial culture—a drive to make money—and therefore a focus on personal achievement and a willingness to push the limits." When Clark dug into the business, he got scared at how little top executives, both at TD and its competitors, understood about how securities dealers made money. It was, he said, a business built on taking tail risk: something highly unlikely and highly destructive. "I started to go through these products and said, 'These products have inherent in them huge risk.' Are derivatives good? Can hedging be good? Of course," says Clark, "but if behind all that someone tells you this only works if the world doesn't change significantly, I don't like that risk." And so, in 2005, TD exited the business of exotic derivatives based on stock indexes and interest rates.

After the wreckage of the financial crisis, TD's decision looked smart. But it would have been smart even without a financial crisis, because it reflected how much risk the organization was willing to tolerate — just as Exxon Mobil's decision to abandon Blackbeard was right even if the Deepwater Horizon hadn't exploded. "It's important to recognize that not all 'right' decisions will be profitable ones," Clark says.

The Canadian government absorbed the lessons of the 1980s and 1990s as well. It created an independent regulator that steadily pushed banks to raise their capital sooner than its foreign competitors did. Today, Canadian banks and their regulators have adopted conservatism as a competitive advantage over their foreign counterparts.

Canada, at the time of this writing, is in the throes of its own housing bubble, and regulators have been steadily tightening lending conditions such as on down payments, loan maturity, and the conditions borrowers must meet. Someday, Canada's housing bubble will burst, just as the bubble in the United States did. The hope is that in the process, it does not take down the financial system.

Foolproof safety is a moving target, with competing prescriptions from engineers and ecologists. Engineers satisfy our desire for control, for eliminating the anxiety that comes with uncertainty and the unknown. They fulfill civilization's need to act, to do something, to take the existing chaotic mess and make it better. Engineers have made car crashes more survivable, enabled people to live and prosper in treacherous places, and devised lifesaving medicine and technology. Economic engineers have figured out how to make recessions and financial crises less severe.

But we should not ask too much of them. We can make disaster and crisis less frequent and more survivable, but we won't end either. Nor should we want to. Periodic crisis is the price we pay for an economic system that encourages, and rewards, risk. Periodic disasters are the price we pay for situating our cities in desirable, productive places.

As ecologists know, forests, bacteria, and economies are irrepressibly adaptable. Every step we take to suppress the risks they present in the short term will provoke some other, offsetting step whose consequences will only show up in the long term. Our leaders naturally look to threats they have seen before and prepare for those, like the French generals waiting for the Nazis behind the Maginot Line. But it's the nature of risk to find the vulnerabilities we missed, to hit when least expected, to exploit the very trust in safety we so assiduously cultivate with all our protection and insurance.

The right tradeoff between risk and stability will maximize the units of innovation we get per unit of instability. It has taken us a century to learn that trying to put out every fire is a recipe for bigger, deadlier fires. The solution is not to let all fires burn, but to make it possible for small fires to burn without hurting people so that we save our resources for the big fires. To combat resistant bugs, we should not ban antibiotics, but use them sparingly — as Stuart Levy does, denying himself their benefit for small illnesses so that they remain effective when a life-threatening bug comes along.

The Federal Reserve is, in its DNA, an organization of engineers tasked with ending panics, recession, and inflation. Yet in achieving precisely that, it often plants the seeds for the next crisis or recession. The Fed should not stop fighting recessions and crises, nor should it have to use its powers for every shock that comes along. Once the biggest banks can fail safely, then the entire financial system will be more resilient.

The engineers and the ecologists in their different ways embody the best of civilization. We do not have to side with either, but we can take the best of both. Our goal should be to eliminate big disasters, not small ones, to accept a bit more risk and instability today in return for more reward and stability in the long run.

ACKNOWLEDGMENTS

This book grew out of my experience covering the global financial crisis and its aftermath. Like most people, I didn't see it coming, though I'd spent two decades covering the economy and markets. In *The Little Book of Economics,* my first book, I tried to explain why: society inoculates itself against the virus that caused the last recession, then the virus "mutates and we're susceptible all over again."

My agent, Howard Yoon of Ross Yoon Agency, suggested that observation could be the germ of a new book. After lighting the initial flame, Howard kept it alive by helping me organize and articulate my ideas, prodding me to keep going when distractions interfered, and providing constant feedback, advice, and therapy. Quite simply, this book would not exist without Howard.

It would take an additional book to properly acknowledge all the people whose time and expertise made this one possible. Here are a few: Paul Volcker, Alan Greenspan, Ben Bernanke, Larry Summers, and Jay Powell for recollections and lessons learned in and out of public service; Gary Gorton, Laurence Meyer, Brad DeLong, Athanasios Orphanides, Michael Bordo, Paul McCulley, Aaron Tornell, Doug Elmendorf, Andreas Lehnert, Lou Crandall, and Steve Kim for their expertise and experience in economics and financial markets; Wally Covington, Jennifer Marlon, Bob Barbee, and especially Stephen Pyne for educating me about forests and fire; Don Arendt for his prodigious knowledge of risk management in aviation and beyond; Arnold Barnett, Linda Connell, and David Wichner for their work on airline safety; Roger Pielke, Jr., Karen Clark, and Carolyn Kousky for their insights into natural disasters and insurance; Sam Peltzman for his research on regulation; George Loewenstein for his findings on emotions and economics; and Stuart Levy for his fight against antibiotic resistance.

At Little, Brown and Company, Geoff Shandler immediately grasped the essence of the book and got behind it. John Parsley, who took over the editing after Geoff, read every word from the perspective of an intelligent, engaged reader, identified gaps in my narrative and my argument, and advised me on how to make the organization more logical and coherent. With inexhaustible wisdom, good humor, and patience, John is everything a writer could want.

Jean Garnett assisted with the line editing, Ben Allen steered the manuscript through production, Chris Jerome copyedited the manuscript, and Malin von Euler-Hogan coordinated countless logistical and production details.

I owe a special thanks to Reagan Arthur, Little, Brown's publisher, for her early and enthusiastic support.

Krista Dugan, my tireless lead researcher, tracked down sources, details, and anecdotes, then fact-checked most of the manuscript under tight deadlines. Boer Deng and Jake Seib also assisted with fact-checking. Any remaining errors are solely on me.

The Woodrow Wilson International Center for Scholars gave me a home during the two most intense months of writing and research. My thanks to Robert Litwak, head of the scholars program, and Jane Harman, the president, for hosting me, and the library's outstanding staff for tracking down obscure articles and books on a bewildering variety of topics.

The Library of Congress, Wikipedia, and the National Library of Medicine at the National Institutes of Health are the embodiment of public goods. By bringing so much of human knowledge together in one place, they are indispensable for this sort of project.

Many of the ideas in this book came to me in the course of my reporting, either at *The Economist,* my home when I started the book, or the *Wall Street Journal,* where I now work. I am grateful for the backing and indulgence of colleagues at both: Zanny Minton Beddoes, now editor of *The Economist,* and John Micklethwait, her predecessor; Gerry Baker, editor-in-chief of the *Wall Street Journal,* Neil King, global economics editor, and Jerry Seib, Washington bureau chief.

Many friends and colleagues provided invaluable comments. Tom Gallagher and Jon Hilsenrath read the entire manuscript; I took their suggestions on tone and content to heart. Kate Kelly and Greg Zuckerman read and commented on various chapters. Alison Fitzgerald shared her knowledge of the BP oil spill; Lennie Friedman shared his experience in the NFL. The Kentbury dads — Andrew, Nick, and Craig — supplied moral support, suggestions, and beer.

For two years this book consumed a good chunk of my evenings and weekends. Too often my children, Natalie and Daniel, took a backseat to its completion. Not only did they never complain, they sweetly checked up on me when I despaired of ever finishing.

My wife, Nancy, has been my biggest cheerleader and most stalwart supporter throughout. She read and commented on the manuscript, was a sounding board, and cheered me on when my spirits and energy sagged.

Nancy is also an inspiration for the book. Like a grizzly bear, she lives to protect her family from harm. She's why we drive more slowly in bad weather, wear helmets on the ski slope, and check the locks each night. In her constant vigilance against danger, she keeps us safe. That's why this book is dedicated to her.

Introduction

3   *Friday, the thirteenth of October*: From William Power and Craig Torres, "The Sell-Off in Stocks: Dow Falls 190 Points; Bucks Safeguards — Special Steps Didn't Cool Fever to Sell," *Wall Street Journal*, October 16, 1989.

3   *The mini-crash was very much on the minds*: The proceedings of the panel discussion are from Lawrence H. Summers, Hyman P. Minsky, Paul A. Samuelson, William Poole, and Paul A. Volcker, "Macroeconomic Consequences of Financial Crises," in *The Risk of Economic Crisis: Proceedings of a Conference by the National Bureau of Economic Research*, Martin Feldstein, ed. (Chicago: University of Chicago Press, 1991), 135–182, http://papers.nber.org/books/feld91-2.

4   *He drew attention to a cartoon*: The cartoon is by Dan Wasserman, "Federal Reserve Issues Money to Calm Nervous Markets," *The Boston Globe*, October 17, 1989.

6   *Fender benders and minor injuries*: Two papers on accidents during winter weather are Jean Andrey and Brian Mills, "Collisions, Casualties, and Costs: Weathering the Elements on Canadian Roads," ICLR Research Paper Series no. 33 (2003), available at http://www.iclr.org/images/Collisions_Casualties_and_Costs.pdf; and Daniel Eisenberg and Kenneth E. Warner, "Effects of Snowfalls on Motor Vehicle Collisions, Injuries, and Fatalities," *American Journal of Public Health* 95, no. 1 (2005): 120–124, available at http://www.ncbi.nlm.nih.gov/pmc/articles/PMC1449863/.

7   *The* Titanic's *crew sailed at top speed*: The description of the *Titanic's* behavior is from Stephanie Barczewski, *Titanic: A Night Remembered*, 100th anniversary ed. (London: Continuum International Publishing Group, 2011), 13.

9   *"An incident-free system"*: René Amalberti, "The Paradoxes of Almost Totally Safe Transportation Systems," *Safety Science* 37 (2001): 109–126.

10   *Banks and their regulators assumed mortgages*: The absence of price declines in housing models is from Kristopher Gerardi, Andreas Lehnert, Shane M. Sherlund, and Paul Willen, "Making Sense of the Subprime Crisis," *Brookings Papers on Economic Activity* (2008), 133, available at http://www.brookings.edu/~/media/Projects/BPEA/Fall%202008/2008b_bpea_gerardi.pdf.

11   *"Europe will be forged"*: Jean Monnet, *Memoirs* (London: Collins, 1978).

12   *As late as 2010, Jean-Claude Trichet*: The comment is from a press confer-
       ence in 2010, available at https://www.ecb.europa.eu/press/pressconf/2010/
       html/is100304.en.html.

Chapter 1

15   *Until then, western settlers accepted fire*: Stephen Pyne, *Year of the Fires: The
       Story of the Great Fires of 1910* (New York: Viking, 2001), 6.

16   *The Panic of 1907 shifted opinion decisively*: Biographical details of Robert
       Owen and his role in the creation of the Federal Reserve are based on sev-
       eral sources, including Mark A. Carlson and David C. Wheelock, "The
       Lender of Last Resort: Lessons from the Fed's First 100 Years," *Federal
       Reserve Bank of St. Louis Working Paper* 2012-056B (2012), available at http://
       research.stlouisfed.org/wp/2012/2012-056.pdf; Wyatt Belcher, "Political
       Leadership of Robert L. Owen," *Chronicles of Oklahoma* 31, no. 4 (1953);
       "About...Robert Latham Owen," *Ten* (Published by the Federal Reserve
       Bank of Kansas City), Fall 2007; and Chad Wilkerson, "Senator Robert
       Owen of Oklahoma and the Federal Reserve's Formative Years," *Federal
       Reserve Bank of Kansas City Economic Review*, Third Quarter 2013.

16   *'panics' with their attendant misfortunes*: From the Report of the Controller of
       the Currency, December 7, 1914, available at https://fraser.stlouisfed.org/docs/
       publications/comp/1910s/1914/compcurr_1914_Vol1.pdf.

17   *Gifford Pinchot, a confidant of Roosevelt*: Gifford Pinchot, *The Fight for
       Conservation* (Seattle: University of Washington Press, 1967, c. 1910), 44–45
       available at http://catalog.hathitrust.org/Record/001312820.

17   *a toll that would be exceeded*: From the National Interagency Fire Center,
       available at http://www.nifc.gov/fireInfo/fireInfo_stats_histSigFires.html.

18   *throughout most of the past two thousand years*: From Jennifer R. Marlon et al.,
       "Long-term Perspective on Wildfires in the Western USA," *Proceedings of
       the National Academy of Sciences* 109, no. 9 (2012), no. 3203.

20   *but as Marshall noted*: Alfred Marshall, *Principles of Economics*, 8th ed.
       (Hampshire: Palgrave Macmillan, 1920): 3–4, 288.

21   *Expertise became institutionalized*: From Robert H. Nelson, "The Religion of
       Forestry: Scientific Management," *Journal of Forestry*, November 1999, avail-
       able at http://faculty.publicpolicy.umd.edu/sites/default/files/nelson/files/Forest
       _Fires/The_Religion_of_Forestry_Scientific_Management.pdf. The Ameri-
       can Planning Association was formed in 1978 but traces its roots to 1909.

21   *financially illiterate*: Edmund Morris, in his biography *Theodore Rex: The Rise
       of Theodore Roosevelt and Colonel Roosevelt* (New York: Modern Library,
       2002), 498, writes: "It was exchanges such as this that persuaded some men
       that Roosevelt was fiscally retarded."

22   *One of his influences*: The progressivism of Woodrow Wilson, his influences,
       and his role in creating the Federal Reserve are from Niels Aage Thorsen,
       The Political Thought of Woodrow Wilson, 1875–1910 (Princeton: Princeton

Notes

University Press, 1988): 55; *Papers of Woodrow Wilson*, February 24, 1898, 440, and December 23, 1913, 65; and Gerald T. Dunne, *A Christmas Present for the President: A Short History of the Creation of the Federal Reserve System* (St. Louis: The Federal Reserve Bank of St. Louis).

22   *Wilson was quite taken*: Woodrow Wilson, *Papers of Woodrow Wilson*, February 24, 1898, 440.

22   *"What we are proceeding"*: Ibid., December 23, 1913, 65.

22   *"The whole country"*: Quoted in "About…Robert Latham Owen," accessed at http://www.kansascityfed.org/publicat/TEN/pdf/Fall2007/Fall07About.Robert Owen.pdf.

24   *"forms of something which has to be done"*: Joseph Schumpeter, "Depressions," in *Economics of the Recovery Program* (New York: McGraw-Hill, 1934).

24   *"liquidate labor, liquidate stocks"*: Whether Mellon actually said this is unknown. It was attributed to him by Herbert Hoover in *The Memoirs of Herbert Hoover, The Great Depression 1929–1941* (New York: Macmillan, 1952), 30.

25   *had to restore prices and end deflation*: Fisher's views are well captured in Robert Loring's *Irving Fisher: A Biography* (Hoboken, N.J.: Wiley, 1993), 240.

25   *It was the engineer's duty*: Hoover wrote this in 1954 in *Engineer's Week*. The article is reproduced by the Hoover Presidential Foundation.

25   *As Warren Harding's commerce secretary*: James Grant, *The Forgotten Depression: 1929: The Crash That Cured Itself* (New York: Simon & Schuster, 2014), 172.

26   *Since the economy was largely*: Even Marshall understood that this might not actually hold in deep downturns; though "men have the power to purchase they may not choose to use it." From Alfred Marshall and Mary Paley Marshall, *The Economics of Industry*, 2nd ed. (London: Macmillan, 1881), 154.

27   *As Stephen Pyne, a historian*: Forest Service policy during the 1930s is discussed by Stephen J. Pyne in *Year of the Fires: The Story of the Great Fires of 1910* (New York: Viking, 2001), 263.

28   *the National Resources Board declared*: From the National Resources Planning Board 1934, Report on Planning and Public Works in Relation to Natural Resources and Including Land Use and Water Resources.

29   *"Floods are 'acts of God'"*: Gilbert White, *Human Adjustment to Floods; A Geographical Approach to the Flood Problem in the United States* (Chicago: University of Chicago Press, 1945).

29   *Leopold's report*: Advisory Board on Wildlife Management appointed by Secretary of the Interior Udall, *Wildlife Management in the National Parks* (National Park Service: 1963).

30   *Macroeconomic engineering faced*: For comparisons between economics, science, and engineering, see N. Gregory Mankiw, "The Macroeconomist as Scientist and Engineer," *Journal of Economic Perspectives* 20, no. 4 (2006): 29–46, and Friedrich August von Hayek, "The Pretence of Knowledge: Prize Lecture to the Memory of Alfred Nobel," December 11, 1974. Edmund Phelps had the same insight as Milton Friedman on the relationship between inflation and employment around the same time.

31   *Hyman Minsky was born in*: For details of Minsky's life and work I have drawn on Minsky's own writings, in particular *Stabilizing an Unstable Economy* (New Haven: Yale University Press, 1986); Dimitri Papadimitrou's *Essays in Memory of Hyman Minsky* (Palgrave Macmillan), in particular Steven Fazzari's "Conversations with Minsky" and Papadimitrou's "Minsky on Himself"; Papadimitrou and Randall Wray, "The Economic Contributions of Hyman Minsky: Varieties of Capitalism and Institutional Reform," in *Review of Political Economy* 10, no. 2 (1998), 13.

32   *Because the financial system*: From Hyman Minsky, "Central Banking and Money Market Changes," in *The Quarterly Journal of Economics* 71, no. 2 (1957), 171–187.

32   *Eric Falkenstein*: Falkenstein gave his recollections in his blog post "Minsky a Keynesian Sock Puppet," September 14, 1999, http://falkenblog.blogspot.com/2009/09/minsky-keynesian-sockpuppet.html, and in an interview with the author.

33   *He predicted the crash*: From Hyman Minsky, "Why 1987 Is Not 1929," available at http://digitalcommons.bard.edu/hm_archive/217/.

34   *yet the economy had chugged along*: Paul Krugman, C. Fred Bergsten, Rudiger Dornbusch, Jacob A. Frenkel, Charles P. Kindleberger, "International Aspects of Financial Crises," in *The Risk of Economic Crisis: Proceedings of a Conference by the National Bureau of Economic Research*, Martin Feldstein, ed. (Chicago: University of Chicago Press, 1991), 85–134, available at http://papers.nber.org/books/feld91-2.

Chapter 2

35   *Richard Ravitch, who headed the state's*: Descriptions of Paul Volcker's career are based principally on two interviews I conducted with him, in 2008 and 2013, plus follow-up correspondence, and his own speeches. I also relied on several secondary sources, including William L. Silber's thorough and authoritative *Volcker: The Triumph of Persistence* (New York: Bloomsbury, 2012) and the Federal Deposit Insurance Corporation's excellent study *History of the Eighties — Lessons for the Future, vol. 1, An Examination of the Banking Crises of the 1980s and Early 1990s*, available at https://www.fdic.gov/bank/historical/history/.

38   *would have been insolvent*: From Robert A. Eisenbeis and Paul M. Horvitz, "The Role of Forbearance and Its Costs in Handling Troubled and Failed Depository Institutions," in *Reforming Financial Institutions and Markets in the United States: Towards Rebuilding a Safe and More Efficient System*, George G. Kaufman, ed. (Boston: Kluwer Academic Publishers, c. 1994).

44   *"shadow banking"*: The term was coined by Paul McCulley, then of Pimco, in 2007.

46   *"contributed to the transfer of credit risk"*: Alan Greenspan, "Remarks on Government-Sponsored Enterprises to the Conference on Housing, Mortgage Finance, and the Macroeconomy, Federal Reserve Bank of Atlanta,

Atlanta, Georgia," May 19, 2005, available at http://www.federalreserve.gov/boarddocs/speeches/2005/20050519/.

48 *"This time it wasn't us"*: From Guillermo Ortiz, quoted in John Bussey, "Mexico's Ortiz Sees Risk in Overregulating," *Wall Street Journal*, http://blogs.wsj.com/economics/2008/01/26/mexicos-ortiz-sees-risk-in-overregulating/.

48 *A study by several Fed economists*: Matthew J. Eichner, Donald L. Kohn, and Michael G. Palumbo, "Financial Statistics for the United States and the Crisis: What Did They Get Right, What Did They Miss, and How Should They Change?," Federal Reserve Board Working Paper, April 15, 2010, available at http://www.federalreserve.gov/Pubs/FEDS/2010/201020/.

50 *had their personal wealth*: The idea that industry insiders profited most from the subprime boom and bust is one of the many myths exploded by Christopher L. Foote, Kristopher S. Gerardi, and Paul S. Willen in their excellent paper "Why Did So Many People Make So Many Ex Post Bad Decisions? The Causes of the Foreclosure Crisis," *Federal Reserve Bank of Boston Public Policy Discussion Paper*, July 2012, available at http://www.bostonfed.org/economic/ppdp/2012/ppdp1202.pdf.

50 *Greenspan took office in 1987*: The events involving Alan Greenspan are based primarily on interviews I conducted with him after his retirement, his speeches, testimony, and books, and my reporting.

51 *inflation slid further, to below 3 percent*: This is based on the consumer price index, excluding food and energy.

51 *"the Great Moderation"*: From James H. Stock and Mark W. Watson, "Has the Business Cycle Changed and Why?," in *NBER Macroeconomics Annual 2002*, 17, Mark Gertler and Kenneth Rogoff, eds., available at http://www.nber.org/chapters/c11075.pdf. The term may have been used earlier, but Stock and Watson are generally credited with popularizing it.

52 *the more investors will pay*: A standard valuation model calculates a present value of a stream of income by discounting future cash flow by some discount rate, which is a function of both interest rates and perceived risk. Lower interest rates and lower risk both reduce the discount rate, which raises the present value of a given stream of future income.

52 *The historical average ratio*: See Jonathan R. Laing, "Abby Says Relax: Here's Why Abby Joseph Cohen Sees This Amazing Bull Market Charging Ahead," *Barron's*, February 23, 1998.

53 *took a beating*: E. S. Browning, "A Year After the Peak—Few Regrets: A Major Bull Looks Back," *Wall Street Journal*, March 5, 2001.

53 *Greenspan himself pointed this out*: From Alan Greenspan, "Remarks Before the Economic Club of New York, New York City," December 19, 2002, available at http://www.federalreserve.gov/boarddocs/speeches/2002/20021219.

54 *"The turn in consumer credit"*: From Gilbert Burck and Sanford Parker, "The Coming Turn in Consumer Credit," *Fortune*, March 1956.

55 *a 2005 study by several Fed economists*: Karen E. Dynan, Douglas W. Elmendorf, and Daniel E. Sichel, "Can Financial Innovation Help to Explain the

Reduced Volatility of Economic Activity?," *Federal Reserve Finance and Economics Discussion Series*, 2005-54, Other papers on this theme were "The Evolution of Household Income Volatility," by the same authors in the same series, 2007-61; and Karen E. Dynan and Donald L. Kohn, "The Rise in U.S. Household Indebtedness: Causes and Consequences," 2007-37.

56 *As Frederic Mishkin*: "Housing and the Monetary Transmission Mechanism," presented at the Economic Symposium of the Federal Reserve Bank of Kansas City, *Housing, Housing Finance, and Monetary Policy* (2007): 393, available at http://www.kc.frb.org/Publicat/Sympos/2007/PDF/Mishkin _0415.pdf.

56 *Brad DeLong, an economist*: J. Bradford DeLong, "Confessions of a Financial Deregulator," *Project Syndicate*, June 30, 2011, available at http://www .project-syndicate.org/commentary/confressions-of-a-financial -deregulator.

56 *One evening in February 2005*: Paul Volcker, "Remarks to the Stanford Institute for Economic Policy Research" (author's transcript), February 11, 2005.

58 *"I wanted to flag it"*: Interview with the author.

58 *"History has not dealt kindly"*: Alan Greenspan, "Reflections on Central Banking," Aug. 26, 2005, available at http://www.federalreserve.gov/Board docs/speeches/2005/20050826/default.htm.

58 *"Even before the crisis"*: Bernanke's crisis preparations are based on an interview with me after he retired, and on my article "Bernanke, in First Crisis, Rewrites Fed Playbook," *Wall Street Journal*, October 31, 2007.

59 *rarely did any of these seem important enough*: Stephen Golub, Ayse Kaya, and Michael Reay, "What Were They Thinking? The Federal Reserve in the Run-up to the 2008 Financial Crisis," *Review of International Political Economy* (2014), available at http://www.swarthmore.edu/sites/default/files/ assets/documents/user_profiles/sgolub1/RIPE%20published%20pdf.pdf.

Chapter 3

61 *"If you don't know if it's pre-packaged"*: Andrea Shalal-Esa, "U.S. Company Recalls Spinach as E. coli Cases Grow," Reuters, September 15, 2006.

61 *When one woman served*: "Shoppers Change Their Buying Habits after Recall of Spinach due to E. coli Contamination," *Associated Press Newswires*, September 16, 2006.

63 *An American supermarket chain*: Malcolm Gladwell, "Some Fear Bad Precedent in Alar Alarm; Scientists Criticize Pulling of Apples Without Proof of Danger," *Washington Post*, April 19, 1989.

63 *a child would have to consume*: Richard W. Lane and Joseph F. Borzelleca, "Harming and Helping through Time: The History of Toxicology," *Principles and Methodology of Toxicology*, 5th ed., A. Wallace Hayes, ed. (CRC Press, 2007), 38.

64 *"What's the difference between"*: From my interview with David Gombas.

65 *"We're abandoning production"*: Annys Shin, "Tomatoes Pulled After Salmo-nella Warning; Three Types Tied to Outbreak, FDA Says," *Washington Post*, June 10, 2008.

65 *By then, the damage*: Dan Flynn, "Tomato Growers Want Compensation for Losses in 2008 Outbreak," *Food Safety News*, August 2, 2013.

66 *In economic terms, the bets*: Here's how the math works. Expected value is arrived at by multiplying the value of a prize by its probability. Since the probability of flipping heads is 50 percent, the expected value of this bet is 50 percent × $1,000 = $500. Another approach is to imagine you flipped a coin 100 times. You'd probably come up heads 50 times and win $50,000, which works out to $500 per coin flip.

66 *Amos Tversky and Daniel Kahneman, two Israeli psychologists*: The findings of Tversky and Kahneman are based on their papers "Advances in Prospect Theory: Cumulative Representation of Uncertainty," *Journal of Risk and Uncertainty* 5 (1992): 297–323, and "Prospect Theory: An Analysis of Deci-sion under Risk," *Econometrica* 47, no. 2 (1979): 263–291, and Daniel Kahneman's book *Thinking, Fast and Slow* (New York: Farrar, Straus and Giroux, 2011). I have modified one of their examples to express the value of the bet in dollars; their original paper didn't specify a currency.

67 *In other words, the typical*: The expected value is the reward, times its proba-bility. So the expected value of the envelope with $500 is $500 × 100 per-cent = $500. The expected value of a $1,000 reward for flipping a coin heads is $1,000 × 50 percent = $500. So this is a fair bet; a risk-neutral individual should be just as happy with $500 in an envelope as a chance to flip a coin and earn $1,000 if it comes up heads. But in fact most people wouldn't take that bet; they'll take the envelope over the coin flip. So how much do we have to make the coin flip worth before they take it over the envelope? We have to offer $2,000 for flipping heads, so that the expected value is $2,000 × 50 percent = $1,000, which is twice the expected value of the envelope.

68 *The economist Richard Thaler*: Richard Thaler, "Toward a Positive Theory of Consumer Choice," *Journal of Economic Behavior and Organization* 1 (1980): 3960.

68 *George Loewenstein, an economist*: Loewenstein described his work to me in several interviews. This experiment appears in the article by Leaf Van Boven, George Loewenstein, Edward Welch, and David Dunning, "The Illusion of Courage in Self-Predictions: Mispredicting One's Own Behavior in Embarrassing Situations," *Journal of Behavioral Decision Making* 25 (2012): 1–12.

70 *Gorton took a circuitous route*: Gary Gorton's story is based on a series of interviews I conducted with him, on his extensive articles, and his book *Misunderstanding Financial Crises: Why We Don't See Them Coming* (New York: Oxford University Press, 2012), a powerful and persuasive account of what causes financial panics.

73 *When Gorton and two*: Gary B. Gorton, Stefan Lewellen, and Andrew Metrick, "The Safe-Asset Share," *National Bureau of Economic Research Working Paper* 17777 (2012).

74 *Lewis Ranieri said the beauty*: Lewis Ranieri, "The Origins of Securitization, Sources of Its Growth, and Its Future Potential," in *A Primer on Securitization*, Leon Kendall and Michael J. Fishman, eds. (Cambridge, Mass.: MIT Press, 1996), 38.

75 *The first big customers to benefit*: AIG's activities are drawn from interviews with Gary Gorton, the report and supporting documents of the Financial Crisis Inquiry Commission (New York: PublicAffairs, 2011), AIG conference call transcript dated Dec. 5, 2007, and the November 2009 and July 2014 report of the Office of the Special Inspector General for the Troubled Asset Relief Program.

75 *AIGFP had begun to worry*: Gorton says the decision was made in 2005 but AIG continued to finish deals in 2006 that were initiated in 2005.

75 *He put those thoughts down in a long paper*: The paper is Gary Gorton, "The Panic of 2007," presented at the Federal Reserve Bank of Kansas City Economic Symposium, *Maintaining Stability in a Changing Financial System*, 2008, available at http://www.kc.frb.org/publicat/sympos/2008/Gorton .03.12.09.pdf.

77 *one of Gorton's PhD students*: Sun Young Park, "The Size of the Subprime Shock," Korea Advanced Institute of Science and Technology, 2012.

77 *"No one wants to pay anything"*: Interview.

78 *to receive the full $62 billion*: For details see report of Special Inspector General for the Troubled Asset Relief Program, "Factors Affecting Efforts to Limit Payments to AIG Counterparties," November 17, 2009, 5, available at http://www.sigtarp.gov/Audit%20Reports/Factors_Affecting_Efforts_to _Limit_Payments_to_AIG_Counterparties.pdf.

78 *After the* Wall Street Journal *reported*: Interview, and Carrick Mollenkamp, Serena Ng, Liam Pleven, and Randall Smith, "Behind AIG's Fall, Risk Models Failed to Pass Real-World Test," *Wall Street Journal*, November 3, 2008, available at http://wsj.com/articles/SB122538449722784635.

79 *sank by a staggering $70 billion*: The estimate is by Lewis Alexander of Nomura Securities International, published in the research note "Monetary Policy and Systemic Risk" on March 18, 2013.

80 *In the 1970s Bent was toiling away*: Most of the information about the Bent family and the Reserve Primary Fund comes from the trial transcript of *Securities and Exchange Commission v. Reserve Management Company, Inc., et al.*, United States District Court Southern District of New York, from October 9 to November 12, 2012. Additional information comes from the Financial Crisis Inquiry Commission report.

80 *The calling card of the money fund*: Regulators permit money market funds to round shares to a dollar if they meet the conditions of Rule 2a-7 under the Investment Company Act of 1940.

81   *only once had a fund*: See Moody's Investors Service, "Sponsor Support Key to Money Market Funds," August 9, 2010.

82   *Within a week, investors yanked*: From the Financial Crisis Inquiry Commission report, 357, and Eleanor Laise, "'Breaking the Buck' Was Close for Many," *Wall Street Journal*, August 10, 2010.

83   *regulators had intervened to protect*: They were First Republic, Bank of New England, and MCorp. See Financial Crisis Inquiry Commission report, 36.

84   *Michael Luciano, a portfolio manager*: See Financial Crisis Inquiry Commission report, 356.

84   *Evidence has since surfaced*: James B. Stewart and Peter Eavis, "Revisiting the Lehman Brothers Bailout That Never Was," *New York Times*, September 29, 2014.

84   *Tim Geithner, president*: Tim Geithner, *Stress Test: Reflections on Financial Crises* (New York: Crown, 2014), 179–180.

84   *One staffer said the Fed*: E-mail from Patricia Mosser, senior vice president of the Federal Reserve Bank of New York, quoted in the Financial Crisis Inquiry Commission report, 331.

84   *Bernanke and Hank Paulson*: According to Geithner.

85   *It later emerged that*: Moody's, "Sponsor Support Key to Money Market Funds," August 9, 2010.

Chapter 4

88   *"They give me a helmet"*: "Despite NFL Crackdown, Dolphins' Crowder Says He'll Use Helmet to 'Knock 'em Out'," *Associated Press Newswires*, October 20, 2010.

89   *When football was first played*: Frederick O. Mueller, "Fatalities from Head and Cervical Spine Injuries Occurring in Tackle Football: 50 Years' Experience," *Clinics in Sports Medicine* 17, no. 1 (1998), 169–182.

89   *The caps were uncomfortable*: William Machin, "The History of the NFL Helmet," *Livestrong.com*, October 30, 2013, available at http://www.livestrong.com/article/341058-the-history-of-the-nfl-helmet/.

90   *"We teach our boys to spear"*: Morton Sharnik, "A Rough Day for the Bear," *Sports Illustrated*, November 26, 1962.

90   *A study comparing football injuries*: Joseph S. Torg et al., "The National Football Head and Neck Injury Registry: Report and Conclusions, 1978," *Journal of American Medical Association* 241, no. 14 (1979): 1477–1479.

91   *In 1968 Bill Masterton, a center*: "Brain Injuries Take Life of Stars' Bill Masterton," (Saskatoon) *Star-Phoenix*, January 16, 1968.

92   *Thereafter the number of head fractures*: For discussion of injuries in hockey and the role of helmets, see N. Biasca, S. Wirth, and Y. Tegner, "The Avoidability of Head and Neck Injuries in Ice Hockey: An Historical Review," *British Journal of Sports Medicine* 36, no. 6 (2002): 410–427; P. D. Reynen and W. G. Clancy, Jr., "Cervical Spine Injury, Hockey Helmets, and Face Masks," *American Journal of Sports Medicine* 22, no. 2 (1994): 167–170.

92   *There is a 'serious concern'*: Lela Jone Stoner and Michael Keating, "Hockey Equipment: Safety or an Illusion?," in *Safety in Ice Hockey, vol. 2*, Cosmo R. Castaldi and Patrick J. Bishop, eds. (1993).

93   *Peltzman grew up in the Bensonhurst*: For Sam Peltzman's life and his work I relied principally on interviews and follow-up correspondence.

94   *In a controversial 1973 paper*: Sam Peltzman, "An Evaluation of Consumer Protection Legislation: The 1962 Drug Amendments," *Journal of Political Economy* 81, no. 5 (1973): 1049–1091.

94   *Peltzman felt his results were*: Sam Peltzman, "The Effects of Automobile Safety Regulation," *Journal of Political Economy* 83, no. 4 (1975): 677–726.

95   *Peltzman didn't stop with autos*: "The Health Effects of Mandatory Prescriptions," Sam Peltzman, *University of Chicago Center for the Study of the Economy and the State, Working Paper #38*, April 1986.

95   *Wilde illustrated his point*: Gerald Wilde, "Does Risk Homeostasis Theory Have Implications for Road Safety? Debate: For," *British Medical Journal* 324 (2002): 1149–1152, available at http://www.ncbi.nlm.nih.gov/pmc/articles/PMC1123100/.

96   *The institute had recruited Robertson*: Information about Robertson's life and work from interview.

96   *He claimed Peltzman's paper*: Leon Robertson, "A Critical Analysis of Peltzman's 'The Effects of Automobile Safety Regulation,'" *Journal of Economic Issues* 11, no. 3 (1977): 587–600.

97   *Peltzman disputed Robertson's adjustments*: Sam Peltzman, "A Reply," *Journal of Economic Issues* 11, no. 3 (1977): 672–678.

97   *"The reification of a theory"*: Leon S. Robertson, "Rejoinder to Peltzman," *Journal of Economic Issues* 11, no. 3 (1977): 679–683.

97   *In his critique of Wilde*: Leon Robertson and Barry Pless, "Does Risk Homeostasis Theory Have Implications for Road Safety? Debate: Against," *British Medical Journal* 324, no. 7346 (2002): 1149–1152.

98   *Clifford Winston, an economist*: Clifford Winston, Vikram Maheshri, and Fred Mannering, "An Exploration of the Offset Hypothesis Using Disaggregate Data: The Case of Airbags and Antilock Brakes," *AEI-Brookings Joint Center for Regulatory Studies Working Paper 06-10* (2006), available at http://www.brookings.edu/~/media/research/files/papers/2006/5/autosafety%20winston/05_autosafety_winston.pdf.

98   *A study in 2001*: Alma Cohen and Liran Einav, "The Effects of Mandatory Seat Belt Laws on Driving Behavior and Traffic Fatalities," Harvard Law School Discussion Paper no. 341, 11/2001, available at http://www.law.harvard.edu/programs/olin_center/papers/pdf/341.pdf.

99   *"the safer, straighter way"*: The original brochure can be viewed at the Old Car Manual Project at http://www.oldcarbrochures.com/.

100 *initial studies of real-life experience*: Aschenbrenner, K. M., Biehl, B., and Wurn, G. M., "Is Traffic Safety Improved Through Better Engineering? Investigation of Risk Compensation with the Example of Antilock Brake

Systems," *Bergisch Glaadbach: Bundesanstalt fur Strassenwesen* (1988), described in Gerald J.S. Wilde, *Target Risk 3: Risk Homeostasis in Everyday Life* (Toronto: Digital Edition, 2014): 93–94. The other paper is Leonard Evans, "Antilock Brake Systems and Different Types of Crashes in Traffic," General Motors Global R&D Operations Paper No. 98-S2-O-12, available at http://www.nrd.nhtsa.dot.gov/pdf/Esv/esv16/98S2O12.pdf.

100 *"We hear it all the time"*: Jim Haner, "Anti-lock Brakes Don't Cut Accidents," *Baltimore Sun*, April 24, 1994, available at http://articles.baltimoresun.com/ 1994-04-24/news/1994114029_1_brakes-taurus-collisions.

100 *In 1998 Leonard Evans*: Evans, "Antilock Brake Systems."

101 *Why, then, was the Peltzman effect*: Interview with Adrian Lund. Lund notes that antilock brakes are used with electronic stability control, which does reduce accidents.

103 *fatalities fell at about*: Sam Peltzman, "Regulation and the Natural Progress of Opulence," speech to the AEI-Brookings Joint Center for Regulatory Studies, September 2004.

104 *Adams notes that in Britain*: John Adams, "Management of the Risks of Transport," in *Handbook of Risk Theory: Epistemology, Decision Theory, Ethics, and Social Implications of Risk,* Sabine Roeser et al., eds. (Dordrecht and New York: Springer, 2012): 242.

104 *When Adams repeated*: Mayer Hillman, John Adams, and John Whitelegg, *One False Move: A Study of Children's Independent Mobility* (London: Policy Studies Institute, 1990), accessed at http://www.john-adams.co.uk/wp-content/ uploads/2013/06/OneFalseMove_Hillman_Adams.pdf.

104 *"They are achieving their higher death rates"*: These remarks are from interview with John Adams.

105 *Once that is controlled for*: Studies of the effect of driver's education on accidents include Raymond Peck, "Do Driver Training Programs Reduce Crashes and Traffic Violations? A Critical Examination of the Literature," *IATSS Research* 34, no. 2 (2011): 63–71, and J. S. Vernick, G. Li, S. Ogaitis, E. J. MacKenzie, S. P. Baker, and A. C. Gielen, "Effects of High School Driver Education on Motor Vehicle Crashes, Violations, and Licensure," *American Journal of Preventive Medicine* (January 1999).

105 *One Norwegian study*: Cited by Ron Christie, "The Effectiveness of Driver Training as a Road Safety Measure: A Review of the Literature," RCSC Services Pty. Ltd., November 2001.

106 *and loans underwritten*: Sumit Agarwal, Gene Amromin, Itzhak Ben-David, Souphala Chomsisengphet, and Douglas Evanoff, "The Effectiveness of Mandatory Mortgage Counseling: Can One Dissuade Borrowers from Choosing Risky Mortgages?," *NBER Working Paper no. 19920* (February 2014, available at http://www.nber.org/papers/w19920.pdf.

107 *hitting one another with twice*: Bertrand Frechede and Andrew McIntosh, "Numerical Reconstruction of Real-Life Concussive Football Impacts," *Medicine & Science in Sports & Exercise* 41, no. 2 (2009): 390–98.

Chapter 5

109 *One economist even speculates*: Keith Chen, "Could Your Language Affect Your Ability to Save Money?," TED Talks, June 2012, available at https://www.ted.com/talks/keith_chen_could_your_language_affect_your _ability_to_save_money?.

109 *"Sell your islands"*: Bild, October 27, 2010, accessed at http://www.bild.de/ politik/wirtschaft/griechenland-krise/regierung-athen-sparen-verkauft -inseln-pleite-akropolis-11692338.html.

111 *"Who would be prepared"*: Quoted in Philip Coggan, *Paper Promises* (New York: PublicAffairs, 2012), 81.

111 *British investors assumed*: John J. Madden, *British Investment in the United States, 1860–1880* (New York: Garland, 1985), 256.

111 *But British savers*: Ibid., 240.

112 *When the state of Pennsylvania*: Ibid., 271, fn 1.

112 *British savers returned*: Ibid., 277.

112 *It was a "good housekeeping"*: Michael D. Bordo and Hugh Rockoff, "The Gold Standard as a 'Good Housekeeping Seal of Approval,'" *NBER Working Paper no. 5340*, November 1995, available at http://www.nber.org/papers/ w5340.pdf.

113 *But the debts Argentina accumulated*: Michael D. Bordo and Harold James, "The European Crisis in the Context of the History of Previous Financial Crises," NBER Working Paper no. 19112, June 2013, available at http://www .nber.org/papers/w19112.

113 *By the eve of the First World War*: J. Bradford DeLong, "Financial Crises in the 1890s and the 1990s; Must History Repeat?," *Brookings Papers on Economic Activity* 2:1999, 261 and 263.

114 *Isn't it absurd to change*: Milton Friedman, *Essays in Positive Economics* (Chicago: University of Chicago Press, 1953), 173.

115 *When Russia was preparing*: Theodore von Laue, *Sergei Witte and the Industrialization of Russia* (New York: Columbia University Press, 1963), quoted in Bordo and James, "The European Crisis."

115 *In the 1970s, families on Capitol Hill*: Joan Sweeney and Richard James Sweeney, "Monetary Theory and the Great Capitol Hill Baby Sitting Co-op Crisis: Comment," *Journal of Money, Credit and Banking* 9, no. 1 (1977): 86–89.

116 *As the economic historian Barry Eichengreen*: Barry Eichengreen, *Hall of Mirrors: The Great Depression, the Great Recession, and the Uses — and Misuses — of History* (New York: Oxford University Press, 2015): 136.

118 *"With their roots in a rural"*: Bordo and James, "The European Crisis."

118 *"Adoption of a single currency"*: M. Emerson, D. Gros, A. Italianer, J. Pisani-Ferry, and H. Reichenbach, *One Market, One Money: An Evaluation of the Potential Benefits and Costs of Forming an Economic and Monetary Union* (New York: Oxford University Press, 1992): 207, available at http://ec.europa .eu/economy_finance/publications/publication7454_en.pdf.

119 *"A common market cannot survive"*: George Soros, "Can Europe Work?," *Foreign Affairs*, September/October 1996.

121 *In the 1990s, governments*: Galina Hale and Maurice Obstfeld, "The Euro and the Geography of International Debt Flows," Federal Reserve Bank of San Francisco and University of California, Berkeley, working paper, December 26, 2014.

121 *A merger or acquisition "within the euro area"*: Ernst Welteke, "The Effect of the Euro on the German Economy—A View from the Deutsche Bundesbank," Speech to the German-British Chamber of Industry and Commerce in London, May 29, 2001, available at http://www.bis.org/review/r010530a.pdf.

123 *As one study documented*: The backsliding on reforms in Greece, Spain, Ireland, and Portugal is examined by Jesus Fernandez-Villaverde, Luis Garicano, and Tano Santos in "Political Credit Cycles: The Case of the Euro Zone," NBER Working Paper no. 18899, March 2013.

124 *That October in Deauville*: Charles Forelle, David Gauthiers-Villars, Brian Blackstone, and David Enrich, "Europe on the Brink: As Ireland Flails, Europe Lurches Across the Rubicon," *Wall Street Journal*, December 28, 2010.

125 *This meant that if a private saver*: The ECB, however, would only buy the bonds of a government that was adhering to the conditions of a reform program hammered out with the rest of Europe. This program was distinct from the "quantitative easing" launched in 2015 under which the ECB bought government bonds as a means of boosting economic growth rather than ensuring that those governments could obtain funding.

127 *"The German economy is competitive"*: Harriet Torry, "Germany Hits Back at U.S. Over Economic Criticism," *Dow Jones*, October 31, 2013.

128 *The head of the IMF repeatedly*: Michel Camdessus, managing director of the IMF, recalls issuing the warning, in an interview with *BusinessWeek* in December 2007, cited in "The IMF Crisis," *Wall Street Journal*, April 15, 1998.

128 *Many of these conditions had*: Independent Evaluation Office, "The IMF and Recent Capital Account Crises: Indonesia, Korea, Brazil" (Washington: International Monetary Fund, 2003): 48.

130 *His fellow governor*: Ben Bernanke, "The Global Saving Glut and the U.S. Current Account Deficit," March 10, 2005, available at http://www.federalreserve.gov/boarddocs/speeches/2005/200503102/.

Chapter 6

133 *Sandy "brought the stakes"*: Michael R. Bloomberg, "A Vote for a President to Lead on Climate Change," Bloomberg, November 1, 2012.

133 *two-thirds of voters*: Thomas Kaplan, "Most New Yorkers Think Climate Change Caused Hurricane, Poll Finds," *New York Times*, December 4, 2012.

134 *But climate change could not*: New York City's post-Sandy report notes that Sandy was no longer a hurricane when it hit. It suggested a few ways climate change might have contributed to Sandy: a one-foot rise in sea levels since 1900 added to storm surge, unusually warm ocean temperatures in the North Atlantic, possibly linked to climate change, added to Sandy's strength, and melting Arctic sea ice may have changed the jet stream and Sandy's direction. *A Stronger, More Resilient New York: Report of the NYC Special Initiative for Rebuilding and Resiliency*, City of New York, June 11, 2013, 12 and 30.

134 *Nicholas Coch, a geologist*: Nicholas Coch's work and findings are from an interview. His findings on the 1635 hurricane are described in "America's First Natural Disaster—The Hurricane of 1635: Implications for Hurricane Damage in New England in the 21st Century," presentation to the Geological Society of America–Northeastern Section, March 25–27, 2002.

134 *Hog Island, a barrier island*: Norimitsu Onishi, "Queens Tried to Be a Resort but Sank in a Hurricane," *New York Times*, March 18, 1997, available at http://www.nytimes.com/1997/03/18/nyregion/queens-spit-tried-to-be-a-resort-but-sank-in-a-hurricane.html.

135 *with eerie foresight*: Nicholas Coch, "The Unique Damage Potential of Northern Hurricanes," presentation to the Geological Society of America, October 22–25, 2006, abstract available at https://gsa.confex.com/gsa/2006AM/finalprogram/abstract_108209.htm.

135 *Compared to previous*: The description of Superstorm Sandy is from *A Stronger, More Resilient New York*, 11 and 21.

135 *Just four years earlier*: Roger A. Pielke, Jr., and Christopher W. Landsea, "Normalized Hurricane Damages in the United States: 1925–95," *Weather and Forecasting* 13 (September 1998): 6, available at https://www.asp.ucar.edu/colloquium/1998/pielke.pdf.

136 *Karen Clark, a prominent*: Karen Clark was founder and CEO of AIR Worldwide. She made the $100 billion prediction to, among others, CBS News, on July 30, 2006, and confirmed it with me later.

136 *Landsea had just*: The paper is by Christopher W. Landsea, Neville Nicholls, William M. Gray, and Lixion A. Avila, "Downward Trends in the Frequency of Intense Atlantic Hurricanes During the Past Five Decades," *Geophysical Research Letters* 23 (1996): 1697–1700, available at http://www.aoml.noaa.gov/hrd/Landsea/downward/.

137 *"It was abundantly clear"*: Details of Pielke's work and life are from my interview with him.

137 *The 1926 hurricane cost*: "Counting the Cost of Calamities," *The Economist*, January 14, 2012, available at http://www.economist.com/node/21542755.

138 *The 1967 fires, they estimate*: Ryan P. Crompton, K. John Mcaneney, Keping Chen, Roger A. Pielke, Jr., and Katharine Haynes, "Influence of Location, Population, and Climate on Building Damage and Fatalities Due to Australian Bushfire: 1925–2009," *Weather, Climate and Society* 2 (October 2010): 305.

139 *Al Gore has compared*: Al Gore, *Earth in the Balance: Forging a New Common Purpose* (London: Earthscan Publications, 1992), 274–275.

139 *his father, Roger Pielke, Sr.*: Roger Pielke, Jr., *The Climate Fix: What Scientists and Politicians Won't Tell You About Global Warming* (New York: Basic Books, 2010), 8. Pielke, Sr., argues that other aspects of human activity such as agriculture and urbanization may contribute even more to global warming than CO_2 emissions.

139 *Kerry Emanuel, a climate scientist*: Kerry Emanuel, "MIT Climate Scientist Responds on Disaster Costs and Climate Change," *Fivethirtyeight.com*, March 31, 2014, available at http://fivethirtyeight.com/features/mit-climate -scientist-responds-on-disaster-costs-and-climate-change/#fn-2.

140 *global hurricane damage will about double*: Robert Mendelsohn, Kerry Emanuel, Shun Chonabayashi, and Laura Bakkensen, "The Impact of Climate Change on Global Tropical Cyclone Damage," *Nature Climate Change 2* (2012): 205–209, available at http://www.nature.com/nclimate/journal/v2/ n3/abs/nclimate1357.html.

141 *Man "cannot tame"*: The quotes are from his *Life on the Mississippi* (Harper & Bros., 1917), 234, and from *Mark Twain in Eruption: Hitherto Unpublished Pages about Men and Events*, Bernard DeVoto, ed. (New York: Harper, 1940).

141 *The Corps went with*: Jamie W. Moore and Dorothy P. Moore, *The Army Corps of Engineers and the Evolution of Federal Flood Plain Management Policy* (Boulder: University of Colorado, Institute of Behavioral Science, 1989), 2–6.

141 *More than two hundred people*: Ibid., 6.

142 *White compiled numerous*: Gilbert White, *Human Adjustment to Floods: A Geographical Approach to the Flood Problem in the United States* (Chicago: University of Chicago Press, 1945), 52.

142 *After Hurricane Betsy*: Joel K. Bourne, Jr., "New Orleans," in *National Geographic*, August 2007, available at http://ngm.nationalgeographic.com/ static-legacy/ngm/0708/feature1/text2.html.

143 *A levee project in Dallas*: Moore and Moore, *The Army Corps of Engineers*, 37.

143 *"We figured this"*: Adam Goodman, "'Our Bubble Has Burst'; Levee Break Dampened Dreams in Chesterfield," *St. Louis Post-Dispatch*, August 8, 1993.

144 *Carolyn Kousky was a teenager*: Details of Carolyn Kousky's life from an interview. Insights into flooding are from a paper by her and Howard Kunreuther, "Improving Flood Insurance and Flood-Risk Management: Insights from St. Louis, Missouri," *Natural Hazards Review*, November 2010, 162–172.

144 *The story has*: Yuriko Koike, "Japan's Recovery Bonds," *Project Syndicate*, March 28, 2011.

145 *A third of Japan's coast*: Norimitsu Onishi, "Seawalls Offered Little Protection against Tsunami's Crushing Waves," *New York Times*, March 13, 2011, available at http://www.nytimes.com/2011/03/14/world/asia/14seawalls.html ?pagewanted=all&_r=1&.

146 *"The northern and southern"*: From my interview with Piet Dircke.

147 *even in Oklahoma's*: Maggie Koerth-Baker, "The Culture of Disaster," Ensia (Institute on the Environment at the University of Minnesota), July 12, 2013, available at http://ensia.com/voices/the-culture-of-disaster/.

148 *a remarkable case study*: From my interview with Robert Meyer.

148 *When I asked the mayor*: My interview with Leo "Chipper" McDermott in 2011.

149 *The plate tectonics*: *Natural Hazards, Unnatural Disasters: The Economics of Effective Prevention* (Washington: World Bank, 2010), 171.

149 *Wallace J. Nichols, a marine biologist*: Wallace J. Nichols, *Blue Mind: The Surprising Science That Shows How Being Near, In, On, or Under Water Can Make You Happier, Healthier, More Connected, and Better at What You Do* (New York: Little, Brown & Company, 2014).

149 *The World Bank estimates*: *Natural Hazards, Unnatural Disasters,* 171–172.

149 *In 2005, all ten*: OECD, RMS, and University of Southampton, "Ranking of the World's Cities Most Exposed to Coastal Flooding Today and in the Future," OECD, 2007, available at http://www.oecd.org/environment/cc/39729575.pdf.

149 *"Five centuries of violence"*: Lewis Mumford, *The Culture of Cities* (Westport, Conn.: Greenwood, 1981): 14–15.

150 *In India, far more*: Robin Burgess, Olivier Deschenes, Dave Donaldson, and Michael Greenstone, "The Unequal Effects of Weather and Climate Change: Evidence from Mortality in India," working paper, May 2014.

150 *"There were still jobs"*: Abhijit V. Banerjee and Esther Duflo, *Poor Economics: A Radical Rethinking of the Way to Fight Poverty* (New York: PublicAffairs, 2011), 138.

150 *One study of Japanese cities*: Donald R. Davis and David E. Weinstein, "Bones, Bombs and Break Points: The Geography of Economic Activity," *American Economic Review* 92 no. 5 (2002): 1281, available at http://www.columbia.edu/~drd28/BBB.pdf.

152 *Two Dutch water experts*: Jeroen C. J. H. Aerts and W. J. Wouter Botzen, "Managing Exposure to Flooding in New York City," *Nature Climate Change* 2 (June 2012): 377.

153 *Climate change was*: Based on my interview with Seth Pinsky and on "A Stronger, More Resilient New York," which Pinsky spearheaded.

153 *That wouldn't have been cheap*: A Stronger, More Resilient New York, 49.

155 *The frenzy of real estate development in Miami*: Robert Meyer, "When Ignorance Can Be Bliss: Miami and the Costs of Climate Change," *Risk Management Review*, Risk Management and Decision Processes Center, (2014): 6, available at http://opim.wharton.upenn.edu/risk/review/WhartonRiskCenter-newsletter_2014.pdf.

155 *While he watched*: Interview with Seth Pinsky.

Chapter 7

157 *was strikingly demonstrated in an experiment:* The experiment is described in a paper by Antoine Bechara, Hanna Damasio, Daniel Tranel, and Antonio R. Damasio, "Deciding Advantageously before Knowing the Advantageous Strategy," *Science* 275 (February 28, 1997): 1293–1295.

158 *But when George Loewenstein:* Based on interviews with Loewenstein and an article by Baba Shiv, George Loewenstein, Antoine Bechara, Hanna Damasio, and Antonio R. Damasio, "Investment Behavior and the Negative Side of Emotion," *Psychological Science* 16, no. 6 (2005): 435–439.

159 *The experiment found:* The authors also asked seven patients with damage to the parts of the brain that did not control emotions to play; they also underperformed the brain-damaged patients.

159 *In one experiment:* L. Busenitz and J. Barney, "Differences between Entrepreneurs and Managers in Large Organizations: Biases and Heuristics in Strategic Decision-making," *Journal of Business Venturing* 12, no. 1 (1997): 9–30, accessed at http://faculty-staff.ou.edu/B/Lowell.W.Busenitz-1/pdf_pro/JBV_1997_Ents%20%20Heuristics.pdf.

160 *Aaron Tornell, a Mexican economist:* Details of Aaron Tornell's life and work based on interviews.

161 *the parts of the economy that depended:* Aaron Tornell, Frank Westermann, and Lorenza Martínez, "Liberalization, Growth, and Financial Crises: Lessons from Mexico and the Developing World," *Brookings Papers on Economic Activity* 2 (2003), available at http://www.brookings.edu/~/media/Projects/BPEA/Fall%202003/2003b_bpea_tornell.pdf.

161 *They answer the question:* Romain Ranciere, Aaron Tornell, and Frank Westermann, "Systemic Crises and Growth," *Quarterly Journal of Economics* 123, no. 1 (2008): 359–406.

164 *The price tag of a nuclear plant:* Bernard Cohen, *The Nuclear Energy Option* (New York: Plenum Press, 1990), chap. 9, available at http://www.phyast.pitt.edu/~blc/book/chapter9.html.

165 *Dread correlates with:* From my interview with Paul Slovic and his article "Perception of Risk," *Science* 236, no. 4799 (April 17, 1987): 280–285.

165 *more deaths can occur:* Peter Burgherr and Stefan Hirschberg, "Comparative Risk Assessment of Severe Accidents in the Energy Sector," *Energy Policy* (February 2014): S53.

167 *Researchers from Stanford:* Jason Gale, "Fukushima Radiation May Cause 1,300 Cancer Deaths, Study Finds," Bloomberg, July 17, 2012, available at http://www.bloomberg.com/news/2012-07-17/fukushima-radiation-may-cause-1-300-cancer-deaths-study-finds.html.

167 *The final death toll:* Eight United Nations–affiliated agencies, including the World Health Organization, International Atomic Energy Agency, and UN Development Program, estimate up to 4,000 (see "Chernobyl: The True Scale of the Accident," http://www.who.int/mediacentre/news/releases/

2005/pr38/en/) and Jim Green, "Chernobyl—How many died?," *The Ecologist*, available at http://www.theecologist.org/News/news_analysis/2370256/chernobyl_how_many_died.html.

167 *Yet these figures, too*: See Clean Air Task Force, "Death and Disease from Power Plants," available at http://www.catf.us/fossil/problems/power_plants/, and World Health Organization, "Ambient (Outdoor) Air Quality and Health," March 2014, available at http://www.who.int/mediacentre/factsheets/fs313/en/. data quoted by http://pubs.giss.nasa.gov/docs/2013/2013_Kharecha_Hansen_1.pdf.

167 *Edson Severnini at Carnegie Mellon University*: Edson R. Severnini, "Air Pollution, Power Grid, and Infant Health: Evidence from the Shutdown of TVA Nuclear Power Plants in the 1980s," Carnegie Mellon University (Heinz College) working paper, December 2014.

167 *Former NASA scientist*: Pushker A. Kharecha and James E. Hansen, "Prevented Mortality and Greenhouse Gas Emissions from Historical and Projected Nuclear Power," *Environmental Science and Technology* 47 (March 15, 2013): 4889–4895, available at http://pubs.giss.nasa.gov/docs/2013/2013_Kharecha_Hansen_1.pdf, page 4891.

168 *One study estimates that an existing*: OECD Nuclear Energy Agency, "Comparing Nuclear Accident Risks with Those from Other Energy Sources" (2010): 39, available at http://www.oecd-nea.org/ndd/reports/2010/nea6862-comparing-risks.pdf.

170 *Ravi Suria, a young*: Jonathan Stempel, "Lehman Urges Investors to Avoid Amazon.com Bonds," *Reuters News*, June 23, 2000.

171 *Tim Stronge, who covers*: Interview with, and data provided by, Tim Stronge.

Chapter 8

178 *When Jennifer Marlon*: Based on my interview with Jennifer Marlon.

178 *Her data shows*: From Jennifer R. Marlon, Patrick J. Bartlein, Daniel G. Gavin, et al., "Long-term Perspective on Wildfires in the Western USA," *Proceedings of the National Academy of Sciences* 109, no. 9 (2012): 3203, available at http://www.pnas.org/content/109/9/E535.

180 *"fire used to burn every five"*: My interview with Tom Swetnam.

181 *Scientists and ecologists*: Hal K. Rothman, *A Test of Adversity and Strength: Wildland Fire in the National Park System*, National Park Service, 101, and interview with Stephen Pyne.

181 *"A national park should"*: Advisory Board on Wildlife Management appointed by Secretary of the Interior Udall, *Wildlife Management in the National Parks*, National Park Service, 1963.

182 *One August day in 2014*: Barbee's life and experience in this section are largely based on a series of interviews that I conducted with him by telephone and in person.

183 *Over the next fifteen years*: Rocky Barker, *Scorched Earth: How the Fires of Yellowstone Changed America* (Washington, D.C.: Island, 2005): 169–170.

184 *Fires spread by*: Rothman, *A Test of Adversity*, 189.

184 *Barbee's staff had predicted*: Barker, *Scorched Earth*, 7.

184 *"I kept hoping maybe"*: Michael Winerip, "Lessons from the Yellowstone Fires of 1988," *New York Times*, September 2, 2013, available at http://www.nytimes.com/2013/09/02/booming/lessons-from-the-yellowstone-fires-of-1988.html?_r=0.

185 *one compared the policy*: Rothman, *A Test of Adversity*, 198.

185 *Park officials fretted*: Kathleene Parker, "Fateful Convergence: Human Policies and Natural Changes Collided to Create Los Alamos 'Super Fire,'" *Albuquerque Journal*, May 9, 2010.

186 *Eventually, 1,400*: Bob Drogin, "Crews Try to Tame Los Alamos Fire Disaster: U.S. Imposes Ban on 'Prescribed Burn' Tactic That Led to Blaze," *Los Angeles Times*, May 13, 2000.

186 *It burned 48,000*: Barry T. Hill, "Fire Management: Lessons Learned from the Cerro Grande (Los Alamos) Fire," United States General Accounting Office, July 20, 2000, available at http://www.gao.gov/assets/110/108587.pdf.

186 *Bruce Babbitt, the interior secretary*: Michael Janofsky, "U.S. Takes Blame In Los Alamos Fire, Which Still Burns," *New York Times*, May 19, 2000.

186 *outraged residents and business owners*: Winerip, "Lessons from the Yellowstone Fires."

187 *"Things happened that"*: Roy Weaver, quoted in Keith Easthouse, "Scapegoat," *Forest Magazine*, May/June 2001.

187 *"a century's worth"*: Pyne interview.

188 *The temporary moratorium*: Sheila Olmstead, Carolyn Kousky, and Roger Sedjo, "Wildland Fire Suppression and Land Development in the Wildland/Urban Interface," *U.S. Joint Fire Science Program Research Reports*, 2012.

189 *Merck & Co. rushed*: Stuart B. Levy, *The Antibiotic Paradox: How the Misuse of Antibiotics Destroys Their Curative Powers*, 2nd ed. (Cambridge, MA: Perseus, 2002), 5.

190 *"One can think"*: Burnet, quoted by Gerald B. Pier, letter to *Scientific American*, October 2008.

190 *Fleming warned that resistant strains*: Levy, *Antibiotic Paradox*, 16.

191 *They estimated that a bacteria*: Ibid., 77.

191 *Resistance appears with*: Ibid., 11–12, 110.

192 *As the microbiologist and physician Stuart Levy says, "Antibiotics select"*: Ibid., xi.

192 *They are, he says, "societal drugs"*: From my interview with Stuart Levy.

192 *photographed pills for sale*: Levy, *Antibiotic paradox*, 291.

194 *one survey by*: Susan Foster, Stephanie Boyd, and Timothy Edgar, "Patient Behaviors and Beliefs Regarding Antibiotic Use," Alliance for the Prudent Use of Antibiotics, Boston, available at http://www.tufts.edu/med/apua/consumers/personal_home_5_2830478716.pdf.

194 *One study of American hospitals*: Michael L. Barnett and Jerey A. Linder, "Antibiotic Prescribing for Adults with Sore Throat in the United States, 1997–2010," *JAMA Internal Medicine* 174, no. 1 (2014): 138–140.

194 *A survey of doctors in Wales*: Sharon A. Simpson, Fiona Wood, and Christopher C. Butler, "General Practitioners' Perceptions of Antimicrobial Resistance: A Qualitative Study," *Journal of Antimicrobial Chemotherapy* 59 (2007): 292–296.

194 *"We as treating physicians"*: Remarks and research of Brad Spellberg are based on personal interview, remarks to Institute of Medicine Panel in Washington on May 12, 2014, and his book *Rising Plague: The Global Threat from Deadly Bacteria and Our Dwindling Arsenal to Fight Them* (Amherst, N.Y.: Prometheus, 2009).

195 *His research in Nepal*: Judd L. Walson, Bonnie Marshall, B. M. Pokhrel, K. K. Kafle, and Stuart B. Levy, "Carriage of Antibiotic-Resistant Fecal Bacteria in Nepal Reflects Proximity to Kathmandu," *Journal of Infectious Diseases* 184, no. 9 (2001): 1163–1169.

197 *Depositors mobbed branches*: Kenneth H. Bacon and Ron Suskind, "Financial Casualty: U.S. Recession Claims Bank of New England as First Big Victim—Federal Regulators Take Over after Company Warned of Large Impending Loss—Depositors Rush to Get Funds," *Wall Street Journal*, January 7, 1991.

197 *On the morning of Sunday*: Powell's recollections based on my interview with him.

197 *Of the $19.1 billion*: *History of the Eighties—Lessons for the Future*, vol. 1, *An Examination of the Banking Crises of the 1980s and Early 1990s*, Federal Deposit Insurance Corporation, 635, available at https://www.fdic.gov/bank/historical/history/.

198 *One prominent columnist labeled*: Anatole Kaletsky, *Capitalism 4.0: The Birth of a New Economy in the Aftermath of Crisis* (New York: PublicAffairs, 2010), 131.

Chapter 9

201 *"while the aggregate"*: D. R. Jacques, "Society on the Basis of Mutual Life Insurance," *16 Hunt's Merchants' Magazine* (1849): 152, 153, quoted in Tom Baker, "On the Genealogy of Moral Hazard," *Texas Law Review* 75, no. 2 (1996): 247, available at https://www.law.upenn.edu/fac/thbaker/Tom-Baker-On-the-Genealogy-of-Moral-Hazard.pdf.

202 *Thai Life Insurance*: It can be viewed here: https://www.youtube.com/watch?v=IkOGwdxcwaw.

202 *which stipulates that a man*: David Rowell and Luke B. Connelly, "A Historical View of the Term 'Moral Hazard,'" *Geneva Association Insurance Economics Newsletter*, January 2012, available at https://www.genevaassociation.org/media/178212/ga2012-ie65-rowellconnelly.pdf.

203 *The term "moral hazard"*: Rowell & Connelly, "A Historical View."

203 *Children's advocates*: V. A. Zelizer, "The Price and Value of Children: The Case of Children's Insurance," *American Journal of Sociology* 86 (1981): 1042.

203 *moral hazard and the Peltzman effect*: My interview.

203 *Car insurance does seem*: For auto insurance see Alma Cohen and Rajeev Dehejia, "The Effect of Automobile Insurance and Accident Liability Laws in Traffic Fatalities," NBER Working Paper 9602, April 2003, available at www.nber.org/papers/w9602.pdf. For health insurance see J. P. Newhouse, "Free for All? Lessons from the RAND Health Insurance Experiment," A RAND Study (Cambridge and London: Harvard University Press, 1993).

204 *demonstrated this incisively*: Howard Kunreuther, Nathan Novemsky, and Daniel Kahneman, "Making Low Probabilities Useful," *Journal of Risk and Uncertainty* 23:2 (2001): 103–120.

206 *people are far more likely*: Howard C. Kunreuther and Erwann O. Michel-Kerjan, "Overcoming Myopia," *Milken Institute Review* (October, 2010): 56.

206 *on thousands of buildings*: "The Northridge, California Earthquake: A 10-Year Retrospective," Risk Management Solutions, May 13, 2004.

206 *four times all the premiums*: Adam Entous, "California Enters New Era of Earthquake Insurance," Reuters, November 29, 1996.

207 *if a $1 million loss*: Kenneth Froot, "Toward Financial Stabilty," in *The Irrational Economist: Making Decisions in a Dangerous World* (New York: PublicAffairs, 2010), 174.

207 *Kenneth Froot, a retired*: "The Market for Catastrophe Risk: A Clinical Examination," by Kenneth Froot, NBER Working Paper 8110, www.nber .org/papers/w8110, Froot, 7–8, and figure 3, page 34.

209 *The rate the authority would have paid*: "California Quake Authority Scraps Bond Proposal," *National Underwriter Property and Casualty—Risk and Benefits Management Ed.* November 25, 1996.

209 *The reaction: the stock market value*: Froot, "The Market for Catastrophe Risk," 13.

210 *"Were a truly cataclysmic"*: "Chairman's Letter," Berkshire Hathaway Inc., February 28, 1997, available at http://www.berkshirehathaway.com/letters/ 1996.html.

210 *Two scholars recall interviewing*: Aaron Doyle and Richard Ericson, "Five Ironies of Insurance," in *The Appeal of Insurance*, Geoffrey Wilson Clark, ed. (Toronto: University of Toronto Press, 2010), 226.

210 *A few years after the California*: "Chairman's Letter, "Berkshire Hathaway, Inc., February 27, 1998, available at http://www.berkshirehathaway.com/ letters/1997.html.

211 *They start with the assumption that*: Carolyn Kousky and Roger Cooke, "Explaining the Failure to Insure Catastrophic Risks," *The Geneva Papers* 37 (2012): 206–227.

214 *Hayne Leland, a professor*: Hayne E. Leland and Mark Rubinstein, "The Evolution of Portfolio Insurance," in *Dynamic Hedging: A Guide to Portfolio Insurance*, Don Luskin, ed. (Hoboken, N.J.: Wiley, 1988).

214 *Around this time, Myron Scholes*: Fischer Black and Myron Scholes, "The Pricing of Options and Corporate Liabilities," *Journal of Political Economy* 81, no. 3 (1973): 637–654.

215 *to boost their returns*: Leland and Rubinstein, "The Evolution of Portfolio Insurance," 7.

215 *By the eve of the October 1987 crash*: *Report of the Presidential Task Force on Market Mechanisms*, Nicholas F. Brady, Chairman (Washington: U.S. Government Printing Office, 1988), http://archive.org/stream/reportof presiden01unit/reportofpresiden01unit_djvu.txt.

216 *Portfolio insurers accounted*: Ibid., 36.

217 *by Leland and Rubenstein*: Leland and Rubinstein argued that portfolio insurance could not explain either the run-up of the stock market in 1987 nor several important aspects of the stock market's behavior during the crash and in its aftermath. They maintain that market panic was a better explanation for the crash. See Hayne Leland and Mark Rubinstein, "Comments on the Market Crash, Six Months After," *Journal of Economic Perspectives* 2, no. 3 (1988): 45–50.

217 *As Gillian Tett recounts*: Gillian Tett, *Fool's Gold: The Inside Story of J.P. Morgan and How Wall Street Greed Corrupted Its Bold Dream and Created a Financial Catastrophe* (New York: Free Press, 2010), 47.

219 *"thrive and grow"*: Nassim Nicholas Taleb, *Antifragile: Things That Gain from Disorder* (New York: Random House, 2012), 3.

219 *Idiosyncratic, or "micro," risks*: From interview and e-mail correspondence.

219 *During a scare*: Esmé E. Deprez, "New York Businesses Get H1N1 Vaccine," Bloomberg News, Nov. 2, 2009, http://www.businessweek.com/bwdaily/dnflash/content/nov2009/db2009112_606442.htm.

220 *Goldman had advanced*: Kurt Eichenwald, "The Day the Nation's Cash Pipeline Almost Ran Dry," *New York Times*, October 2, 1988.

220 *Naturally, such a policy*: This is based on an interview with a former Goldman Sachs official.

220 *Goldman prepares*: From the Goldman Sachs Group, Inc., Form 10-K Annual Report, for the fiscal year ended December 31, 2013, 95–96.

221 *Goldman protected itself*: This description of Goldman's subprime mortgage activities and its role in creating and using the ABX index is drawn from the report by the United States Senate Permanent Subcommittee on Investigations, "Wall Street and the Financial Crisis: Anatomy of a Financial Collapse," 400–406; Senate Subcommittee report, page 9.

221 *"our profitable year"*: Senate Permanent Subcommittee on Investigations, "Wall Street and the Financial Crisis," 413.

222 *Goldman's demands were based*: Serena Ng and Carrick Mollenkamp, "Goldman Details Its Valuations with AIG," *Wall Street Journal*, August 1, 2010, accessed at http://www.wsj.com/news/articles/SB10001424052748703787904 575403423902297954?mg=reno64-wsj.

222 *In 2011, Nancy Wallace and Richard Stanton*: This is based on an interview with Nancy Wallace and the paper she co-wrote with Richard Stanton, "The Bear's Lair: Index Credit Default Swaps and the Subprime Mortgage Crisis," *Review of Financial Studies* 24, no. 10 (2011): 3250–3280, available at http://faculty.haas.berkeley.edu/stanton/papers/pdf/indices.pdf.

223 *it later claimed*: Goldman Sachs Group, "Overview of Goldman Sachs' Interaction with AIG and Goldman Sachs' Approach to Risk Management," available at http://www.goldmansachs.com/media-relations/in-the-news/archive/aig-summary.html.

223 *But $170 million*: "AIG External CDS Notional by Counterparty as of 9/15/08," document submitted by Goldman Sachs to Chuck Grassley, available at http://www.grassley.senate.gov/sites/default/files/about/upload/Attachment-1.pdf.

224 *After 9/11, its policy was canceled*: Testimony of Chicago CFO Walter K. Knorr to the Senate Banking Committee, October 24 and 25, 2001, available at http://www.gpo.gov/fdsys/pkg/CHRG-107shrg83472/html/CHRG-107shrg83472.htm.

224 *"All of us in the industry"*: Warren Buffett, letter to shareholders of Berkshire Hathaway, February 28, 2002, available at http://www.berkshirehathaway.com/2001ar/2001letter.html.

225 *one survey found*: Kip Viscusi, "The Hold Up Problem: Why It Is Urgent to Rethink the Economics of Disaster Protection," in *The Irrational Economist: Making Decisions in a Dangerous World* (New York: PublicAffairs, 2010), 147.

225 *"We can never insure"*: Social Security Administration, "Historical Background and Development of Social Security," available at http://www.ssa.gov/history/briefhistory3.html.

227 *So the federal government*: Officially, it was called the National Insurance Development Program. It is described by the Government Accountability Office in testimony by Richard J. Hillman, "Terrorism Insurance Alternative Programs for Protecting Insurance Consumers," October 24, 2001, available at http://www.gao.gov/assets/110/109046.pdf.

227 *The Treasury reported*: ProPublica, "Bailout Tracker," available at http://projects.propublica.org/bailout/.

227 *Amy Finkelstein, an economist*: Based on interview with Amy Finkelstein and the article by Amy Finkelstein, Sarah Taubman, Bill Wright, et al., "The Oregon Health Insurance Experiment: Evidence from the First Year," *Quarterly Journal of Economics* 127, no. 3 (2012): 1057–1106, and Katherine Baicker, Sarah L. Taubman, Heidi L. Allen, et al., "The Oregon Experiment—Effects of Medicaid on Clinical Outcomes," *New England Journal of Medicine* 368 (2013): 1713–1722.

228 *But those reminded*: Orit E. Tykocinski, "The Insurance Effect: How the Possession of Gas Masks Reduces the Likelihood of a Missile Attack," *Judgment and Decision Making* 8, no. 2 (2013): 174–178.

Chapter 10

231 *As Don Arendt, a veteran safety*: Personal interview with Don Arendt.

232 *A sulfurous-smelling smoke*: The description of Flight 9's loss of power and the experience of the passengers on board is from Betty Tootell, *All Four Engines Have Failed* (London: Pan Books, 1985).

232 *Volcanic ash consists*: Thomas J. Casadevall, "Volcanic Hazards and Aviation Safety: Lessons of the Past Decade," *Flight Safety Digest*, May 1993, available at http://flightsafety.org/fsd/fsd_may93.pdf.

233 *In 2001 aviation's global*: International Civil Aviation Organization, "Doc 9691 Manual on Volcanic Ash, Radioactive Material and Toxic Chemical Clouds, Second Edition," 1-3-19.

233 *It was not a particularly*: According to Ed Poole of the Air Safety Consultancy, quoted in Thomas Withington, "Clearing the Air: Reconsidering How to Respond to Ash Clouds," *Aerosafetyworld*, November 2010.

233 *All told*: Oxford Economics, "The Economic Impacts of Air Travel Restrictions Due to Volcanic Ash: A Report Prepared for Airbus," available at http://www.oxfordeconomics.com/my-oxford/projects/129051.

234 *I met Barnett*: The discussion of Arnold Barnett's work is based on his papers and articles, a personal interview in Boston, telephone calls, and e-mail correspondence.

236 *Trips less than that length*: Arnold Barnett, "Flying? No Point in Trying to Beat the Odds," *Wall Street Journal*, September 9, 1998.

237 *Barnett has crunched the numbers*: Arnold Barnett, "Moving Up," *Aerosafetyworld*, January 2014.

238 *In the 1920s, a pilot had*: Nick A. Komons, "Bonfires to Beacons: Federal Civil Aviation Policy Under the Air Commerce Act, 1926–1938" (Washington: U.S. Department of Transportation, Federal Aviation Administration, 1978), 25.

239 *"One of the severest handicaps"*: Both Cabot and the Manufacturers' Aircraft Association are quoted in Komons, "Bonfires to Beacons," 28.

239 *The industry could also observe*: Mark Hansen, Carolyn McAndrews, and Emily Berkeley, *History of Aviation Safety Oversight in the United States, Final Report* (Washington: U.S. Department of Transportation, Federal Aviation Administration), 1.

240 *He concluded that*: Chauncey Starr, "Social Benefit vs. Technological Risk: What Is Society Willing to Pay for Safety?" *Science* 165 (1969): 1232–1238.

240 *On that diagram*: Paul Slovic, "Perception of Risk," *Science*, new series vol. 236, no. 4799 (1987), 280–285.

240 *flying still combines*: Interview with Lucas van Gerwen.

241 *insurers find it prohibitive*: Geoffrey Heal and Howard Kunreuther, "IDS Models of Airline Security," *Journal of Conflict Resolution* 49, no. 2 (2005): 201–217.

241 *a term popularized by*: See Karl E. Weick and Kathleen M. Sutcliffe, *Managing the Unexpected: Assuring High Performance in an Age of Complexity* (San Francisco: Jossey-Bass, 2001).

242 *Every day, more than*: The work and description of the Aviation Safety Reporting System, including the Burlington HANAA incident, is based on my visit to its headquarters in Moffett Field, California, and interviews with Linda Connell, ASRS director, and David Wichner of Booz Allen Hamilton. Additional background comes from Rex Hardy, *Callback: NASA's Aviation Safety Reporting System* (Washington: Smithsonian Institution Press, 1990).

244 *"When you consider"*: Callback, December 2013, available at http://asrs.arc.nasa.gov/docs/cb/cb_407.pdf.

244 *he was showing his iPad*: Callback, September 2012, available at http://asrs.arc.nasa.gov/docs/cb/cb_392.pdf.

245 *Errors are much harder*: The problems of replicating aviation's success in incident reporting in the field of medicine are discussed by C. W. Johnson, "What Will We Do with the Data? Issues in the Reporting of Adverse Healthcare Events," Department of Computing Science, University of Glasgow, available at http://www.dcs.gla.ac.uk/~johnson/papers/qhc.pdf, and Charles Billings, MD, whose remarks are quoted by Richard I. Cook, David D. Woods, and Charlotte Miller in *A Tale of Two Stories: Contrasting Views of Patient Safety Report from a Workshop on Assembling the Scientific Basis for Progress on Patient Safety*, National Patient Safety Foundation at the AMA, 1998.

245 *airline share prices*: Nancy Rose, "Fear of Flying: Economic Analysis of Airline Safety," *NBER Working Paper* no. 3784 (July 1991).

245 *In the weeks after*: Arnold Barnett, John Menighetti, and Matthew Prete, "The Market Response to the Sioux City DC-10 Crash," *Risk Analysis* 12, no. 1 (1992): 45–52.

245 *domestic Taiwanese airlines*: Jinn-Tsai Wong and Wen-Chien Yeh, "Impact of Flight Accident on Passenger Traffic Volume of the Airlines in Taiwan," *Journal of the Eastern Asia Society for Transportation Studies* 5 (2003): 471–483.

246 *Airlines blanched*: Arnold Barnett, "North Atlantic Data Link Value Proposition," unpublished PowerPoint presentation.

247 *The National Highway Transportation*: U.S. House of Representatives Committee on Energy and Commerce Majority Staff, "Memorandum for Hearing on the GM Ignition Switch Recall: Why Did It Take So Long?," March 30, 2014, accessed at http://docs.house.gov/meetings/IF/IF02/20140401/102033/HHRG-113-IF02-20140401-SD002-U2.pdf.

247 *NHTSA learned in 2005*: David Friedman, Acting Administrator, National Highway Traffic Safety Administration, "Statement Before the U.S. House of Representatives Committee on Energy and Commerce Subcommittee on

Oversight and Investigations," April 1, 2014, accessed at http://docs.house
.gov/meetings/IF/IF02/20140401/102033/HHRG-113-IF02-Wstate
-FriedmanD-20140401.pdf.

247 *When a plane crashed in 1931*: Hansen, McAndrews, and Berkeley, *History of Aviation Safety*, 4.

248 *As Alan Greenspan was fond*: Alan Greenspan, Remarks on Bank Super-vision, Regulation, and Risk, October 5, 1996, available at http://www .federalreserve.gov/boarddocs/speeches/1996/19961005.htm.

248 *One morning in 1986*: Robert Samek, "Tampa Airport Warned Pilot 4 Times about Fog," *St. Petersburg Times*, November 22, 1986.

249 *"To emulate the airline"*: Larry D'Oench, "Letter to the Editor," *Wall Street Journal*, Jan. 6, 2013.

249 *general aviation accounts*: Comparisons between general and commercial aviation are based on per 100,000 hours flown. Comparisons between commercial aviation and automobile fatalities are based on fatalities per 100 million miles traveled, three-year averages. The data are from the Bureau of Transportation Statistics, U.S. Department of Transportation.

250 *Fly-by-wire, as this became known*: A great history of the technology is by William Langewiesche, *Fly by Wire* (New York: Picador, 2009).

251 *Shortly after the autopilot*: Details of the events leading up to the crash of Air France Flight 447 are from Bureau d'Enquêtes et d'Analyses pour la sécurité de l'aviation Civile, "Final Report on the accident on 1st June 2009 to the Airbus A330-203 registered F-GZCP operated by Air France flight AF 447 Rio de Janeiro–Paris," 2012, 173.

251 *pilots had never trained*: Ibid., 204.

251 *he may have ignored the stall warning*: Ibid., 180. "He [the pilot then flying the aircraft] may therefore have embraced the common belief that the aero-plane could not stall, and in this context a stall warning was inconsistent."

251 *"Airbus said their aircraft"*: Andy Pasztor, "Air France Crash Report Likely to Alter Pilot Training," *Wall Street Journal*, July 28, 2011, available at http://online.wsj.com/news/articles/SB10001424053111904800304576474234278567542.

253 *later told Congress*: U.S. House of Representatives Subcommittee on Avia-tion of the Committee on Transportation and Infrastructure, "Hearing on Child Safety Restraint Systems Requirement on Commercial Aircraft," August 1, 1996.

254 *That drew the attention*: From my interview with Thomas B. Newman, from Newman's article "The Power of Stories over Statistics," *British Medical Jour-nal* 327, no. 7429 (2003): 1424–1427, and from T. B. Newman, B. D. John-ston, and D. C. Grossman, "Effects and Costs of Requiring Child-restraint Systems for Young Children Traveling on Commercial Airplanes," *Archives of Pediatric Adolescent Medicine* 157 (2003): 969–974.

254 *in an editorial*: http://rds.epi-ucsf.org/ticr/syllabus/courses/4/2012/11/29/Lecture/ readings/airplane%20seats%20editorial%20101303.pdf. David Bishai, "Hearts

and Minds and Child Restraints on Airplanes," *Archives of Pediatric Adoleschent Medicine* 157 (2003): 953–954.

255 *The FAA's decision*: Ralph Nader and Wesley Smith, *Collision Course: The Truth about Airline Safety* (Blue Ridge Summit, Pa.: TAB, 1994).

255 *added travel time*: Steven A. Morrison and Clifford Winston, "Delayed! U.S. Aviation Infrastructure Policy at a Crossroads," in *Aviation Infrastructure Performance: A Study in Comparative Political Economy*, Clifford Winston and Gines de Rus, eds. (Washington: Brookings Institution, 2008): 7–35.

255 *federal air marshal program*: Mark G. Stewart and John Mueller, "Risk and Cost-Benefit Assessment of United States Aviation Security Measures," *Journal of Transportation Security* 1, no. 3 (2008): 143–159.

255 *increased traffic following*: Gerd Gigerenzer, "Dread Risk, September 11, and Fatal Traffic Accidents," *Psychological Science* 15, no. 4 (2004): 286–287.

256 *As the agency's administrator*: John S. Pistole, TSA Administrator, address to Homeland Security Policy Institute, George Washington University, May 28, 2013.

256 *"That begs the question"*: "TSA Chief, Facing Skeptical Lawmakers, Defends New Rule on Small Knives," *CQ News*, March 14, 2013.

Chapter 11

260 *traveled to Cambridge*: Interview with Larry Summers.

261 *they are two sides*: Lawrence Summers, "Beware Moral Hazard Fundamentalists," *Financial Times*, September 23, 2007.

263 *we cannot endure*: Tyler Atkinson, David Luttrell, and Harvey Rosenblum, "How Bad Was It? The Costs and Consequences of the 2007–09 Financial Crisis," *Federal Reserve Bank of Dallas Staff Paper* no. 20, July 2013.

265 *graduated driver licensing laws*: See, for example, Robert D. Foss, John R. Feaganes, and Eric A. Rodgman, "Initial Effects of Graduated Driver Licensing on 16-Year-Old Driver Crashes in North Carolina," *Journal of the American Medical Association* 286, no. 13 (2001): 1588–1592.

266 *As one senator*: Quoted by Marian Moser Jones and Ronald Bayer, "Paternalism and Its Discontents: Motorcycle Helmet Laws, Libertarian Values, and Public Health," *American Journal of Public Health* 97, no. 2 (2007): 208–217.

266 *intermittently rationed credit*: Douglas J. Elliott, Greg Feldberg, and Andreas Lehnert, "The History of Cyclical Macroprudential Policy in the United States," *Federal Reserve Finance and Economics Discussion Series Working Paper* 2013-29, May 15, 2013, available at http://www.federalreserve.gov/pubs/feds/2013/201329/201329pap.pdf.

270 *maintain a perimeter*: According to Stephen Pyne, quoted in *Audubon Magazine*.

270 *"pompous and aloof"*: Matthew Pearcy, "After the Flood: A History of the 1928 Flood Control Act," *Journal of the Illinois State Historical Society* 95, no. 2 (2002): 172–201.

270 *"The loss of life and property"*: "Flood Control in the Mississippi Valley Message from the President of the United States, Transmitting Letter from Dwight

Davis, Secretary of War, with Favorable Recommendation of the Report of Maj. Gen. Edgar Jadwin," December 8, 1927.

271 *"There are two types of levees"*: The expression is common among flood experts. It is cited here by Renée Jones-Bos, the Netherlands' Ambassador to the United States, in "As the Mississippi Floods, Follow the Dutch Model," *Washington Post*, May 26, 2011.

273 *Houses built immediately*: Berrin Tansel and Banu Siziric, "Significance of Historical Hurricane Activity on Structural Damage Profile and Posthurricane Population Fluctuation in South Florida Urban Areas," *Natural Hazards Review* 12, no. 4 (2011): 196–201.

273 *As Gordon Tullock*: Richard B. McKenzie, "Professor Gordon Tullock: A Personal Remembrance," *Library of Economics and Liberty*, December 1, 2014.

273 *"One can be a particularly"*: Donald G. MacGregor and Paul Slovic, "Perceived Risk and Driving Behavior: Lessons for Improving Traffic Safety in Emerging Market Countries," in *Transportation, Traffic Safety and Health*, Hans von Holst, Åke Nygren, and Åke E. Andersson, eds. (Berlin: Human Behavior, 1996).

274 *The Deepwater Horizon had*: The National Commission on the Deepwater Horizon Oil Spill and Offshore Drilling, "Final Report: Deep Water, the Gulf Oil Disaster and the Future of Offshore Drilling," January 11, 2011, 6, accessed at http://cybercemetery.unt.edu/archive/oilspill/20121211010250/http://www.oilspillcommission.gov/sites/default/files/documents/OSC_Section_I.pdf.

274 *BP had a culture*: Stanley Reed and Alison Fitzgerald, *In Too Deep* (Hoboken, N.J.: Bloomberg Press, 2011): 18, 59, 76, 111, and 132.

274 *For years afterward*: According to author Steve Coll, quoted by Terrence Henry in "How Exxon Learned from Its Mistakes: A Conversation with Steve Coll," *State Impact: A Reporting Project of NPR Member Stations*, July 6, 2012.

274 *Glenn Murray helped*: Interview with Glenn Murray.

275 *bee stings, paper cuts*: Elizabeth Souder, "ExxonMobil Touting Its Safety Program after BP Spill," *Dallas Morning News*, June 22, 2010.

275 *Worried that such*: Reed and Fitzgerald, *In Too Deep*, 128–129.

277 *The early 1990s*: Material on Ed Clark's career and experience is based principally on my interview with Clark and Clark's speech "Final Major Address as TD's CEO," September 16, 2014.

GREG IP is an award-winning journalist and the *Wall Street Journal*'s chief economics commentator. He's spent two decades in financial and economic journalism, including eleven years at the *Wall Street Journal* and six years at *The Economist*. He appears frequently on television and radio, including National Public Radio, PBS, MSNBC, and CNBC. He lives in Bethesda, Maryland.